assignment: **PRISON RIOTS**

assignment:

Peg and Walter McGraw

PRISON RIOTS

ILLUSTRATED WITH PHOTOGRAPHS | HENRY HOLT AND COMPANY
NEW YORK

To
Terry Olga
and
Olga Senior

acknowledgments

In giving acknowledgments, as in giving name credit any place, the problem is always with that one name you remember so well that you omit it. To that person, advance apologies. To the following, however, our deepest thanks for all their help in putting together the radio program, "The Challenge of Our Prisons," and this book:

Ruth Astor, Charles "Bud" Barry, Charles "Chuck" Beardsley, Charles Bennis, Mitchell Benson, Arnold Bransdorfer, Joan Bennett Calin, John Cleary, Stanley Colbert, Fred Collins, Dudley Connolly, Chester "Bud" Dickinson, Martin Enghauser, Don Fitch, Louise Fogarty, Ray Gray, Robert Hannum, Audrey Hanse, Arthur Hjorth, Theodore Kupferman, Bernard Lenrow, Morris Mamorsky, Joseph McDonald, Kermit Murdock, Leona Nevler, Ray Perry, Ken Roberts, Robert Sosman, Edward Stanley, Davidson Taylor, Luis Van Rooten, Albert Vitucci, and Roberts Wright.

And of course no list of acknowledgments would be complete without tossing a nod to Johann Gutenberg and Guglielmo Marconi, without whose inestimable help we could never have gotten into quite so much trouble.

Peg and McGraw

contents

Note:
Asterisks in the text indicate the first
appearance of a word that has been
included in the glossary.

assignment: **PRISON RIOTS**

1

assignment: prison riots

. . . McGraw Reporting

"FIND OUT WHY THERE ARE PRISON RIOTS. GET THE OFFICIAL points of view, talk to the inmates, and bring back the truth. We want the real story, not a whitewash."

This was the assignment given Peg and me by Charles "Bud" Barry, vice-president in charge of programs for the National Broadcasting Company. From Canada to Mexico, from New Jersey to Oregon, prisons had been going up in riot. Guards had been held hostage. Blood had flowed in prison yards. Prisons had not only hit the headlines, they had become a matter of such public interest that NBC, always on the lookout for important public-service programs, felt the time had come to find out "why." This we hoped to be able to answer in two or three half-hour documentary radio programs.

Instead we brought back more than enough material for nine full-hour shows that went on the air as "The Challenge of Our Prisons." We had enough material to fill a book. Prison riots turned out to be more than a story; we found a frightening indictment of our prison system. We cannot say we had a scoop, because everyone in prison work knew what was going on. Our problem was to fight the many people who benefited by keeping the public in ignorance.

That we won the fight is a tribute to the high-minded attitude of NBC, to the sincere prison men, and to the many inmates and ex-inmates who at times literally endangered their freedom to give us the facts. Some of the last we still cannot name; others we cannot even quote directly because their stories—found to be true after careful checking—would reveal their identities and leave them wide open for further imprisonment. But the facts they gave us can be revealed, and, if anything is to be done about the staggering crime picture in this country, of which prisons are an integral part, those facts must not only be revealed—they must be publicized and acted upon.

To find material that had authenticity and truth, Peg and I used a technique we had developed some years before (and since often flattered by imitation) of taking tape recorders to spots where news had happened. There we had the actual people involved tell their own stories and, more important, the "why" behind those stories.

We find that this method has an added value when we tape someone, whose monologue gives an unconscious picture of his inverted thinking, whose accent betrays his environment, or whose expressions verge on a sort of natural folk poetry. And in the pages to come we have tried to preserve some of that color as we let inmates and prison officials, governors, and John Does speak. Put together, these stories reveal a national scandal.

Peg and I are Mr. and Mrs. Walter McGraw in private life and McGraw Associates professionally. We are "packagers"— we create and produce radio and television programs. Peg writes the shows, I direct them, and the white elephant of a country home we deluded ourselves into buying uses up what we earn.

When, at five-thirty on a Friday afternoon in November, 1952, the call to cover the prison story came in, we found that we had not only an important assignment, but an almost unbeatable deadline. Prison riots were news. NBC wanted to get the show rolling while riots were still making headlines, and there was no telling how long that would be. Despite the need for haste, we also faced a problem that is unique with radio. While a newspaper or magazine can take an editorial stand, a radio station, in order to keep its license to broadcast, must present all sides on any public issue with which it deals. Since we would be working for a radio network, we could never be satisfied only to interview the representative of one side of the prison question, even if we wanted to. We had to follow up on all points of view. This, we knew, takes time and sometimes presents problems. But we had to have the answers fast.

We got the call on Friday, and the meeting to discuss program approach and all the details was set for Monday morning. We had a whole week end to relax and research everything there was to know about prisons, prisoners, and prison riots. It was a week end full of surprises.

Our first surprise came from the history books.[1] We discovered that prisons, as we know them, are only about a century and a half old. Until the nineteenth century there were dungeons for holding political prisoners and jails for keeping prisoners until such a time as they were tried and punished, but the concept of prisons as punishment is a fairly recent innovation.

England, from whence come most of our legal traditions, solved many problems by killing off criminals, usually in public demonstrations, in the hope that this would deter potential malefactors. Not only did the English hang and burn their criminals in public, but they branded them, cut off their hands, feet, and tongues, tore out their eyeballs and testicles for such minor crimes as pocket picking. The failure of this "deterrent" theory of punishment can be seen by the fact that the English called off these public exhibitions because they could not handle the wave of pocket picking in the crowds attending each preventive lesson.

About the time of the American Revolution, with fewer and

---

[1] The best of these, the standard text in the field, is *New Horizons in Criminology*, by H. E. Barnes and Negley K. Teeters (Prentice-Hall, 1951).

fewer colonies in which to dump what criminals she did not kill, England evolved the prison system. The age of reason had come and its reformers, both in Europe and in the newly liberated United States, looked on imprisonment as a new, enlightened method of handling convicted criminals.

Over here, the Quakers in Pennsylvania brought about vast legal and penal reforms, which provided for reformation by contemplation. To accomplish this they built a couple of monstrosities called The Western and Eastern State Prisons. The theory behind these edifices was to keep every convict in solitary confinement. He worked in his cell, had his own private, walled-in yard, and saw no one save religious reformers who preached at him regularly. If he had to go out of his cell, it was with a hood on his face so no other prisoner could recognize him.

In New York State they went a step further, and some prisoners were locked up seven days a week with no work at all to do in their cells. Some of the others got out three days a week, and first offenders got out six days to work on congregate jobs. But a rule of silence always held, and corporal punishment, which prison was supposed to replace, followed the convict into the new prison, where he was beaten and tortured for breaking its new and "humane" rules.

Both the Pennsylvania and the Auburn, New York, systems broke down. It was found that keeping a man by himself was too expensive. And bit by bit, despite the fact that one prison followed the practice of pardoning a prisoner for each new enrollee who came along, they found that they could not build prisons fast enough to hold all their increasing prison populations in solitary confinement. Thus, doubling up of prisoners in cells came into practice, and more congregate work was provided for them, especially since the state officials found out that this work could help defray expenses. It is only fair to add that a few people objected to the solitary system on the grounds that too many prisoners went stark, raving mad, but these radicals were the figurative ancestors of the "country-club penologists" of today.

Incidentally, some of the cells constructed in those first prisons—cells built to conform with the solitary theory of penology and considered in their day to be too small for one man—are still in use today. They now house two, three, and even four men. However, solitary confinement in dungeons for months, and even years, at a time is still in practice. Such a dungeon is now called "the hole." *

Nor has corporal or physical punishment disappeared. As of 1940 (when the last attorney general's report was made on this subject) seventeen states continued to authorize whipping up to twenty-five strokes. "Stretching," hanging men from the ceiling and pulling on their legs, is still in use in much of the South, as is the "hot box." * True, the change from corporal punishment is coming, but the reforms begun in 1776 are not yet in universal practice.

Also, although the theory of reforming or rehabilitating criminals is supposedly the first objective of today's prisons, the older idea of punishment for the sake of punishment still influences a lot of our thinking. The oldest-known theory of criminal treatment, revenge, is still behind many of our laws and prison practices. And, although it has been shown that fear of punishment does not deter crime, we are still influenced by the "let's show 'em" school. Unfortunately, anyone who tries to throw off these shackles is accused of mollycoddling prisoners and of running country clubs. This is no new charge. As far back as the 1890's there were condemnations of "collegiate" and "hotel" prisons.

Starting from scratch on the subject of prisons, Peg and I had no preconceived ideas. We were vaguely aware that there were two schools of thought in penology, but we neither knew how violent that split was, nor even what either school really stood for. We merely had heard them described as the "hit 'em alongside the head" and the "let's grow flowers in the gun turrets" schools.

So it was that our first phone call for lessons on practical penology was to a warden we had worked with on our earlier series, "Wanted." While I was reading history (I am the student in this combination; Peg, the salesman), Peg put in a long-

distance call to our friend. As usual, I got on another phone.
We explained the situation. We were greeted by a silence,
then some sputtering.

"For God's sakes, stay away."

We were stunned. The warden had always been most co-
operative, and we liked him personally. Furthermore, we felt
we were doing him a favor. We would show that his prison
hadn't gone up in riot and that his prison was good. What
made?

"Look," he went on, "you can't say my house is good. Do
me a favor. I'll tell you anything you want, but keep me off
this series. I'm close to pension time and I'm sitting on a keg
of dynamite. This joint might go up any minute. If you go on
the air and say this place is good, then it will go up for sure."

"You mean the convicts might riot there?" Peg asked.

"Any day!"

"How come?" I asked, "after all . . ."

"Look," came across the phone, "the bastards hate my guts.
This place is a stink hole. I can't do anything about it. I just
want to finish my time and retire with no problems."

"But you're such a good warden," said Peg.

"Christ, have you kids got a lot to learn! Go talk to people.
Go to the federal prison system first; then go into your riot
spots. Then call me and ask me anything you want to—off the
record!"

Peg and I decided maybe there was going to be more to this
job than we had thought at first. But our friend had never given
us a bum steer, so we looked into the Federal Bureau of Prisons. Quickly we found out from Bob Wright of the American
Prison Association that "Federal" is the vanguard of what is
called the "progressive" school of penology, which was made
famous by Thomas Mott Osborne.

Osborne, the son of a wealthy publishing family was volun-
tarily a prisoner at Auburn Prison, then became an adviser to
the warden. As such he revolutionized penology by pointing
out that prisons were doing nothing to make citizens of their
inmates. He set up what is now usually called "an inmate
council," gave the men token money and commissary privi-

leges, and in general turned over much of the running of the institution—including inmate discipline—to the convicts in an attempt to teach them to handle responsibilities and train them for life in a community.

Successful at Auburn, he was sabotaged as warden of Sing Sing, but again he showed that his plan could work when he took over the Portsmouth Naval Prison. When he retired in 1920, he founded what is now the Osborne Association, which investigates prisons and helps ex-convicts adjust to outside life.

Osborne's influence hit the federal government in 1929 when the Department of Justice decided that their prison system was getting out of hand due to the increasing number of prisoners foisted on them by prohibition. Three men were brought in to guide the destinies of the Federal Bureau of Prisons. One of them was Austin MacCormick, who had trained under Osborne at Portsmouth. He was made an assistant director. James V. Bennett was brought in from the Bureau of Efficiency. He had been assigned to do a survey on the federal prison system, and the report was so good that the government also made him an assistant director.

Over these two men, as director, was Sanford Bates, who had run the Massachusetts prisons under Governor Calvin Coolidge, had been president of the American Prison Association, and was the admitted leader, after Osborne, of the progressive school of penology.

By 1952, when Peg and I set out to study prisons, these men had gone their separate ways. However, we were told that these still were the big three in prison work. No report on prisons would be complete without each of them. By this time, Bennett had become the director of the Federal Bureau of Prisons. MacCormick, acknowledged to be the country's foremost prison investigator, was head of the Osborne Association and a professor at the University of California at Berkeley. Bates had become the Commissioner of Institutions and Agencies for the State of New Jersey.

Despite the fact that the man called "the father of modern penology" was handling its prison system as part of his department, New Jersey had the first of the great riots. So we killed two birds with one stone. We went to New Jersey to investigate the first riot and to get our first lesson in modern progressive penology.

And get it we did.

the assignment starts

· · · Peg Reporting

WE MET SANFORD BATES. COMMISSIONER BATES IS A HAND-
some man. Well over sixty, his Irish ancestry is clearly marked
in his face and his eyes, his quick wit, his warmth. Tall, heavy
set, square-faced with sparse strands of gray hair fringing his
forehead, he knows how to talk.

We had spent a couple of hours with the commissioner ar-
ranging our first recording session. He had given us a ream of
mimeographed material on the riot to digest prior to our recording date. We studied the riots, which had rocked the State
of New Jersey and seemed to have set off the other riots across
the nation.

On April 16, 1952, at ten in the morning, sixty-eight convicts seized control of the Trenton prison print shop, a small
building located inside the walls, and barricaded themselves
inside. This was the prison's second major riot in one month.
The first riot had broken out in the isolation ward and had
been quelled with water hoses and tear gas.

But tear gas was no weapon against the sixty-eight men who were safely barricaded in the stone fortress of the print shop building. Those men had four hostages, two guards and two instructors, and they screamed they would spare the lives of those men in exchange for an investigation of prison conditions by an independent outside body. They also demanded the ouster of William H. Carty, principal keeper.[1]

Machine guns were trained on the concrete fortress; two hundred armed officers waited outside for what they feared might be a mass break. Water and electricity were cut off inside the riot-torn print shop, while floodlights illuminated the scene of action.

Then the rioters were off on a tear of violence and destruction. Seventy-seven hours later, Commissioner Bates brought the riot to an end and saved the lives of the hostages by bringing Robert Hannum of the Osborne Association to talk to the inmates—with one condition: first the inmates had to surrender; and they did.

Twenty-four hours after Trenton's print shop subsided, a second riot, this time at the Rahway Prison Farm broke out. There 231 inmate rioters barricaded themselves in a Rahway dormitory and screamed defiance at officialdom. Pictures of inmates, with banners hanging from their windows, asking for an Osborne investigation of all of New Jersey's prisons, occupied front-page space, while the inmates rampaged hysterically inside. This costly display came to an end 116 hours later.

Charges and countercharges occupied front-page space and made spicy reading for New Jersey's voting public.

With this sketch of the events as they had occurred, we arrived in New Jersey's Department of Institutions and Agencies. Frankly, I was nervous about this first session. We knew a lot about the commissioner. He was the man who had first pointed out that better than 97 per cent of all men imprisoned will some day return to the streets.* They will come out better or worse. It was the commissioner's contention that the way they come out depends on the job the prison does. Treat men like beasts and they'll act like beasts. Give them a break, work

---

[1] Jerseyese for *warden.*

with them, help them, provide education, trade training, and
psychological help, and you'll improve your chance of success.

McGraw and I had both puzzled over what approach we
could use with the commissioner. Any official whose penal system has gone up in riot is sitting on a political volcano. The
politicians, without caring very much about prisons, like to see
them out of the headlines. What could we say to Bates? How
could we start? How to ask a man of the commissioner's stat-
ure, "Did your inmates riot against you?" Evidently the commissioner had an answer and one that he thought was important.

Commissioner Bates came in followed by Dr. F. Lovell Bixby,
who is in charge of prisons for the department. During our
brief research we had heard almost as much about "Bix" as
we had about the commissioner himself. Dr. Bixby[2] was also
a one-time member of "Federal" and had been the warden of
one of the best institutions in the country, the Federal Reformatory at Chillicothe, Ohio.

Then McGraw opened up. "Suppose we start off with a little
history, commissioner. Fill us in on the New Jersey system."

"From 1917 on," the commissioner explained, "all institutions
have been coordinated under the jurisdiction of the Department of Institutions and Agencies, with two notable exceptions." Those exceptions, he told us, were New Jersey's
maximum-security* prison at Trenton and its branch, the State
Prison Farm at Rahway. These two institutions were little king-
doms, both ruled solely by one principal keeper or warden.
That warden was appointed by the governor of the state. "In
many cases a man was appointed warden as a reward for
political activity rather than on the basis of prison experience."

We could well understand that a politically appointed warden didn't make the commissioner's life very easy.

"However, in 1947," Commissioner Bates explained, "the
old constitution was abolished and Trenton State Prison as
well as the prison farm at Rahway became part of the department. But this change was only on paper." It wasn't until some
years later—1951 to be exact—that the old Warden George W.

---

[2] He is most famous as a pioneer in classification* in the federal system.

Page resigned because of ill health. Now the commissioner, Dr. Bixby, and the department were free to go out and get a top-notch prison administrator. But soon they learned top-drawer men did not want to be involved with the dirty, creaking, ancient institution. After months of searching, the department decided to give the job to an old-line officer in Trenton.

His name was William H. Carty. Carty knew Trenton, the ins and outs, the politics, the problems, the inmates, and, most important of all, the prison personnel. He had served New Jersey, faithfully and honestly making a career of penology, and the department felt he deserved to be rewarded. With Carty at the prison, the department took over and a new administration began.

Eighteen months later, both Trenton and Rahway went up in riot. The newspapers made sure Commissioner Bates, the department, and the board of managers took the rap. The years of work Bates had put in trying to free Trenton and Rahway of the political strangle hold were forgotten in the hot news of the day. We couldn't help but sympathize with the commissioner, who felt he was being fed to the wolves for the sake of a couple of headlines.

McGraw stuck to the story: "During the year and a half you and the department were in charge, how many changes did you make in Trenton and Rahway?"

Bates answered in an even voice, "We reorganized. We set up a book of rules and regulations so that Trenton and Rahway would be run on the same basis as the rest of the institutions in the department."

Suddenly the commissioner signaled to us to cut the recording. He didn't want to go on the air and make apologies, he said. After all, there was nothing to apologize for, but from the moment the department took over they were bedeviled with problems. First of all, there was the problem of money. A bill that proposed an allocation of funds for the entire department of institutions and agencies was turned down in 1949, because it included a sum of money for modernizing the state prison.

Then Warden Carty, the key man, had an unfortunate accident. The day after he became warden, he was in the prison talking to a psychopathic prisoner when the prisoner suddenly

attacked him and broke his jaw in five places. Warden Carty
ended up in a hospital.

Then, according to Bates, Franklin Gregory, of the Newark
Star Ledger, came out with a series of prison exposés. We knew
all about Gregory. He had grabbed headlines with hot stories
about prison scandals: "Floating crap games, dope, sex, homebrew and homerule by the convicts . . . that's the picture of
New Jersey's maximum-security prison at Trenton as drawn
for this reporter by six disgusted prison guards." Gregory's
article alleged that these six guards had come to him volun-
tarily, asking for an exposé of prison conditions.

"This exposé kicked off a Senate investigation, didn't it?"
McGraw asked.

The commissioner did not go into detail about the Senate
investigation. But he pointed out that his department was
requested to appoint a special committee to investigate the
charges. They did a thorough job, and Bates reported to the
governor: "A careful examination of the sworn testimony of
twenty-eight eyewitnesses failed to reveal any evidence to substantiate the serious allegations made in the newspaper article."

"Did you ever talk to any of the guards who were Gregory's
informants?"

Evidently this was a touchy question, because the commissioner replied with some heat, "It's a prized American tradition that a man be faced by his accusers. But the facts were
that these anonymous guards had been invited to appear before the committee to make their charges in person, and none
of them showed up."

"What about the riots?" I pushed the microphone over to
Dr. Bixby to give Commissioner Bates a rest.

"Let's start with the first riot at Trenton."

Dr. Bixby was a good talker, and he knew his material. He
launched into a simple account of the Wing* Five riot. It seems
Wing Five is an isolation wing where certain inmates are kept
for reasons of health or behavior. The riot had started when
an inmate called a guard over to his cell and demanded to be
taken to a hospital. The guard checked the inmate's condition
and found there was no reason for hospitalization. The inmate
was infuriated and kicked up a rumpus. Emotional outbursts

in any institution are contagious. The other inmates took up the cause and started on a campaign of yelling, breaking up the furniture in their cells, and smashing cell bars. Wing Five is an ancient wing, and before long the inmates had broken out of their cells and were loose in the corridor. The inmates had no demands and no hostages, and the affair was put down quickly with tear gas.

Once again, McGraw returned the microphone to the commissioner. "What's the story on the second riot?"

The commissioner described the affair much as we had reconstructed it. But it was his feeling it was a spontaneous explosion. He said:

Remember only sixty-nine men out of a total population of thirteen hundred inmates had participated. But I think thanks should be given to that large majority of inmates who are well behaved, well intentioned and desirous only of serving out their sentences and getting another chance at normal living.

McGraw pressed on, turning to the subject of the outside investigation. "What were the inmates' demands?"

The word *demand* was like waving a red flag at the commissioner. He was the first man to fight for improved conditions for inmates; but, he pointed out, "Felons have long since forfeited the right to demand anything." His department took the position then, as it does now, that if there were any infractions, any violations of the department's rules, these violations would be corrected.

"We read a lot about the inmates' complaints of the food at Trenton. Was it pretty bad?" I asked.

The commissioner looked disgusted, then amused. "Mrs. McGraw, have you ever heard of a rooming house or boarding school where people don't complain of the food?"

I told him frankly I never had, and Dr. Bixby produced a chart of the prison fare. There was a breakdown of calories and vitamins, proteins and starches. Each inmate received a carefully balanced diet that totaled some three thousand calories per day per man, and Dr. Bixby pointed out that this cost the State of New Jersey $.58 per man per day. The chart conclusively proved the inmates were actually getting a balanced diet and plenty of it.

McGraw moved on to the next item we had listed. This was marked as "The ouster of Carty." The inmates wanted him fired at once.

The commissioner said there was no doubt that Warden Carty had done a competent job, there was also no doubt that he was a sick man, and Commissioner Bates didn't feel it was fair to criticize him.

McGraw now went down the list of complaints: sanitation, lack of educational and recreational facilities, the bedding in the institution, poor medical facilities, lack of reading matter, lack of a program of rehabilitation. The commissioner made no comment; he just shook his head and looked wearily toward Dr. Bixby. We didn't press for an answer—instead, I loaded a question, "Commissioner, would you say the riots were kicked off by a need for reform at Trenton?"

The commissioner smiled at me and answered, "I think it could be more properly said that an enlightened system, such as we had at Trenton State Prison, made the riots possible. It was not so long ago when each man was locked up in his cell twenty-four hours a day. This did nothing toward preparing a man for his eventual release but it did prevent mutinies and riots."

We felt the commissioner had a point. His policy, considered liberal and humane, one that had gotten him international recognition, certainly allowed inmates freedom. But this answer avoided the question: why a riot at that particular time? If the riots were not motivated by a need for reform, what was the motivation?

The commissioner thought it out carefully. The answer was not an easy one. "I think it's spring fever."

McGraw and I were startled.

The commissioner smiled. "You can quote me on that any time. I mean it. Spring fever. The riots were a symptom of the general unrest in the world today; another symptom of that same unrest could be the panty raids that are epidemic on college campuses. What explanation can you find for panty raids?"

Dr. Bixby stepped in. "The riots are over. What should interest you now is the current situation at Trenton."

It did. We knew that Warden Carty had gone on extended sick leave.

Bixby added, "A very competent man named McCorkle has taken over."

"Wasn't there a riot or a near riot since McCorkle's been in charge?" McGraw asked.

The commissioner nodded, "It was more of an escape attempt. Actually, it was put down very fast."

We had read of the last riot and the way it was put down. Warden McCorkle had ordered the guards to let loose with machine guns. We asked about the report that two inmates had been wounded by gunfire.

Commissioner Bates said that was an accident. "The bullets ricocheted off the ceiling." He pointed out, however, that outside of that one incident we would find the morale of the entire institution much improved since McCorkle's advent. He granted us permission to visit the Trenton prison, and Dr. Bixby volunteered to conduct us.

McGraw produced our standard release form. Before we can use anyone's voice on the air, we must have a signed release. The commissioner scanned it carefully and said, "I wonder if it might be too much trouble for you to return and play back my statements after you've cut and edited them to time?"

It seemed very little to ask, and we were more than happy to comply.

I made one more request. "While we are at Trenton, would it be possible for us to talk to the inmates? I'd like to get opinions from both nonrioters and rioters."

My request upset him. "The prison is still in a state of high tension. I'd like to give you permission to talk to the men, but it is my feeling that allowing reporters to wander around inside could only cause trouble. Perhaps another riot. I want your promise that you'll not talk to them."

The commissioner's request seemed logical enough, so we promised, even though we were disappointed. Dr. Bixby beckoned and led the way.

Trenton State Prison occupies an area of about four square blocks. This huge, dirty-looking, brick-walled monstrosity is located in the middle of a poor residential section in Trenton. Facing the prison on three sides are rooming houses and three-story flats. The fourth side is reserved for prison industries. They occupy another block and are walled off by wire fences.

Dr. Bixby took us inside. A tired-looking guard in a wilted uniform admitted us. We passed through a battered reception room to a long narrow conference room. Bix suggested we set up and he'd tell the warden we were there.

Then Warden McCorkle came in, followed by Dr. Bixby. McCorkle, a severe-looking young man with a heavy shag of black hair, wasted no time greeting us. We had heard a great deal about Warden McCorkle. He had served during World War II in Japan, where he conceived and put into practice a theory of group therapy. He was drawn into New Jersey's Department of Institutions and Agencies and given the job of taking over the rehabilitation center at High Fields (a delinquency-control group). The *Reader's Digest* had given him their award for his work, and because of this McCorkle had become as popular as chlorophyll in New Jersey.

Dr. Bixby left the room to ferret out some eyewitnesses.

"Let me say one thing," Warden McCorkle began as soon as we were alone. "I don't approve of this sort of thing. I don't like having you here." He eyed me coldly. I started to smile at him and then withdrew the effort. Possibly, I reasoned, if our positions were reversed, I'd feel the same way.

Dr. Bixby returned, and he had two officers with him who had been on duty when the print-shop riot broke out. They were stiff and formal. I perched on the table facing the men while McGraw held up the microphone. I suggested that the officers tell the story directly to me as if they were telling a friend about it. But the atmosphere in the conference room was not conducive to relaxed storytelling.

Dr. Bixby did everything he could to relieve the tension, but it was thick as the first officer assumed his place in front of the microphone. His story, halting and formal, coincided in every detail with that of the commissioner's: "The riot was a spontaneous uprising."

Our next informant, Officer Warren Pinto, who looked very handsome in New Jersey's white-hatted outfit, was a better storyteller. He described the print-shop building where the riot took place:

> The print shop is composed of three units. On the first floor we have the bindery and the press room. On the second floor we have the composing room. At the entrance to the bindery the inmates had started a blockade. We broke through the blockade and pushed the inmates back. The inmates had a second blockade at the entrance to the print shop, and it was a good one. The inmates that were holding this blockade began throwing pig leads[3] at us, and threatened to kill the hostages if we tried to come through.

Officer Pinto and the men withdrew and waited for orders.

That was the story they had to tell. We produced the release forms and they signed them. Now Dr. Bixby appeared with a third eyewitness. We wanted a hostage, and he had one in tow. The hostage took one look at the microphone and tried a strategic retreat. "I don't want to talk. The inmates treated me well enough. I have nothing to say." He was still shaken from his experience.

I tried my usual high-pressure salesmanship.

"What if the inmates hear me on the air?" he asked.

McGraw suggested that he withhold his name and just detail for the microphone his reactions to being a hostage. He agreed to talk, as long as his name was not used. Between nervous giggles he pictured himself and his fellow hostages locked in a room on the second floor of the print shop, a scene of violent insurrection outside, with men screaming and yelling on a spree of destruction. He was most concerned, however, with the food he had been served while a hostage. "A small square of a sandwich and a cup of coffee. Oh me, I never tasted such awful coffee! But it was coffee, even if you couldn't call it such."

When our hostage finished his story, he signed his release and ran.

Now we were ready for Warden McCorkle. McGraw and I

---

[3] Pieces of lead crudely cast for storage purposes.

had a lot of questions to ask him, but he had one statement to make for publication and he made it. It was his opinion that the entire morale of officers and inmates was greatly improved since he took charge.

With that, Warden McCorkle suggested our stay at Trenton was over.

We wanted to go through the prison. We requested permission to talk to the food steward, the prison doctor, a sociologist, the man in charge of rehabilitation, and the head of their educational system. Our requests were denied.

We wanted to see the setup in the prison industries. We were particularly interested in the print shop. The rioters had destroyed it; was it going to be rebuilt or not?

Dr. Bixby interrupted. He was sure we could get all that information from the department. He thanked Warden McCorkle for giving us so generously of his time.

Dr. Bixby confided that the print-shop situation was ticklish. The prison needed it to help keep the inmate body busy. Prison industries are one of the important factors in helping a man prepare himself for his eventual release. More than that, it gave him a trade he could follow later on. But New Jersey's printers were objecting to the rebuilding of the print shop because of the old bugaboo, familiar to prison men, of prison labor's being unfair competition. Bix promised to get us a man from the department who would explain the situation for us.

We returned to the department and recorded an official explanation of the print-shop problem. Then we were ready for the counteropinion. We asked Dr. Bixby who would make the best spokesman for the printers. He disappeared for a hurried conference with Commissioner Bates. On his return, he said, "The commissioner agrees that perhaps it might be better all around if you ignore that facet. Talking to the printers might stir up a lot of trouble."

McGraw explained that it was our job to get all sides of the question. I pressed for the name of the man who had represented the printers, but Dr. Bixby remembered only that the man we wanted had something to do with a graphic-arts group in New Jersey.

We had taken a good deal of Bix's time. We thanked him

for all of his courtesy, and he assured us that we could call him at any time.

Out in the hall, McGraw said, "Graphic-arts group . . . let's go some place and begin tracing the spokesman down."

Henry Cossalino received us in his print shop on the second floor of a ramshackle building. McGraw and I were in sympathy with Dr. Bixby on the subject of prison industries. If trade groups and unions refused to allow the prisoners to set up economically feasible on-the-job training programs, how then could inmates prepare themselves for life outside? The official explanation was that inmate printing is not competitive, since the prison prints for tax money only—and a very small amount of printing at that.

Cossalino, a small, intense worker, gave us an extremely cynical eye. "Jus' set up the microphone and lemme answer."

We set up.

"First of all," said Cossalino, waggling a finger at us, "the prison printing program for the rehabilitation of prisoners is not doing a job. In the past thirty years only one man, *one,*" Cossalino stressed, "paroled from the state prison ever applied for a job in the printing trades in Essex County. I know, because I happened to be the man who hired him. He was supposedly trained, but I found that he didn't even understand the fundamentals of the printing business. I had to teach him myself."

This was a tangent we had not expected. He was waiting for a protest from us. He had another argument against the rebuilding of the print shop: he felt that it would place a double burden upon printers. In addition to being taxed for rebuilding the plant, they were penalized by not getting the work that is done in prison industries.[4]

The office already was busy when we arrived the next morning after four refreshing hours of sleep. While we had been in New Jersey, Joan, our assistant, had spent her time getting angles on the prison riots from all the reporters, including

---

[4] California's union leaders have found the solution to the problem. See page 231.

Gregory of the Newark *Star Ledger*.[5] She had the material that had been sent in neatly stacked on her desk. McGraw and I read through it.

Gregory certainly was hitting hard in his exposé. There was a copy of a letter to him from one of the prison guards which I found interesting. It was an answer to Trenton's latest riot or escape attempt.

Gregory insisted that we withhold the name of the man whose signature the letter bore. Once again we sympathized with the commissioner. Here was another nameless critic, but it was pointed out to us that this nameless critic could very well lose his job if his identity were known. The guard wrote:

> I have always admired Governor Driscoll, but his stock with me as well as many others has dropped to a rock bottom low when he publicly commended the prison authorities in the handling of this riot and he made the statement "future disturbances would be treated with the same type of force," a departure from the "wait them out" methods used to deal with the earlier revolts. In other words, if I am held as a hostage by one of the many psychopathic criminals in our prisons, I would have to take my chances with the convicts as well as bullets from my fellow officers and call it "all in a day's work." I do not agree with this policy and I'm sure that the public would not agree with this policy of disregard for the lives of decent citizens doing a job that very few want. I do not wish my name used on any of the above, and trust that you will keep my confidence. I simply wanted to give you the officers' slant on how we feel about any possible future outbreaks where . . . our lives are not even taken into consideration."

We filed the letter.

"Did you talk to the inmates?" Joan asked.

We explained the situation in New Jersey and put Joan to work to help us get the inmate point of view. Our first lead was an old friend of McGraw's. This was a man McGraw had met in his bachelor days. He was an ex-convict, whom we named

---

[5] Both Reporter Franklin Gregory and City Editor Arthur Heenan of this paper were most helpful in supplying background information on New Jersey prison riots.

Smitty.[6] At one time Smitty had walked away from Trenton State Prison and hidden out in New York where he supported himself by part-time or fill-in work as a barber. McGraw had met Smitty years ago but their friendship was rudely interrupted when Smitty was picked up and returned to what he called "Boys School" at Trenton with an additional three years for escape. Smitty had come out flat* about a month previously.

Smitty was one lead. Our second lead was a small office on East Thirty-eighth Street in New York City. This is the Osborne Association. Austin MacCormick, the head of this penal-reform group, was teaching at the University of California, and Bob Hannum, his assistant, was in charge in New York.

From the moment we set foot inside the brownstone building, we were aware of a very sincere missionary spirit. The first floor bustles with activity. The second is "Hannum's Heaven." It is occupied solely by Bob Hannum and a co-missionary spirit fortuitously named "Miss Christmas." The second floor, which consists of two large rooms with a hallway between, is sparsely furnished. Mr. Hannum and Miss Christmas have the front office. On the walls are two huge oil paintings, one of the founder, Thomas Mott Osborne, the other of Austin Mac-Cormick. Bob Hannum is a modest man, small, slight, wiry, and energetic, with the kindest eyes I've ever seen. His honesty cannot be questioned. Constant contact with former inmates has colored his speech, and he punctuates each sentence with convictese.

He greeted us warmly and gave our project an enthusiastic nod. "Yep, the truth should be told."

Since Hannum had talked to the rioting inmates, we felt that he was the one to present the inmates' demands. He shook his head. "That's not for me. It was my job to listen, record, transmit, and relate all of the inmates' beefs. I turned all of my material over to my boss, Austin MacCormick."

Then Bob explained that Governor Driscoll of New Jersey had requested Mr. MacCormick, together with Stanley Ashe, former head of Western State Penitentiary in Pennsylvania,

---

[6] Another nameless critic, but, for the sake of this man who could very well wind up back in Trenton, his name is withheld.

and New Jersey's Supreme Court Justice, Justice Heher, to
make a comprehensive report on the entire penal system of
New Jersey. We wondered if we could get a copy of that report. Bob was sure we could, but we'd have to wait until it
was released by the governor.

Bob felt he could be of genuine help in securing former inmates of Trenton to talk to us. "I'll expose the proposition to
them when they come in here." Bob started to think—he already had in mind one boy. "Very fragile.* He's just out."
Bob described him as a colored kid who had spent most of his
life in the New Jersey penal system. "He'll give you the inmate point of view, that I promise. I wouldn't use his real
name, since this boy will undoubtedly get into trouble again.
Let's call him 'The Professor.' "

Bob promised to send over any men who wanted to talk.

We had a third source. We paid a visit to a former inmate
who had written a book. He said, "New Jersey ex-cons? I
know a million of 'em. I'll pass the word you're in the market."

Now that we had laid the groundwork, we waited for results and results came. Within forty-eight hours our office was
flooded with a variety of former convicts, who quickly punc-
tured the legend that convicts don't talk.

Smitty was the first. He is a heavy-set, good-looking Irishman
whose face is littered with freckles.

"Long time no see, chum," he enthusiastically greeted Mc-
Graw. Then he turned to me. "So you're Peggy." He clucked
nicely at me and I clucked back. Smitty was a big question
mark. "What's it all about—what's this I hear about your investigating a riot?"

McGraw explained. "Look, Smitty, I've known you for a
long time. Don't peddle me any pumped-up stories. I want
facts, real down-to-earth facts. Think you can help me?"

Smitty wagged his head happily. "You're the boss, Mac. I'll
tell you anything I can." Smitty paused uncomfortably. "Only,
look—see, I'm different than most guys. I got along swell with
everyone. I was the prison bootlegger. That's how come I
walked away from the place the first time. Usually, I got better sense than to drink my own stuff, but I was thirsty. When I

woke up, I was in New York. That's the truth, Mac, so help me! After serving seventeen years—with two years to go—why would I walk off if I wasn't drunk?" He shook his head.

McGraw held the mike up and we started questioning.

"You see, chum," Smitty said, "one thing the public don't know. There's elements in prison. Now the real element don't riot. They behave themselves. They don't care nuttin' about the fact Trenton ain't got no rebilitation or edshacation. They don't worry about the food either. They're only waitin' to get out to make a buck. Besides, the real element don't eat in the mess hall."

McGraw pressed, "What do you mean?"

Smitty shifted his weight uncomfortably. "You think this is good for people to hear about?"

McGraw nodded.

Smitty sighed and talked. "After all, no one can eat that stuff they serve in the mess. The food is lousy."

I began to argue with Smitty. "Three thousand calories a day per man. Look, Smitty, that's more than I eat, and believe me, it's much better balanced."

Smitty looked at me as if I had rocks in my head. "Maybe you like to eat calories. It ain't the amount, it's the way it tastes. You can't swallow it—beans boiled, mashed, tasteless— all them beans is full of calories. Day in, day out, the food comes out tasteless. Besides, you can tell what day of the week it is by the food they serve, and the only utensil we got is a spoon. That means everything is sort of a soup." He went on. "But if you got a few bucks you buy what you need at the commissary."

"What's that?"

"It looks sort of like a cigarette counter. But they sell raw eggs, canned spam, all sorts of things."

"Where do you cook it?"

Smitty grinned as he talked about prison cookery. Inmates cook the food in their cells. He explained that the big shots get steaks and chops—the best. "We use swag stoves," Smitty pointed out. "Of course, everybody can't afford swag stoves. They cook their food by pullin' back the mattress and cook the food on the springs. They use the *Saturday Evening Post* as kindling. It gives out the best flame."

It was a colorful description of penal culinary art, but McGraw and I were curious how Smitty would explain the official reaction.

"Buyin' raw food in the commissary is allowed," Smitty answered. "But if you're caught cookin' the stuff, it's a pinch. Five days in lockup. A man with a stove gets ten days. But a guy with connections don't get pinched."

Smitty was happy to explain that connections are everything. He pointed out that the guards are badly underpaid. "Look, Mac, they don't make enough to pay rent. They have kids, families—they gotta make a buck."

McGraw took out a list of questions and started going down the list.

"What about hooch?"

Smitty answered promptly. "The best. I made it."

"The *Star Ledger's* accusation of bossism?"

"You kiddin'? Money talks. Same in as out. Big shots are big shots."

"Dope?"

"Nahhh!" Smitty replied. "I never saw dope. There's very little dope in Trenton."

"Sex?"

Smitty looked down shyly, and then glanced toward me as he shifted his weight. "Geez, Mac, men got instincts. What are you gonna do? The she-boys* are there and— You know what she-boys are for?"

We had heard.

McGraw turned to Commissioner Bates' rehabilitation program. He asked, "What educational facilities were there at Trenton?"

"Nah. None in Trenton."

"None?"

Smitty grinned. "We used to have a hobby shop—I worked in it. But some of the inmates began makin' real dough sendin' stuff outside. That got Carty's goat; he stopped it.

"There was a fellow once at Trenton who started his own

self-rebilitation program. He was writin' stories about wild-
life. This is an interestin' story because he knew from nothin'
about birds when he went in. But he studied. They stopped
him. You see, they said a doctor can't be a doctor inside, a
lawyer can't practice law—why should a writer write? He was
paroled, but he was sent back on a forgery rap."

Smitty began to work up quite a temperature as he said,
"Some of us fellows wondered if he'd a been sent back if he'd
been allowed to rebilitate hisself."

McGraw turned to Warden Carty. "What do you think of
him?" Smitty had an opinion of Carty:

> He was awright, but he was accident prone. On a hunting trip
> he had a foot shot. Then one day before he became warden he
> was showin' an inmate how to run a press. He slipped and lost a
> finger. Then the poor guy made a bad mistake. One day after he
> became warden he was talking to a psycho inside the walls. Now,
> no one who's got good sense ever turns their back on a psycho,
> but this psycho comes up to Carty and asks a favor. Carty turns
> him down and then turns around, and with his back to the guy
> he starts to walk away. The psycho jumps him and breaks poor
> Carty's jaw in five places. But Carty was awright.

McGraw gave me the nod to start the questioning on the
riots. "What was the inmate version of the Wing Five affair?"
Smitty settled back:

> Wing Five—that's where they keep guys in isolation.* You
> know, not with the general population.* Mostly homosexuals.
> There was an inmate who wanted to get out of his cell late at
> night, one o'clock in the morning, to go see his girl friend in the
> hospital. He was refused, so he broke out of his cell and began
> letting the others out. It's easy to break out of those old cells.
> So they went on to destroy the wing and just raise any kind of
> hell they could think of. There was a seventeen-year-old boy in
> there for protection from hardened criminals like myself, which
> none of us could understand why they put him in there with a
> lot of homosexuals, and it proved that our way of thinking was
> right that night.
> The riot went on till Warden Carty called in the fire depart-
> ment and the state troopers. The fire department turned the hose
> in on them, and the guards and troopers shot gas in. One funny

thing happened: right in the middle of the troopers' shootin' the
gas in, the wind changed direction. It blew the gas right back in
the troopers' faces. The rioters stopped rioting and began to sing,
"We cried for you, now it's your turn to cry over us."

Smitty concluded that Wing Five riot "was nuttin'. The only
thing that did go wrong was that seventeen-year-old boy. He
got raped."

McGraw moved on to the inmate version of the print-shop
affair. "What happened, Smitty? What kicked it off?"

It didn't just get kicked off, Mac; it was planned. No hit-and-
miss affair. For weeks before, them guys in the print shop were
storin' up water, food, cigarettes, in the bindery. The officials
had word of it. There's always a leak—stool pigeons. They en-
courage stool pigeons at Trenton—they got no council or inmates
to tell 'em what's going on. Carty tried to break up the riot. As a
matter of fact, he picked up about half of the leaders and had
them transferred to Rahway. But the important leaders were still
inside. The arrest of some of the leaders hurried the riot on,
y'know. And it was because they hadda hurry, it was botched. All
the food was in the bindery, and right from the start the guards
broke down the first barricade and cut the boys off from most of
their food supply.

Smitty paused. "Mac, honest—that's all I know about it." He
got up and walked around the room nervously. We cut the
recording equipment and gave him a chance to rest. Then we
started again. Smitty sat down, protesting, "Y'know, Mac, I
still don't think all this stuff is good for the public."

McGraw ignored Smitty. He started off with, "Smitty, what
is Trenton like now since Warden McCorkle took over?"

He took away bananas and gave us peanuts. But McCorkle is
trying. He put down that last riot with a machine gun, and the
guards don't like that much. They can get killed. Everyone calls
him "Machine Gun McCorkle." Y'know, I don't think there's
much he can do. Trenton is Trenton. They got everything in
there all mixed up: young, old, sick, everything. Like the case of
another kid, seventeen too. They had him in with a bunch of ho-
mosexualists. These men kept after him—you know—all the time

tellin' him what they were gonna do to him. Next thing y'know
the kid hung himself. He had no right to be with those men.

"How do you know about that?"
Smitty looked at us. "In prison you know everything from
the grapevine."
We finished recording at six that night. Now we had two
versions, the official version and the inmate version. The question was, how much of Smitty's story was true? Any of it?
That's what we had to find out.
We took Smitty out to dinner and at midnight saw him off
to Pennsylvania.

Now we turned to a second foray into New Jersey to see if
we could check Smitty's story with a copy of the MacCormick
report. But the report wasn't ready, so Driscoll's office promised
to send us one as soon as possible.
We paid a call on the head of the parole board, Chairman
Zink. We had discussed the possibility with Commissioner
Bates of recording the parole board in action. The commissioner's secretary handed us a letter that speaks for itself:

November 19, 1952

MEMORANDUM

To: Mrs. Feehan

Yesterday, at Leesburg, the Board discussed the advisability of
permitting Mr. and Mrs. McGraw to attend the hearing at the
State Prison next Thursday, bringing a tape recorder. The members all feel strongly that the effect of such a recording, when produced, might be unfortunate, even though it were to be carefully
edited, as suggested.

The Board recognizes the delicacy of the situation and under-
stands that outright refusal might result in bad publicity. . . ." [7]

---

[7] Dictated over telephone to C. L. Ayres.

The board didn't want bad publicity, something we could understand, so we settled for what we thought would be a straight questioning session of the three members. Actually, once they started talking, we had little chance to get a word in edgewise. McGraw and I knew what the ex-convicts meant when they said they had had the same trouble. Chairman Zink and his colleagues were more than willing to cooperate. The parole board had come in for a heavy share of criticism by the rioting inmates. "Unfair parole policy," the rioters had claimed. Our question was, "What is the parole policy of New Jersey?"

Chairman Zink was a full-time member. His two associates were part-time. All three were experienced lawyers. They were aggrieved by the criticism of their policy. In many cases it was true that inmates received only a two-minute interview before the board, but Chairman Zink pointed out, "Many times the inmates have nothing to say during those two minutes. We have to prod them into talking." Chairman Zink explained the board always studies every case for a considerable period of time before talking to the inmate. They have the man's complete record, his penal record, his prison record, and his family history. With that on hand, they said, there is very little a man can say or add. We recorded all three members.

Now we were ready for a man hunt. We were looking for the mother of the boy that Smitty claimed had committed suicide inside Trenton. Our only lead was her name and the fact that she lived somewhere near Clifton, New Jersey.

After circling Clifton for hours, we found the street and began a house-to-house canvass. McGraw and I are old hands at this business. The canvass took two hours of ringing doorbells and asking questions. It was almost 10:00 P.M. when a corner drugstore yielded a clue. The druggist jerked a finger toward a flight of rickety wooden stairs. "Sure, they live upstairs, the second flat in the back."

We went upstairs and rapped on the door. We waited for five minutes, and then the door opened a crack. A woman was on the other side. "What do you want?" McGraw and I had learned the efficacy of putting a foot in, and I talked as we applied a gentle but firm weight. The door opened and we asked permission to come in.

This was probably one of the toughest assignments we had. Whatever do you say to a mother whose son has recently committed suicide? How do you even approach the subject?

The woman, a big-boned, heavy woman in her early forties, had an old wrapper hastily tied around her. We had awakened her. I stumbled clumsily trying to explain why we were there.

"I have other children," she said simply, sitting down at a table. "Other children . . . I must think of them."

We agreed. We didn't want to use her name. We merely wanted a denial or corroboration of Smitty's information. I pulled up a chair and sat opposite her at the table. She sat there dully, staring at me. "My boy?" She looked at me. "I don't know—all I know is what he wrote me, what I heard from other inmates . . . he's dead." Her voice was almost a whisper.

She got up from the table and turned away from us. "I want to ask my husband." She disappeared into another room. We were left alone. We couldn't talk. I wanted to get up and get out of there, but we needed the facts. Bits of cake crumbs and half-eaten fruit littered the table.

Suddenly a door flew open. A man, unshaven, with a huge scar running from his eye to his throat, stood at the door. He had been asleep. He brushed past us toward the conveniences and then came back. He stood there. "Which of you guys are asking for it?" He was hot.

"I'm the talking member of the group," I interrupted. "Won't you sit down and let us explain?" He hesitated and then joined us at the table. Once again, we went through the story. He looked down, then toward his wife. She was crying. "I don't care," he muttered. "It's her kid. We've had enough trouble. We even went down to the commissioner's office and testified about the kid. Seventeen years old. How do you like that?"

His wife sat there dimly staring straight ahead. Then she started to talk, and I heard the whir of the machinery recording in the background.

I don't want to tell you my name because I want to protect my family. My son was sixteen years old. He got into bad company and went on a four weeks' spree. And he was sent to Annandale for an indeterminate[8] term.

While there, he had a good record, but he was not segregated from second offenders, and he got in with boys that had been in trouble before. He became involved in a plot to escape. There was no violence—they just simply walked off. And he got involved in auto larceny and attempted holdups.

He was sentenced to state prison at Trenton. He was only seventeen. He was told by the judge that he was beyond hope of rehabilitation.

While there, certain things happened of which I have partial knowledge and have been told since then. My son is dead now, but if he had been segregated,* if he had been allowed to see the chaplain when he wanted to, I have full belief that he would be alive today.

And I say this in the hope that somewhere, somehow, something will be done to prevent it ever happening to another boy his age.

Now her story dissolved into sobs and we cut the tape.

"How the hell can we say he committed suicide because he was put in with a bunch of queers? We got no proof! I know a lot of fellas inside. I'll get that proof someday," her husband added.

We gave her our usual release. She signed it and left the room. McGraw attempted to give the release payment to her husband. He waved it aside, but in midmotion he stopped. "What the hell, it's money."

He stood watching us pack up. He was thoughtful. "Seventeen . . . good or bad. Seventeen. A kid is still a kid."

After our jaunt to Jersey, we received from the governor's office a copy of the investigating committee's report. Here, in one hundred seventy-four pages, Austin MacCormick, of the Osborne Association; State Supreme Court Justice Heher; and Stanley Ashe, of Western State Penitentiary, submitted their findings. They had not concentrated completely on the riot, but they had investigated all of the penal institutions under the direction of New Jersey's department.

We had spent the better part of the past two weeks inter-

⁸ See Chapter 7, page 233.

viewing the inmate population. Some twenty-seven former inmates of Trenton and Rahway had come to us, each with a story. The stories were good; how farfetched, how embroidered for their own purposes we did not know, but we felt that if they were good for nothing else, we could use them to show the inverted thinking of the convict.

Report in hand, McGraw and I closeted ourselves in NBC's editing room. We had an enormous job ahead of us with miles of tape and one hundred seventy-four pages of considered information. It was interesting to remember that Austin Mac-Cormick, the chief investigator, at one time had been Commissioner Bates' assistant in the Federal Bureau of Prisons. MacCormick paid his respects to the commissioner in the first pages, outlining the career of the man he too considered the father of modern penology.

The report went into detail on New Jersey's entire penal system, not only on the two institutions recently integrated into the department, but on all institutions. They commended the department for the fine work done at Menlo Park (psychiatric center), for the high quality of performance at High Fields, for the excellency of the Women's Prison, and for the high rating of both Annandale and Bordentown. Then they turned to other institutions, to Rahway, Leesburg, and Trenton. Although we were interested in the other institutions, our assignment limited us to Trenton.

The plant itself was the first subject under scrutiny. We played through the inmate tapes looking for their comments. Since the inmates all agreed with each other, we choose three to be spokesmen for the group: Smitty, the professional; "The Professor," the colored boy sent to us by Robert Hannum; and a small, slight, dark-haired, dark-eyed, stuttering thirty-year-old nicknamed "The Dancer," whose specialty was picking pockets.

The Dancer described the plant:

It-it-it stinks in T-T-Trenton. The service tunnel leaks sewer gas. It's awful. Worse in summer. They have f-f-four men in one cell which isn't big enough f-f-for one man. One man goes to sleep, all the other m-m-men have to go to sleep. Th-th-the whole

place is broken down, filthy, and they have r-r-rats. It just ain't
a s-s-sanitary place to be.

The official report states:

> The prison buildings are in the bad condition one would ex-
> pect from their age, and are badly in need of paint. Proper sani-
> tary conditions are difficult to maintain. Rats infest the build-
> ings, sewer gas escapes from the service tunnel between the cells
> in Wing Seven.

Commissioner Bates and the department had not described
the prison to us, but we gathered that, since they had tried to
get an allocation for a completely new prison, they agreed.

The inmates complained at length about something they
called "general population." The Professor vividly described
the problem.

> They got sixteen-year-old boys locked up with seventy-year-old
> men. They got fellas in there doin' two to three years with fellas
> doin' seventy to eighty. They got guards who don't care, an' when
> a fella is doin' that much time anything goes. That's why they got
> so much homosexuality in there.

The report talks of the heterogeneous population inside
Trenton:

> (They had) in addition to the "ordinary" prisoners who con-
> stitute the majority of the population, insane and near insane,
> mental defectives, unstable psychopaths, some of them highly
> assaultive, prisoners convicted as sexual psychopaths, passive
> homosexuals, aggressive "wolves"* with long records of fights and
> stabbings, escape artists, agitators, and "incorrigibles" of all ages.
> This would constitute a serious problem in any institution, but
> coupled together with the age and inadequacy of the plant, the
> lack of constructive activities and the personnel situation at
> Trenton, it becomes a problem of paramount importance.

The inmates had lingered at length on the lack of something
to do, something to keep a man busy. The report also went into
this subject at length. Nearly four hundred out of a total

population of thirteen hundred prisoners at Trenton were idle. One third of that four hundred were idle because of illness, quarantine, or inability to work. On April first, the date under consideration, seven prisoners were assigned to the school (as teachers), and to the library (as research librarians for study hour); but the daily work report showed not one prisoner assigned as a student.

McGraw and I reread that portion. Were the jobs assignments merely paper assignments? What does a teacher do with no one to teach? As for other work assignments, the committee reported that they found two or three men assigned to a job that was barely capable of keeping one out of trouble.

Inmate thinking had an interesting side opinion on the entire subject. The Dancer spoke for all when he said, "Yeah— s-suure, y-y-you have to know s-s-someone to get an assignment. It t-t-takes pull. Y-y-you don't mind not havin' anything to d-d-do so much if you get outside enough. B-B-But in Trenton mostly you're locked in the c-c-cells."

"Yard out" * was important to every inmate, a chance to go outside, breathe, stretch, walk around, and relax. The report verified this complaint. At Trenton State Prison there was a limited yard out for both the working and idle population. They had examined the actual yard time and found a fascinating fact. The idle inmate, who sat in his cell all day, was allowed to go out only from one-thirty to three-thirty in the afternoon. He was also allowed to go out from five to seven in the evening, but during the summer the inmates had to pay their keepers for this second privilege. The money to pay the guards came out of the inmate welfare fund.[9] Commissioner Bates and the department had been questioned by the committee about this practice, which it considered "questionable."

Commissioner Bates pointed to the budget. The State of New Jersey couldn't afford to pay a necessary guard force overtime. "It would have been impossible to provide a summer yard period from five to seven," the commissioner pointed out, "without inmate funds."

The report said it almost seemed impossible to the commit-

---

* Monies the inmates contribute for special equipment for the benefit of all.

tee that the State of New Jersey couldn't raise some money to
do something "that the Federal Prison System and all our
better State Prisons provide for routinely."

The report also scrutinized educational and vocational activities, which they concluded were "virtually nonexistent,"
and were "in particularly sharp contrast to the situation in the
Federal Prison System."

McGraw and I were puzzled. This three-man board had
pointed out time and time again the contrast between the system that was instituted in Trenton by Commissioner Bates
and the department and the system that Commissioner Bates
had begun over twenty years ago in federal prisons. Why the
difference? Were his hands tied politically? Why was he defending an institution that the committee found indefensible?
We went on with inmate testimony and the report.

The inmates were at their colorful best when talking of the
guards who were in charge. Smitty said they were "stupid, but
they hadda make a buck." Little Dancer said, "The inmates
h-h-had it b-b-better than the g-guards." But The Professor
launched into this bit of inmate-guard life:

> They couldn't get a job any place else. They don't pay 'em, so
> that's why they gotta make money offa the convicts. Some of
> them officers wrap up the suits in the tailor shop and take 'em
> home. I don't know what possible good they are, because when
> the rain hit 'em they shrink up seven yards, but they carry home
> bolts of cloth, they carry home a ham, and yet they have me locked
> up for stealin'. They're stealin' every day, and I'm supposed to
> help 'em steal! I'm supposed to help bring a ham out and stick
> it in the back of his car when he's drivin' in the yard—and he's
> honest. If I did it, I'd go to the hole!

Fact or fancy—with The Professor we weren't sure—but the
report gave us no room for doubt. It detailed the turnover in
the guard force during the previous year. Of the total force
64 per cent had changed. In 1952 the guards received an entrance salary of $2,160 per annum. At the time of the riot an
entrance salary of $2,400 was paid. At $200 a month, minus
taxes, that comes to approximately $40 to $45 a week take-
home pay.

New Jersey evidently expected to get the highest type of men for this money. A guard's job is as difficult a job as there is anywhere. And to be a guard in New Jersey, a man must pass the Civil Service exams. But at the time of the riot 50 per cent of the guards had been unable to pass the Civil Service qualifications and were on a temporary basis.

Evidently the examining committee of Heher, MacCormick, and Ashe had questioned the department's spokesman concerning this situation, and the spokesman had explained, "There have been so few applicants for the job of correction officer it was necessary to accept applicants who weren't qualified." The committee found that one of the correction officers had been an inmate of a state mental institution. The department admitted it, but explained, "We took anything we could get."

The inmates maintained that the result of unqualified guards meant more than crookedness. The convicts had a certain sympathy toward the underpaid men, but they charged the guard staff with brutality. The Professor had a rousing sample to give:

I done six months in solitary. You get a meal every third day. The rest of the time they give you bread and water. For toilet facilities you got a pail, and you get it whenever the guard feel like handin' it to yuh. Other than that you can do it on the floor if yuh wanna. But you gotta sleep in there. They give you one raggedy blanket, and I mean raggedy. They got one window. When it's warm, they close it. When it's cold, they open it—at least that's the way it appear to me.

This one guard while I was in isolation made a mistake. He gave me my tray and then told me, "You're not supposed to eat today."

An' I said, "As long as that tray's sitting up there for me, I'm going to eat."

And so he tried to keep me from going to the tray. So I walked across him and went and got my tray. Course I knocked him down and stomped on him a little bit, and I went on up there and I got my meal. So when he got up, I went back and closed the door to the cell.

So he went downstairs and blew his whistle. And when they blow the whistle, that mean they need some help. So they came

up there, and they was going to beat me, but they couldn't get in
the door, because I had the bed jammed in the door so
they couldn't get in. And then one got in, and every time one
would come in, I hit him in the mouth so they couldn't get in.

So I went to sleep that night, and that's when they got in. And
that's when the six of them dragged me out. They did a good job
that time. I remember that one, because I had bruises all over.
And then, you see, when you don't have any people, there's no
one there can see you; and they just lay you up there till you get
a little better, then they let you back out into the population, as
they call it.

The Professor's account of his own actions leaves the listener
no doubts as to his own behavior problem, and you may say
he deserved the beating he got. But penologists of the Sanford Bates school of thought pointed out, "Violence encourages
the inmate to repay you in its own kind." Smitty gave us the
inmate version, "Violence gets yuh nuttin', inside or out."

Commissioner Bates was vehement when the committee
questioned the possibility of brutality on the part of the
guards. He hotly denied the use of any physical force, and he
was quoted as pointing out that the department had issued a
handbook of rules, in which it is clearly stated, "There shall
be no corporal punishment and no officer or employee shall
strike or lay hands on an inmate unless it be in defense of
himself or necessary to prevent escape or serious injury to person or property, or to quell a disturbance."

The report allowed that, "In considering this conflict between prisoners' and officials' statements, the Committee chose
to accept the word of the officials." The report pointed out,
however, that the committee "could not . . . dismiss the possibility that there have been instances in which physical force
was used beyond the degree necessary to bring the prisoner
under control and beyond the limits of the Department's
rules."

The report scanned the problems of the fire menace, inefficient housing, and homosexuality.

Little Dancer explained the last without mincing words. "If
a f-f-fellah is young and small, he's led to homosexual
tendencies. They usually approach y-y-you, give you stuff—

c-c-cigarettes, candy—and promise to protect y-y-you. They
t-t-talk to you nice."

All of the inmates had charged that certain inmates got the
best deal. Smitty admitted it. He had been one of the lucky
ones. The report told of this unevenness in discipline. Commissioner Bates, in rebuttal, denied it. The report, however,
had investigated a meeting that had taken place between Dr.
Bixby, Warden Carty, and the guard force. Deputy Commissioner Bixby is quoted in the report as saying to the guards,
"A 'no fix' policy should be adopted so that charges have to
stick. So-called 'big shots' should not be bailed out by 'ANY-
ONE.' Informers[10] should be paid off in other ways than by
leniency in disciplinary matters."

To quote the report, "The statement and its implications,
considering the source, must be assumed to have some basis in
fact."

As for food—the food, which Commissioner Bates maintained was good and which the inmates maintained was
"lousy,"—the committee said: "The meals were served so close
together that many men were eating all three meals within
eight hours or less. Breakfast was served . . . between . . .
5:40 and 7:30 A.M., and the evening meal between 3:00 and
4:30 P.M."

The committee, as we did, found the inmates' complaints
were based more on preparation than quality. Warden Carty
had explained that, unfortunately, for one period of sixteen
months during the years 1950-1951, Trenton Prison had no
real cook since the head cook was ill.

They concluded the food story with one fact: "The prisoners
were not permitted to have knives or forks in the mess hall, although it is a standard practice in the federal prison system
and in all but a minority of state prisons, to provide them. It is
manifestly inconsistent to talk of a balanced diet if the prisoners are to have nothing but spoons to eat with."

Now New Jersey's parole policy was placed under scrutiny.
Without exception all of the prisoners had complained about

---

[10] New Jersey had no inmate council. Therefore, informers were important.

parole policies. The Professor, again, most colorfully describes
his experience:

> They got four people in there. And you got two minutes to
> talk. They got sixty, seventy, eighty, ninety guys comin' up in a
> day. When you walk in the door, he say, "Sit down, what have
> you got to say for yourself?"
> What can you say for yourself? You got nothin' to say. All you
> say is, "I'd like to be turned loose."
> And so then they say, "We'll let you know." They give you one
> minute to tell them what you think of them, and you can't pos-
> sibly tell them what you think in one minute. Oh, they got a
> favorite question, "If you were in our place would you parole
> yourself?" They got your record on the table, and there is nothin'
> you could possibly say in one minute that could convince anyone
> to turn you loose.
> They used to tell you right there what you got. I think the first
> time they met they told a fellow he had ten years, and he climbed
> right across the table, and they had quite a little jumble up in
> there. So now, they make a practice of not telling you what you
> get, they send a piece of paper. In the old days, the old parole
> board—they call that the Board of Pardons—they hadda see you
> every two years. But now they don't have to see you at all if they
> don't feel like. You can write 'em letters, but they don't an-
> swer. If you got twenty years to go, you might do the whole
> twenty if they feel like.

The entire business of parole is a complicated subject, which
McGraw takes up later. Parole complaints were similar in all
the riots. In New Jersey the parole problem was complicated
by what the committee called "the inequities in the law itself."
They cited an example. In New Jersey a fourth offender is not
eligible for parole. However, a murderer is eligible even if the
murder was a fourth offense. This could give a lot of nonviolent fourth offenders pause to think. Not only is the law con-
fusing, but the committee pointed out the board's interpreta-
tion of the law sometimes confuses the issues even more so.
They further pointed out that they felt perhaps the two-
minute interviews were not quite ample.

For 117 pages the committee detailed their findings. They

made twenty-two recommendations that would eliminate what they called, "Basic and Contributory Factors in the Disturbances at Trenton and Rahway." They touched on everything from finances and sanitation to supplying eyeglasses and wooden legs free to inmates who need them, and outmoded prison practices, such as the punishment of standing the inmates under a clock for all to see. Foremost in their list was a brand-new prison. Trying to patch up, improve, or change the old plant was, the committee thought, a waste of money.

Fifty-three pages at the end of the report were provided for Sanford Bates and the department to comment on the riots. We read through those comments and found the same answers they had recorded for us: the history of the prison, the problems of disentangling it from political control, the reference to the job Trenton had done despite the problems. New Jersey pointed an amiable finger at itself and announced:

> The recent disturbances in New Jersey State Prison system, and the tremendous amount of publicity surrounding them, might well confuse the public and lead people to wonder how these things could happen . . . in a State where the penal and correctional system has generally been hailed as one of the best State systems in the country. . . .

"There you have it, Peg," McGraw announced after we had listened to the final tape.

"We have what?" I was miserable. "We have a story that makes no sense. McGraw, why—why does Commissioner Bates defend the prison? Why doesn't he just come out and say it's a rat hole and ought to be eliminated? Why doesn't he use the publicity to get rid of it and get funds to put in a new prison?"

"Maybe he has to, Peg."

"Why?"

"Politics. Bates, after all, isn't the final word in New Jersey. The department is responsible to the board of managers. And everyone is responsible to Governor Driscoll."

"But we don't say that in the script, McGraw."

"We don't know if it's true."

I thumbed through the report idly, thinking. McGraw

looked at me. "We have to return to New Jersey to get the release on the tapes from the commissioner. Let's give him another crack at answering the questions. Maybe he'll reverse his stand."

We went back to New Jersey with hope.

The commissioner was anxious to listen to the material he had recorded. We played it back.

"You left out some of my statements, didn't you?" He was particularly unhappy about the omissions, especially the statement concerned with "the vast majority of well-intentioned inmates who did not participate." The commissioner wanted that part in. "You said you liked it at the time."

At the time I did. But ex-convicts we met did not participate for reasons that had little to do with good intentions. McGraw gave me the nod to begin trying to sell the commissioner on another stand. I led carefully into it. We started the whole process of rerecording. Once again I returned to the problem of why a riot at Trenton. Could it possibly have been that the ancient, broken-down institution was inadequate for modern penal methods? The commissioner began to look at us in a new light, and he didn't like what he saw.

"You've been talking to Gregory," he said.

That was neither here nor there, we pointed out. Reporter Gregory wasn't the only one who had said the Trenton Prison was a rat hole. As a matter of fact, the governor's committee had actually reported that the prison was rat-infested.

The commissioner's face turned red. "They saw one rat! One rat can conceivably enter any institution! As a matter of fact, any home."

I quickly changed the subject. "Commissioner, what has happened to the riot leaders? Are they in Trenton now?"

My choice of subject was ill advised—the commissioner didn't want to talk about them. But we learned that some of the riot leaders had been committed to an institution for the insane.

By this time Commissioner Bates was working himself up to a fine case of indignation. "The trouble with you reporters," he started, "you just want to say anything you can that's bad. All this talk of Trenton's problems can only lead to another riot."

McGraw pointed out we also like to say anything that's good, but what was good about Trenton?

The commissioner pointed to the changes that had been made. Amusingly enough, on his list of improvements was the fact that Warden Carty was on sick leave. He didn't mean it that way, but that's the way it came out. The population had been reduced. The entire institution was being painted, with inmate work crews doing the job. The entrance pay of the guards was now up to $3,240. The position of the library was being changed to make it more accessible to the inmates. They had plans to rebuild the print shop.

Once again McGraw returned to our original line of questioning. "Would you say this improvement was a result of the riot?"

Bates snapped, "It was not."

"Is it a result of the MacCormick report?"

"We are carrying out the plans that we have had for a long time." The commissioner paused. "If you were doing a real public service, you'd go to see such institutions in our department as Menlo Park, rather than concentrating on Trenton." With this the commissioner closed the subject of Trenton.

We had heard a great deal about the fine diagnostic center at Menlo, but it wasn't part of the riot assignment.

"Menlo is a real step forward in penology. It services our entire penal setup. That's a facet you ignore. A great many of the prisoners have had the benefit of a thorough psychiatric examination at Menlo."

McGraw looked at me. Perhaps Menlo was a part of the riot assignment. It serviced Trenton and, as a service, it should be included. Our report, so far, was devoted to tearing down the penal system. Here was an opportunity to build it up.

"When can we see Menlo?" McGraw asked.

The commissioner left the room and made arrangements. When he returned, he suggested that we meet Dr. Bixby and he'd take us there.

We had one other request. We had never actually seen the

inside of Trenton and it was now or never. The commissioner was surprised. He could easily arrange a tour of the prison. As a matter of fact, a tour at this point might be a good idea: we could see for ourselves how the entire attitude of the personnel had changed.

"Of course, you'll do no recording of the inmates while you're there," he said once again.

Once again we agreed. McGraw handed me a release form and I gave it to the commissioner. "We still need the release, sir."

He was thoughtful. He walked past me to his secretary. "I don't like your release." He dictated a release of his own giving us permission to use the material that he had recorded for us. He signed his name.

To my unpracticed eye, Trenton had not changed since our last visit. Warden McCorkle hadn't changed either—he still didn't like us. Dr. Bixby had deserted us, but he promised to rejoin our party at Menlo.

McGraw and I waited uneasily for the warden in his anteroom. The warden came in to announce that our escort was ready. "Of course, Mrs. McGraw, you cannot go inside. You'll wait here for the men."

I could hear the tour beginning in the outer hall, as the guide started the tour with a thorough explanation that the outer foyer was an outer foyer.

Warden McCorkle disappeared into his office. I sat watching his secretary work. I decided to open a conversation. "How do you like working for Warden McCorkle?"

"My father used to be a warden here years and years ago," she informed me. "I've been here through a lot of wardens. But McCorkle's trying. He's trying to make a lot of changes. He's educated, y'know."

I was interested.

"Some of the guards don't know what he's talking about here, y'know? He talks over their head. Y'know, things have gone on the same way for a long time, and the people here, they're used to doing things the old way, but . . . well, I like him."

I settled back quietly, watching her type.

"How's the food?"

She looked up at me; now I had found a subject dear to her heart. "It makes me mad. I had hot dogs for lunch yesterday and I had the same thing for dinner."

"Do the inmates have the same thing for lunch and dinner?"

She looked disgusted. "No."

"What did they have for dinner?"

She shrugged her shoulders. "You'd think they'd feed us decently—after all, we're not inmates."

I sympathized. "How is the inmate food?"

She wasn't too interested in what they got, but she said the food has changed. "The problem isn't what they give you to eat, it's what they do to it. They torture it, inside. One thing has changed—you can no longer tell what day of the week it is by what you're eating. They switch it around." She said this as if the switching was kind of tricky.

I didn't have a chance to pursue the subject since McGraw had returned. They had been gone about twenty minutes.

"You saw all of Trenton?" I asked.

"I got the Cook's Tour. I saw what they wanted me to see, nothing more." McGraw shook his head and then, half grinning, "My guide had orders, Peg. He did, however, offer to take me to death row. He suggested I might want to try the electric chair."

We arrived at Menlo a little later than we had planned. Dr. Bixby was waiting for us in Dr. Brancale's office.

Menlo is impressive. The spotlessly clean, busy institution is up to date. The personnel is even better. Originally, Menlo was built as a maximum-security hospital, with plenty of stone, tool-proof steel, and concrete. Dr. Brancale apologized for the maximum-security appearance, "since we have only children here."

"Children?" asked McGraw. "I thought Menlo served as a diagnostic center for the inmates of all New Jersey institutions. This is supposed to be the key institution!"

Dr. Bixby assured us it was. By law Menlo must examine every sex offender released from all New Jersey institutions, but the adult services are a separate function of the institution. The inmate population is some fifty to sixty youngsters who spend three months under treatment at Menlo. Prevention of criminality is the basic function of the center.

Probably more than any other institution in our tour of the entire country, Menlo Park represented the best in modern penal philosophy in its treatment of the disturbed delinquent. We spent the day watching psychologists, psychiatrists, therapists, and physicians at work. We heard case histories of children who had been dramatically cured. Here was the future of penology. We toured the entire institution and returned to Dr. Brancale's office, agreeing with the commissioner that here was something the department justifiably could point to with pride.

But our story was not the treatment of delinquents. Our story was why the riots. What part had Menlo played in the treatment of disturbed inmates inside Trenton? For instance, McGraw stated that several of the riot leaders had been confined in mental institutions. Prior to the riot, how long were they at Menlo for diagnosis?

"Prior to the riot?" Dr. Brancale shook his head.

"They weren't here," Dr. Bixby said. "Menlo is small and can't possibly treat every inmate—only the man who is a severe risk."

McGraw and I nodded. That was understandable. Prior to the riots, perhaps, these leaders had given no indication how deeply disturbed they were. But since the riots, that was another story.

"Would it be permissible," McGraw began, "for us to see the result of your diagnostic department's examination of the riot leaders that led to their being committed to mental hospitals?"

There was a long, uncomfortable pause.

Dr. Bixby took over. "They've never been here." Then he changed the subject. "There's a case history I'd like Dr. Brancale to tell you about. It's a story of one of his most interesting inmates, a seven-year-old child."

We listened, we recorded. The story was fascinating, but we filed it for future use. Menlo Park was not part of our riot story.

The effectiveness of a prison system is best judged by the end product. Here is an end product, the colored boy we called "The Professor." We do not vouch for or endorse any statement he makes. Possibly it's riddled with inaccuracies. But remember, New Jersey prisons have had eleven and one-half out of his twenty-eight years of life to rehabilitate him, and this is the result.

I'm twenty-eight years old. I can't remember too much about my family life. In fact, I can remember prison days better than I can family life because I've been in prison the best years. The only thing I can remember is my mother and father having a fight. And my father pushed—tried to push—my mother down the steps, and my brother stopped him, and they got into a fight. But it didn't make any difference to me if they both hadda fell down the steps, because I didn't care nothing about them and I never had any love for them.

The next thing I can remember, I was around nine or ten years old and I ran away from home and I went to Scranton, Pennsylvania. And a truant officer came and got me. That was the first time I went before the juvenile judge, and he asked me, why did I run away from home? An I tell 'im I didn't like home. I don't know. . . .

The Professor looked around, confused, and then continued, skipping the years:

And so, 'bout twelve years old, I went to the juvenile court in Newark, and the judge sent me away because my people didn't come to court to get me. I went before the judge and they said, well, they'd had trouble with me in school for a long time and I was always fighting, and every time I got in a fight I was trying to kill somebody, and so the judge told me I had "murderous instincts."

And so he sent the probation officer round there to investigate my home conditions, and he said they weren't of the best, but they would do if I meant to do good. So he asked me if I meant to do good, and I told him yes (naturally I told him yes—not that it'd make any difference), but I said, "If you want to send me to jail, send me to jail; if you want to send me home, send me home. I don't care what you do, 'cause whatever you do is all right with me."

And so then he said, "Well, I'll give you to next week to get your parents back here to appear in court with you. And if your parents don't come," he said, "I'll see what we'll do then."

So then I wrote two or three letters home to my mother and my father, but they didn't come. And so the next week, when I went before the judge, he sentenced me to Jamesburg.

Jamesburg was a real good place. When I say real good, I mean real nice. Oh yes, they cut all your hair off your head when you go there. You get a bald head when you go in there. In fact, all the jails you go in, you get a bald head. And, to me, that's the worst thing in the world can happen to you. But anyhow, I went to Cottage Six, and I got along pretty good there, 'cept my usual number of fights that I usually have everywhere I go. And you have to fight in jail, because, if you don't, the older fellas will take advantage of you and make a girl outcha, whether you wanta be one or not. You got to fight the guards, too, to let 'em know that you don't care enough about anything.

Oh, I got beat about two times, one time by a guy Muller,[11] who threw me off a coal ramp in the coal shed where I was shoveling coal because I threw some coal and the wind blew it on him. I lost something out of my ear, because I couldn't hear out of my ear for about a year.

Another time two screws* double-teamed* me. They put me in a little small closed room where they have clothes at, because I'd insulted him, so he said. So anyhow, they double-teamed me in there, and they beat me pretty bad. Then they took me over to the hospital and told 'em I got inta a fight with another inmate.

I was thirteen years old when these two men beat me. That was in Jamesburg. But other than that, as jails go, it wasn't too bad.

And then I left Jamesburg when I was sixteen years old, and I went home—if that's what you can call it. I started back to school, and then I got into a little trouble. It was because in study period some fellow, he had a *National Geographic Magazine,* and he opened a book up, and he had a picture of some African women, the Ubangi tribe with the large lips, and he said, "There's your mother." And right in the schoolroom I just climbed across six desks, and there it was—all up and down that study hall we had one. I won the fight but lost the battle, because I got expelled.

So I got a job in a hospital. There's where I met the fellow

---

[11] The name is changed.

that was the cause of me going to Annandale. He wanted to get
sharp to go out, so I lent him my brand-new shoes; and, when I
tried to get my shoes back, he wouldn't give them to me.

Every time he used to wash dishes, he would take his watch off
and hang it up on a nail. So I just took the watch off the nail and
put it on my wrist and wouldn't give it back to him. The next
thing I know, there was some cops looking for me with a warrant
for robbery. In fact, at first I couldn't even think of what I had
robbed, cause I—I just forgot about the watch. So they carried
me down to headquarters in Newark, and then they tried to clear
the books on me.

"Clearing the books" is when you go down to headquarters,
any crime that they got on the books down there that they can't
find the actual guy that done it, any guy that go in there that
don't have any lawyer or no connection or people to come
and look after him, they'll beat you until you sign a confession
to take two or three of them things off the books. You just sign
a blank confession, and they'll fill it in later on with the amount
of crimes they want to put on you. They tried that on me, but I
had a good ability to stand whippings, and so after they beat
me three nights at headquarters in Newark, they brought me up
to the county jail, and I went before a judge and he sentenced
me to Annandale Reformatory, indefinite sentence. After that
and another term at Rahway, when I got finished, I was twenty-
eight years old, which is how old I am at the present time.

I was released with $12 in my pocket with no relatives around
here, no one to turn to, and I took it and paid $7 for room rent,
and then someone stole all my clothes the first day I moved. So
I rode the subways for about six days. For about five days I didn't
have anything to eat, and then at the end of three weeks
I couldn't get a job anywhere.

Society pays taxes to make jails and to hire guards to keep
people in jails and hire cops to catch people—put 'em in jail—
and then, when they turn 'em loose, society doesn't want any
part of you. At least, that's the way it appeared to me, because I
wouldn't have this job where I'm at now, washing pots in
a kitchen for sixteen hours a day for $110 a month if he knew
that I'd ever been locked up.

The first time I had a job, when I first came out, actually I
told the man I was in jail, and he asked me how long I'd been
in jail, and I told him. Brother, he started picking up things
around his office! I guess he thought I was going to steal some of
them things. Boy, I'm telling you the truth—you could see he

visibly drew back like I done hurt him, or something. Boy!
Outside, the average person has a tendency. When you tell him
you been in jail, they think that's the worst thing in the world for
a person, and if they ever knew how long I been in jail, they
know there's no good to me! And yet, it's a funny thing . . . I
don't think I done anything to warrant all this time.

And I should be mad at somebody, but I can't pick out anybody to be mad at! I mean, I can't put my finger on no one
definite person. See, I can't get mad at the jail, because going to
jail—jail didn't come out and get me, I went to jail, so I can't
get mad at the people in jail. That's why I can't bear no grudge
against any of the people that kicked me around in the place,
because if I hadn't went there, they couldn't kick me around.

What my plans are for the future, I don't know, but I know
one thing—that I can't stand another trip in jail. And what the
future holds, I'm not going to let it worry me too much, because
if I can stand eleven years of jail, I don't believe there's anything out here could be any worse. But right now I look like I'm
standing on a treadmill—I'm walking, but I'm not moving. I
don't like the job I got, but I can't do any better. I don't like
the smell of hot pots, but I got to wash 'em if I want to make the
$110. One hundred and ten dollars minus what the government
takes off me, it's not going to leave me much.

I would like to be able to get dressed up and look "sharp" as
they say. I would like to read the best of books. I would like to
be able to listen to the best of recorded music—I don't even have
a radio that I can listen to. And yet they tell you to go straight!

It's funny—words. Words is everything, and words is nothing.
It all depends on what you mean when you say it and what you
do. And that's all they ever done for me, was give me words. No
one helps. Oh, brother . . .

This man is one end product of Jersey's prison system. It is
interesting to note that later on The Professor came to us for
money. When we refused, he decided to go to New Jersey and
offer to retract everything he said if *they* would pay off. Naturally the commissioner was not interested.

We wrapped up the Jersey report and stored it, as we prepared for a two-month trip of American penal institutions.
Our first stop was Michigan. We had succeeded in penetrating
official thinking in Jersey. In Michigan, we needed a riot
leader and the inside story of a riot.

3

portrait of a riot leader

. . . Peg Reporting

We met the leader of Michigan's million-dollar riot. No ordinary inmate, Earl Ward is twenty-nine years old, tall, well built, extremely handsome. He frankly admits, posturing best profile forward, that he ought to be in Hollywood. Only his eyes are disconcerting. They have a touch of fanaticism.

We had arranged this meeting with Ward through the amiable, easygoing sheriff of the local jail in Pontiac, Michigan, where Ward was held awaiting trial for his part in the million-dollar blowup. He had been transferred to Pontiac after displaying dissatisfaction with a previous jail by ripping out the plumbing and decorating his keeper's face with his food. The officials told us Earl had launched into this rampage because some visitors, who were going through the jail, had laughed at him.

The sheriff advised us, "You can see Ward if you want, but at your own risk. If he gets excited, get out." McGraw led the way up to the fourth floor where Ward was confined. Interestingly enough, the first three floors of Pontiac's prison were packed with the usual assortment of jail humanity: drunks, pickpockets, erring husbands, and a sprinkling of federal cases being held for trial. But the fourth floor was as deserted as a department store at midnight. The only prisoner up there was Earl Ward, who had an entire section of the jail to himself. He could roam easily in and out of four cubicles and a bull pen. For company Pontiac had provided a guard who had instructions to mollify their highly volatile prisoner and protect the prison's plumbing.

As we approached, Earl opened the door to the corridor and invited us in to join him. The guard just grinned at us as Ward led the way to the bull pen table and suggested we make ourselves comfortable on the hard wooden benches. For our refreshment he produced cigarettes, matches, cough drops, and cough medicine.

Then Ward settled himself across the table from us and we started questioning him. He talked for four hours straight, detailing his life and times from childhood through his participation in Michigan's riot. How much of the Ward story was fact, how much of it was fiction, was what we had to determine.

Never before had anyone had the opportunity (and the money) to travel around and prove or disprove the life story of what officials call a "psychopathic personality," and yet the psychopathic personality is the most puzzling of inmate mentalities, and perhaps the least understood. The term is a catch-all, the garbage can of medico-criminal terminology. Psychiatrists explain the so-called psychopathic personality has no deep or real attachments. He knows the difference between right or wrong, but doesn't care. Legally, if not medically, he is sane. He frequently has powers of leadership, a high intelligency, a disarming personality. The psychopath constitutes one of the worst of prison problems. These men, frequently dangerous, have tremendous ability which could be channeled inside the walls. But, more often than not, the brilliant psychopath is thrown into the hole and allowed to rot, only to emerge either into prison society or back on the streets as a dynamic maker of violence, destruction, and death. Such a man lives in brilliant

hysteria. Why? We were looking for an answer. There wasn't
a prison riot without a psychopath behind it.

Earl Ward was the textbook example. He had been likened
by some to Hitler and by others to a madman on a tear. But
all admitted that he, through sheer force of a magnetic personality, had what amounted to a genius for leadership. Austin
MacCormick said it best when he described Michigan's riot
leader as "a psychopath with a strangely well-developed sense
of social responsibility."

We listened to Ward's story literally hundreds of times,
checking and cross-checking what he said and how he said it.
About 70 per cent of what he said was true or only slightly
embroidered. Ward's memory was impressive, but after a
while we found we could almost always spot a lie by listening to his vocal inflections. When Ward deserted the truth
and soared into fantasy, he took the flight with ease. But when
his fantasy was over and he was searching for some way to
wend his way back to the facts, he would stop, lick his lips,
giggle, hesitate uncertainly, and then steady down as he picked
up his story.

Eyes down, voice modulated, tones dulcet, Earl began:

My childhood was not a happy one. Why? In the first place I
did not get along in school. That might seem strange to some
people, since in later years I developed such a high IQ and other
aptitudes.[1] But I resisted dislepin. I was a dreamer and, as a
dreamer, I was punished. I was hit on the head with yardsticks
and sometimes with the hand by teachers and I rebelled against
physical violence. Naturally, when I rebelled at school, I would
have to be punished at home and I rebelled against that. My
mother was a dislepinarian, and she was sadistical in some of her
punitive measures, forcing me to strip and beating me with a
leather paddle. Each time the paddle episode came up, I became
more resistive and more rebellious. Consequently I started running away at the age of ten and continued to do so until my
sixteenth year. I have traveled all over the country in these runaways to avoid beatings at home. When I was fifteen I ran away
to New York City, and it was there I met a young lady who later

---

[1] Ward's IQ at eleven was reported to be 99 (normal-dull). During his imprisonment a subsequent IQ showed Ward with a rating of 112 (college level).

became my first wife. Her name was Marnice Richardson. I was stealing cars at the time and naturally doing quite well through a fence. Although I never supported her and she never supported me, we had what you might call an agreement. She became pregnant in 1939.

This was the first spot in the tape where Ward's voice tipped off one of those flights of fancy. His voice evened off afterward as he returned to what we supposed was fact:

And in 1939 I was arrested for a fatal false fire alarm.

We checked our hunch. Our lead was the name Marnice Richardson. We never found her or any trace of the child Ward claimed she bore him. But we did find variations of this tale scattered through his life. He had given various officials in different institutions many variations of the same story. One version was the story Earl told of his adventure with a wealthy New York girl. He claimed he had impregnated her and she had paid him a good deal of money to lend her his name. Another version was Ward's claim that he had a liaison with a highly connected gun moll who had born him a daughter. None of these stories could be run down.

But we learned a great deal about Ward's early life during our search for Marnice. We talked to Ward's family, his teachers, his friends, the neighbors, and the officials, and this is the story as we pieced it together.

The Ward family lived on a tree-lined street in a nice neighborhood where a working man could enjoy modest luxuries and where his children could play in the fields nearby. Well-kept lawns, neatly painted houses, everything familiar to young Earl was certainly far from a breeding ground of juvenile delinquency.

Earl's father was known as a go-getter. The neighbors described him as "a hard-working man who, if he wasn't busy in business, was busy with club work. He's a big club man." Both Mr. and Mrs. Ward were socially active people, constantly on the go with church and civic activities.

One neighbor remarked, "I don't know how she did it. Busy and all, and trying to bring up three children."

Earl was the second child. There were a brother and a sister. There were also Earl's maternal grandparents, who took care of the children when the parents were busy.

Earl was an exceptionally beautiful baby. He had no unusual childhood diseases, but he did have one accident. When he was two and a half years old, he fell off a concrete wall and struck his head. He was rushed to the hospital, X-rayed, stitched, and returned home none the worse for the experience.

At four, Earl seemed babyish. He was a spoiled, petulant child used to having his own way. He stole a brooch from his grandmother and was roundly punished for it. "But surely, a child stealing a brooch is no indication of juvenile delinquency," Ward's parents pointed out.

From the earliest years the two Ward brothers clashed. Not just childish battles, but hot arguments, one after another. "I could always beat him up," Earl's brother told us. "He was weak, and a coward."

When Earl went to school, he became a problem student. The usual preschool medical check up showed Earl to have a pronounced speech defect, bad eyesight, and poor teeth. He was a scrawny underdeveloped youngster.

He flunked the first grade. He managed to get through it the second time around. In the fourth grade he lagged so badly behind his fellow students that he was put into a special class for backward children.

He went through the next years with a series of fights, hysterics, constant complaints of head pains and heart pains. His physical check-ups showed no physical reasons for them.

When Earl was eleven years old, he had another accident. He was run over while playing outside. For three days he was semiconscious in a hospital, but he pulled out of it. On his release, the physicians agreed that Earl's injury would have no aftereffects.

Because of the accident, he missed several weeks of school. When he returned to the classroom, he found that he was now the center of attention. He liked it, and he played the drama of his near demise for all it was worth. When the attention died down, Earl looked around for another and less painful attention-getting device. He took to drawing lewd pictures. Soon he picked up the vocabulary to go with his art. He flunked the seventh grade since he was not concentrating on his school work. Then some of his artistic creations hit the faculty and the faculty hit back. He was expelled.

Mr. Ward started a pattern which he continued all through Earl's subsequent career. He went to school and pleaded with the authorities to take Earl back, promising to exercise a good influence on the boy if they would give him another chance. Earl was given the chance, but the reinstatement lasted less than a week. He was caught suggesting certain lewd practices to the girls in school, and he was expelled for good.

Now the Ward family decided that there was "something wrong" with Earl's head, and started on a tour of the doctors in the city. But they could find nothing wrong with his head.

But Earl was on his way. The family sent him to Harding Junior High School. After the briefest of intervals the school faculty realized that Harding could function better without Ward. Feeling that tough discipline would do the trick, the Wards sent Earl to the Daniel Boone school for incorrigible children. The school had a system of thermostatically controlled heat. Earl went on a two-hour tear and smashed more thermostats than have ever been smashed before or since in an equivalent amount of time. Daniel Boone authorities also found they could live without Earl.

When Earl had free time, he spent it joy riding. He ran away too. Once he took a runaway trip to Virginia; another time he went to the New York World's Fair. But these runaways were neither as long nor as glamorous as Earl pictured them.

Earl had another hobby. He liked to pull fire alarms. The police suspected him but couldn't prove it. Once, when an officer who was a friend of the Ward family found Earl near a firebox that had recently been tampered with, he hauled Earl into the precinct station house to give him a scare. He didn't know his customer. Earl pulled a temper tantrum of titanic proportions. He screamed at the top of his lungs that his father would have the officer demoted. Then Earl tore around the station house wrecking equipment. The police called the

Wards in to help them protect the precinct. The storm passed
as suddenly as it had blown up, and Mr. Ward took Earl
home.

After many adventures in misbehavior, he was finally caught
pulling a firebox. There was a fatal accident in Philadelphia
when a fire truck ran amuck in answer to a false alarm, but
Ward was never charged with that. At fifteen Earl was sent to
Glen Mills, a reform school out past Chester, Pennsylvania.
Earl talks of his life at Glen Mills:

> My admittance was a shocking one. Perversion was wide open
> in the cottages. Young boys were forced to commit acts against
> their wills. Other men who were not liked by the monitors were
> beaten. I foolishly confided to another boy I was going to run
> away. Not knowing that any inmate who ran away caused the
> entire cottage to lose their movie rights, I tried running away.
> The next evening the brother monitor, who was a big boy almost
> eighteen years of age, told me to come up front.
> He wanted to introduce me to the other men. All the others
> had rifles in their hands. They were standing at attention, present-
> ing arms. We started walking down the aisle. Then all of a sudden
> the brother monitor pulled back and the men started beating me
> on the head and body with the rifle butts. I had two teeth knocken
> out, my eye gashed, two ribs broken, and I wound up uncon-
> scious in the hospital.

Ward's story of his experience climaxes with an heroic account of his appearance before the authorities. They questioned him in order to find out how he got his bruises, but
Earl claimed he observed the criminal code: he didn't talk.
After he was returned from the hospital, Ward explains:

> I ran away again. I was caught, but I continued to run away.
> Each time I was brought back I was beat by the cottage boys,
> and consequently I developed a bitterness against them. The offi-
> cials at the institution had punitive measures like making you
> bend over and touch your knees till you pass out. And beating
> you with a long leather strap. As a matter of fact, Mr. MacCormick
> of the Osborne Association investigated the institution and had
> the officials arrested for their treatment of the boys.

His voice cracked, lips smacked, and Ward giggled. Austin
MacCormick, the prison investigator, does not investigate juvenile institutions, and, although he admits he has heard "a lot
about Glen Mills," he never has conducted any official investigation of it.

Now Ward discusses his final act at Glen Mills:

> I attacked one of the officials who I thought was responsible
> for some of the brutalities on myself and other inmates. I was
> handcuffed to a bedspring and forced to lay nude upon it for
> four days without anything to eat but soup. I won't say my mind
> snapped, but I will say my mind turned bitter.

Ward emphasized his last words, since he hotly disputes the
idea that there is anything wrong with his mind.

How close to the truth was Ward's entire account of Glen
Mills? We went to the institution and met Major Hickman,
headmaster.

Glen Mills is located in the lush, lovely, rolling countryside
outside of Chester, Pennsylvania. It looks like any private
boarding school to the casual observer, a red brick, ivy-covered
administration building flanked by three- and four-story brick
cottages. There are no walls or fences.

Major Hickman believes, "Psychiatry is dangerous. Pretty
soon it will just excuse away all bad boys." If a boy behaves
himself, he'll do all right. If not, he'll be taught the road to
honesty.

Major Hickman pointed out to us that one of the worst offenses at Glen Mills is running away. This is dangerous not
only to innocent folks who live nearby but it's even more dangerous for the runaways. A runaway boy acting out of panic
can commit much worse crimes than those for which he was
originally sentenced. This, explained the major, is why a runaway faces severe punishment. The major described routine
punishment at that time as follows:

> A boy is given a pack to wear on his back. He does guard duty
> outside the cottage during the time which is usually allocated as
> a play period. The cottage as a whole is also punished if one of

their members runs away, since the cottage's movie rights are forfeited.

We were convinced as we talked to the major that the story
Ward had told us of the beatings with the rifle butts was a
classic example of his brand of fiction. But this was no fiction.
We saw the racks of wooden rifles. We were told that they are
used as props for military drill.

Major Hickman took us to see a cottage in which he said
Earl Ward had lived. As we entered the cottage, there was a
small homey parlor for the personal use of the cottage "mother
and father." The parlor opened into a huge, barren hall and
dining room. All the wooden floors had a polish that was almost diamond-hard, kept that way by the children who wore
padded stockings—not shoes—on their feet. And with their
stocking feet they shuffled back and forth over the floor, working the candle wax into the floor until their soles were hot
with friction. This device, we were told, was not only practical,
but "an excellent lesson teacher."

The cottage didn't sound like a cottage where children
lived. There was little talk and no laughter. It was the school
of any child's nightmares.

We were led downstairs through a stairwell that was enclosed by iron grillwork. Major Hickman apologized for the
grillwork, saying, "Some people think it looks too much like
a jail, but the ironwork is done right here in the school. We
think it's handsome." Handsome work it is, but he was right—
it does look like a jail.

Major Hickman didn't remember very much about Ward's
stay at Glen Mills. "He wasn't here very long."

I asked him if he could give me a list of boys who used to be
in Earl's cottage. Perhaps they'd remember Earl better than
the major did. The major was delighted to help out. He gave
us the list and wished us well. He hoped that we would not
follow the lead of some "ill-advised" newspaper reporters who
always criticized his institution for being so strict, but we made
no promises.

The list contained fourteen names, and we checked them
out. Eight of the names on that list were boys who had died

in service. Two of the boys lived out of state. The others were scattered around the state of Pennsylvania. We tracked them down and talked to them. We also talked to their friends.

None of the boys we talked to had been in Ward's cottage, but they remembered him vaguely as a boy who was always fighting and always trying to run away. He was described as a skinny, lonesome kid, who made friends with the colored boys rather than the whites.

Although they did not remember Ward too well, they vividly recalled their own experiences at Glen Mills and agreed with Ward on the facts. Here is the testimony of one boy, who now owns his own successful tailor shop on the west side of Philadelphia.

> Glen Mills is an awful place, really. Earl exaggerated some, but not much. I don't believe that story about being handcuffed to a bedspring, but it could be! They did worse. They used the cat o'nine tails till your fingers bled. The beating with the guns, that happens all the time. The older boys enjoy beating the younger ones. And they got a lot of sadistic people too. One of the instructors used to like beating the boys up. Some of those little colored kids he used to beat until they cried like little babies. A Chinese boy once ran away. They dunked his head in a toilet and kept flushing the toilet until he was 'most drowned. It's the officials who make the boys bend over. Lots of times the boys pass out, 'cause the blood rushes to their head. Glenn Mills doesn't make a boy better, but it teaches him to hate. You never forget how much you hate after Glen Mills.

On May 1, 1953, shortly after we broadcasted the story on Glen Mills, Wendell Fewell became superintendent after Major Hickman resigned. According to Robert Beatty, chairman of the board of managers, Glen Mills is *now* "an institution for reform, not punishment." Psychiatric care is being introduced, new treatment positions created, and the over-all policy is being brought into line with the standards set for reform schools by the United States Children's Bureau. Beatty admitted that in the past some Philadelphia judges had refused to send boys to Glen Mills, but he felt the new policies would change their attitudes. According to all reports, while progress is necessarily slow there, as it is at all penal institutions, it is being made.

The police blotter contained the verification of Ward's next story. Earl ran away from Glen Mills one more time. But this time during his escape he attempted a burglary in order to get funds to go home. He was charged with breaking and entering and sent to an institution for older boys at Huntington.

We checked Ward's next story with the Huntington authorities. Ward said:

> Huntington was built in 1700 or 1800. When I arrived there with this bad record, I was more or less condemned from the start. It was really juvenile adolescence, but a lot of violence as far as they were concerned. So I started carrying a knife when I realized I was in a place where older men were and that's the way they fought. I became known as a shiv* boy, one who carries a shiv or a knife, and I would use it at the slightest provocation.

Huntington authorities confirmed Earl's boast that he was a shiv boy. He stole a knife from the mess hall shortly after he arrived. They took it away from him but he found another.

> I became involved in several serious incidents with some inmates in which I cut them, but they never cut me. One time, I was asked to commit an act which I resisted. Consequently I almost killed a boy, and although I never told people the real reason, it worked on my mind that I would always have to resist as long as I was in prison.

There is a notation on Ward's record at Huntington that the authorities suspected Ward of having definite homosexual tendencies.[2] Earl Ward from his first day at Huntington became an acute problem. The authorities conferred about his case and decided Ward would do better in a different institution. They recommended his transfer to a new industrial training school known as Camp Hill.

Camp Hill had a brand-new laundry when Earl arrived. He was there only a short time when he and a fellow inmate, who was game for anything, decided to sabotage the equipment. They stole knives and slashed the conveyor belts. They dumped two hundred and fifty dollars' worth of laundry soaps, starches,

---

[2] Michigan inmates called him a "punk." *

and bluing down the drain. Ward was punished and placed in the isolation ward.

After he was returned to general population, Earl decided to ingratiate himself with the authorities, and before long he was forgiven for his past behavior. Earl's father, true to form, had visited the institution and pleaded for his boy. Impressed by the obvious sincerity of the father, the officials gave Ward a chance, and Earl Ward became a hall boy. He also became popular with his fellow inmates and took over as a leader.

Ward goes on:

As a hall boy, I had a lot of liberty. I was in charge of the inmates' cards. Well, these men from Eastern State employed my aid in switching the cards which showed the men who were allowed to come out of their cells and the men who were not. I switched the cards when a relief guard was on duty during dinner hour. I told him the men were allowed out for some water.

They came out and we hit the guard. I assisted in tying the guard up, and the wound was fatal to the guard. Then we ran for it. We reached the yard of the prison and ran for the fence to the outside. It was noontime. We were fired upon before we hit the fence, and we were caught in a continuous cross fire from the four towers.

One of our boys was shot dead. I was wounded three times. We were taken to the prison hospital and confined there. I was there four or five weeks when politics came into the picture. My father played a very important part, and I was given a pardon and released.

It's a funny thing to say, but I was not fit to be released. I should have gone through some habilitation before I was turned loose, because I was bitter. I knew I wasn't going to live up to my parole or any other agreements right from the start.

Camp Hill remembered that incident vividly. Their version differed only slightly from Ward's. Earl was the hall boy who had engineered the deal, but he had had nothing to do with tying up the guard. The guard who had been attacked suffered nothing more than acute embarrassment from a subsequent investigation.

The four inmates started for the fence, and the institution, in an attempt to stop them, opened fire. They never thought the boys would try to run past that line of fire, but the four escapees ran into it. One boy was killed. This supposedly was a vicious kid whose own family was frightened of him. Two of the other boys were wounded, one on the inside of the wall and the other when he climbed the fence and reached the outside.

Earl Ward suffered only acute cuts of his hands from scaling the barbed wire. Ward could have made good his escape attempt, but he stopped to help his injured pal. A guard got there before the two boys could get away, and all the fight went out of Ward. The two boys gave up.

The reports of Earl made by the medical and psychological staffs at Camp Hill are interesting. They found:

> This boy is normal. But for his age he is conceited and spoiled by the attention of others. There must have been something wrong with his early upbringing. He says he ran away from home to show he was as good as his brother. He hates his father. He likes his mother better, but he has no great affection for her. He is crude, shiftless, and immature. He has an IQ of 112 (college level).

The escape attempt returned Earl to the isolation ward. At that time there was no pardon. But several months later, for reasons that cannot be explained, Earl Ward was considered fit to be released.

Now his family was faced once again with the return of the prodigal. Ward tells of that return:

> When I got home, the first rule was this: I had to be home by 10:00 P.M. I could not go out unless I had my brother or sister with me. Oh, the rules my parents tried to lay down! I ran away the first day. I've never been home since. I came home that evening to get my clothes, and my brother and I got in a very serious argument. I tried to kill my brother. I did not succeed. My grandmother stepped between us, and I escaped because the police were at the front door.

The Ward family gave us a different version of that story. They said that the first evening Earl started an argument with his brother in the family bathroom. Grandma stepped between

the two boys in an attempt to break it up. Earl raced downstairs to the kitchen and grabbed a knife. He raced back upstairs and slashed the air madly, missing his brother by inches.
The older brother knew this was no longer a kid he was dealing with. Bigger and stronger, he picked Earl up and flung him
down the stairs.

There were no police involved in this episode. The family
resolved the problem by deciding Earl would go to live with
his maternal grandmother. Earl agreed with this plan and he
packed his clothes. Although Earl never mentioned his grandmother when he talked to us, he evidently felt a true attach-
ment for her. During the time he was in her home, his violent
eruptions and hysterical displays were at a minimum. Earl
promised his grandmother that he'd get a job. But he spent
more time loafing on street corners than inhabiting employment agencies.

He claimed he was "pushing dope at the time." He also returned to his old story of Marnice Richardson. "She had some
big connection," he said, "and that's how I got mixed up with
dope and medicine and one thing and another."

These activities are not recorded on a police blotter. But the
police blotters do state Earl was picked up driving around in a
stolen car with a fellow ex-inmate. Once again he was hauled
into court, and once again his father appeared by his side.
Drawn, haggard, confused, he heard his son sentenced to
a second indeterminate period at Camp Hill.

Ward picks up the story with his second arrival at Camp
Hill:

> At the gates of Camp Hill I was refused admittance by War-
> den Hill. He would not take me back into his institution, so they
> had to take me back to Philadelphia. Then they called Hunting-
> ton, but Huntington didn't want me. It just seemed that no place
> wanted me, even at that early age.

Earl Ward was right. He was shuttled back and forth between the institutions until the courts decided he was to be
committed to Huntington.

> Well, when I got back up in there, I was immediately placed
> in solitary. For six months I stayed in solitary. And this guard

continually ruled me. He tore up my letters, cut down my food, aggravated me, wrote reports on me for things I didn't do, and one thing and the other. Finally I could take it no more.

Now Ward comes to probably the most important story he has to tell, because this is the story that the officials at Jackson Prison believed to be true during the riot there.

I had a knife smuggled into the hole there, and I did what some people may call a very dastardly deed. I saved up some urine, and, when that guard came by that evening, I threw it in his face, knowing that he would come into my cell for that act. This, you see, was the only way I could get at him. When I did the act, he went and got some other officers and then came back and came into my cell. I took the knife, I lunged at him and I hit him in a very vital spot in his stomach. I ripped him all the way down, and he died of complications that set in there.

The official report of Huntington, Pennsylvania, gives this version of the attack. Officer Calhoun was the officer reporting. The date: May 18, 1943.

When passing this boy's cell during the count, he tried to throw a tin cup full of water on me and remarked, "Now I'll give you sons of bitches something to write a check* about." I reported this to Sergeant Kepner. We escorted the sergeant to the barber-shop cell. When I opened the door to go in, Ward hit me on the head with a hairbrush.

Search as we did, looking for a dead guard, there was none. But the institution supplied us with a full copy of the prison's report of Ward's activities while he was there:

DISCIPLINARY RECORD—EARL WARD #B-1794

8/24/42 *Reported by Mr. Van Ormer:*
         Ward admits stealing a knife from the dining room. When
         questioned, he said he took the knife to "get" Mr. Ken-
         nedy in Ward D.
         B-4 CLOSE CUSTODY. BRING BEFORE BOARD IN SEPTEMBER.

9/3/42   *Reported by Officer H. E. Quinn:*
         I report this boy for wasting food, insolence, and threat-
         ening two officers with death. This boy refused to eat all

his food and became insolent when told he would have to clean his tray, saying, "I won't eat it and you can't make me." Mr. Roth and myself entered his cell. He drew back his tray to hit us. We were forced to handle him pretty rough. We relieved him of his tray. He took his shoe and advanced toward us, threatening to kill us both. This boy has had a surly attitude ever since he was confined to this ward.

FIVE DAYS B&W* IN SEGREGATION. AFTER THIS SENTENCE RETURN TO B-4 FOR CLOSE CUSTODY.

4/1/43   I report this boy for being disorderly while in segregation, for using profane language in reference to Ward B officers and for stealing a razor blade with the apparent intention of cutting Officer Wagner.

THREE DAYS B&W IN SEGREGATION CELL.

4/29/43   *Reported by Officer Calhoun:*
While making the count,* this boy complained about his mail being lost and requested to go out and see the captain. I instructed him to write Mr. Brant a letter, to which he replied, "The hell with Brant, I want to see the Goddamned captain." He yelled those remarks at the top of his voice.

24 HOURS B&W IN SEGREGATION.

5/16/43   *Reported by Officer Calhoun:*
This boy was whistling out of his cell and deliberately throwing his tin cup on the floor. He also remarked, "Every officer in this place is a sonofabitch."

24 HOURS B&W, 4th TIER (segregation).

5/25/43   Released this date from segregation cell and returned to Cell 131, 4th Tier Ward B (close segregation).

Now Ward was examined by a two-man commission, Dr. Bernard Alpers and Dr. Robert Matthews, who advised immediate commitment to a mental institution: "He is extremely bitter and almost vituperative against his father. His brother infuriates him." Although, they conclude, this man does not have a clearly defined and well-developed mental condition at this time, he has had a "distorted personality since childhood with a gradual development of persecutory ideas, all of which should be considered as constituting a psychosis of in-

sanity of certifiable degree. In addition, he has criminal tendencies."

Ward was sent to Farview State Hospital for the criminally
insane, July 16, 1943. He was nineteen years old. We contacted
the staff of Farview in order to check the following story with
their records. Farview claimed Earl was an ideal inmate from
the moment of his admittance through his entire stay. In addition, they said, he lived in a dormitory with other well-
behaved prisoners.

Ward's version differs:

> I knew what state hospitals were like, but I'm no dummy and I
> played it cool. If you resist up there, they can kill you and call it
> justifiable homicide.
>   I'll never forget the gravity of the hour when the four guards
> came out for me:

Ward stated the guards' names correctly. Farview verified them.

> I was sitting naked on the floor. They asked me my name . . .
> and when I tried to get up, I was down again. They put the
> boots to me. They kicked me.

(Ward himself later denied that he was ever kicked or beaten,
except once.)

> Then they took me to a little peanut of a cell, which was about
> seven feet long and four feet wide. There was a window which
> could be opened from the outside where the cold air came in. It
> seemed to me they had one idea: to weaken me mentally, mor-
> ally, and physically.

Fact or fiction, we have only Ward's word. However, Farview
State Hospital does have small cells for close confinement where
they keep unruly inmates.

> I was finally let out of this little peanut and taken to the hos-
> pital. I was then given a spinal, against my will. I know the law.
> I knew they couldn't give me a spinal unless I had syph or any
> signs of it, which I didn't have. But this doctor bound me and
> tied me and threw me up on the table. He hit me three different

times to give me that spinal and each time a crippling pain went through me. Afterwards they took me to the hospital hole.

There is no such cell designated as a "hospital hole." The spinal tap as described by Ward, officials claim, is a highly colored description of a routine medical examination. They take a sample of spinal fluid.

> About two months later, I was taken to the ward. Most of the people just deteriorate in there. You have nothing but soup and fluid to eat. Everything is limited. I was assigned to a bench. Six straight months I sat there. I was allowed to get up only three times: to wash, to go to the lavatory, or to eat. Other inmates had the same seats assigned to them. Those who had been there for some time were allowed to walk around and do little jobs. While I was there, I saw four men beat to death, kicked to death.

Earl's preoccupation with violent death is apparent throughout his narrative. The death of the inmates, according to the staff, is an outright lie. However, Farview officials have dismissed guards from their staff for undue cruelty.

They described Ward's life in the hospital as routine. He was given wholesome food, which they describe as soups or nourishing stews. Furthermore, they claim, all patients have a prescribed treatment of occupational therapy. We questioned the Farview staff about the occupational therapy given Earl. After much hesitation they told us, "Well, he made beds."

As for Earl's claim that he sat on a bench for six straight months, one doctor said, "Nonsense, no one sits on a bench at Farview—except, well—now and then, once in a while. We have them sit on a spot as punishment for misbehavior, but Earl never misbehaved."

The boy who never misbehaved gives a sample of his exemplary behavior at Farview:

> I knew I had to get away. There were three men there who, if they are still living, I think they're still sane to a certain extent. There was nothing wrong with them. One of them had been serving time at an eastern penitentiary. It seems he was sent up from Eastern State Penitentiary. When they can't handle you in a penn, they "bug" you and send you to a mental hospital for a

lesson. If you go insane in the mental hospital, that's just one of
those frailties you have to suffer. So I started talking to these men,
and we had a plot up, a very good escape plot, I might say. But
one of the inmates got wind of it.

Farview officials both denied this story and admitted it. They
couldn't decide which. Finally they settled their dilemma by
saying, "We heard something of an escape plot, but Earl wasn't
serious. He was kidding."

The old kidder continues:

> My father came to visit me. The superintendent told him I was
> planning to escape. My father says to the superintendent, if there
> is something wrong with Earl, what it is?

Ward's father confirms part of his story. He went to Farview
to find out how Earl was doing. However, the father's version
and Ward's version of this visit differ from here on. Mr. Ward
says he was called to Farview to discuss Earl's problems.

But Ward reconstructs his father's meeting with the superintendent in highly dramatic terms. He says that Ward Senior
stalked into the office and denounced the institution, lacing
them roundly for their lack of corrective therapy. He threatened
to call in a commission of doctors who would challenge the
findings of previous commissions. Ward's story climaxes when
he says a guard was called in and forced to admit the truth.
Head hanging, the guard confessed, "Ward don't blow his top.
He don't talk to himself like some other inmates. I am with
him most of the time—I know."

Now Ward's voice evens off, as he continues calmly:

> After my father left, they promised to do something for me.
> They did. I got an ass-whipping I'll never forget. I was laying on
> the floor asleep when a guard kicked me, saying, "You will get
> hand happy" and all this business, and he accused me of trying
> to start a fight. He went and got some other guards and they
> really puts the boots to me. But I will say this: outside of this one
> time, I was never beaten.

Now Ward tells of a second visit his father and brother supposedly made to Farview. The family denies a second visit. Be-

cause of this visit and his "political pull," Ward claims the
superintendent decided he was ready to be released. Ward
launches into the story of his release:

> At six o'clock the next morning, . . . I had a nice breakfast
> of bacon and eggs, something I hadn't seen since before I came
> in. Then they took me out and removed me to Huntington,
> back to the place where all the trouble started. I said to myself,
> well—this isn't going to work. They're waitin' for me. You know
> what I mean—who's kiddin' who?
>
> Sure enough, when we got inside Huntington, they didn't want
> me. But there was a court order and they had to take me. Com-
> mander Pennington let me know right away he wanted to send
> me back. I was frightened because I had come so far and yet
> really gotten nowhere. So I got into an argument with an officer
> and I tried to do him up. I was put in the hole for that. Right
> away they called a sanity commission in again.

Ward's version of his return to Huntington is half the truth.
We pieced together the full version of this return trip from
the stories of various officials.

Earl Ward was chastened and subdued when he returned.
As far as Commander Pennington was concerned, two years in
a state hospital for the criminally insane was no cure-all, and
he eyed Ward's return with doubts. But the commander awaited
developments, and they came in the form of an abject letter
from Earl, a strong plea to let bygones be bygones. Earl con-
tended that he had grown up and was now ready to take his
place in an institution and behave himself. He pleaded for an
opportunity to prove himself.

Commander Pennington had Ward brought to his office for
a talk. Ward can be charming and convincing. Scrubbed and
immaculate, he was at his best. He faced the commander and
threw himself on his mercy, insisting that no one in the world
quite understood him the way Commander Pennington did.
His future was in the commander's hands.

Commander Pennington could hardly believe his ears, but,
if the boy was sincere, the commander was going to see that he
got a chance. He ordered Ward housed in desirable Ward F,
which allowed inmates maximum freedom within the enclosure.
He scheduled a work program for Ward that made other in-

mates envious: the laundry detail in the morning and the gym detail (the one every inmate wanted) in the afternoon. The commander gave orders to give Ward the benefit of every doubt. He himself kept a friendly eye on the boy.

The first week Ward's activities caused the commander to wonder if Farview had truly worked miracles. He alternated between this assumption and another idea. Perhaps, reasoned the commander, harsh treatment had caused the earlier eruptions.

Ward was making friends among the more desirable inmates. He was gaining prestige. He was exhibiting his ability as a leader. He began doing favors, not only for inmates but for the guards. Inmates flocked around him. His head swelled. One day in a fit of generosity Earl decided to launder clothes for his special friends. The fact that he had no permission dismayed him not at all, and he was reprimanded for taking matters into his own hands.

This reprimand brought a hot retort from Ward. He briefly told the instructor that he had pull, the Ward family had connections that would allow him to do exactly as he pleased. The instructor sent in a disciplinary report, and Ward was returned to close segregation; his privileges were cut. This punishment inspired Ward to try to get even. He stole a knife from the dining room and attempted some plain and fancy knife throwing. A second disciplinary report resulted in Ward's return to the hole.

Commander Pennington appealed to the juvenile courts. After some thought he had decided that Earl Ward could not possibly benefit from incarceration in a penal institution, and he insisted that Earl Ward needed medical care. Once again a lunacy commission was appointed. Ward says:

> This commission was either honest with itself or something, because they decided I could get along in any environment except that of a prison. In a prison, something just went wrong. I blew up.
> They took me back to court, and the court psychologist ruled on me. But, in the meantime, my father had got to work and paid quite a bit of money to have me removed to Byberry. Who's kidding who—he had political pull.

The Wards' political pull was nonexistent. The court decided Byberry might help Ward, for Philadelphia authorities were getting desperate. Byberry is a huge institution for
the retention of the insane. We spent considerable time at Byberry talking to the doctors, the technicians, and the nurses.
Earl, they said, responded to their treatment, and Earl agrees:

Dr. Zeller of Byberry did what no one else could do. He rebili-
tated me.

I was admitted to the institution with shackles on and everything else. Dr. Zeller called me on the phone. He said he had
talked to my father and to the judge and would like to see me
personally. He told me to walk over by myself. Well, it was a
ten- to fifteen-minute walk over, and I believe I did take
my time. I knew I was not being followed. There was an urge
in me to run. I can't explain why, but this was the first time in
years I had been free.

Somehow or other I got over to the administration building,
and I was ushered into Dr. Zeller's office. There was another
doctor there, Dr. Pierce. They treated me as one of them, offered me a cigarette, asked me to sit down. They didn't talk about
any neurosis or phobias or anything like that. They acted like I
was normal.

They told me I could pick out my own assignment after I was
there a while. What did I want to do? What could I do? Well, I
was taken back. I was shocked. I had never been treated like
that before. Then I was told to wander back to the male division
on my own. No one seemed alarmed that I was loose. I was
treated normal even though it is a mental hospital.

Undoubtedly the treatment Ward received at Byberry was a
startling contrast to his treatment at Farview. He was given a
room in the administration building away from the other inmates, a lovely room with a fine view of the grounds. Ward was
happy at Byberry. He was given more freedom than he had
ever been given before. This is fact. But the authorities weren't
sure whether Ward actually wandered around the grounds that
first day or not. It was possible, they conceded.

Ward continues with his adventures at Byberry:

An officer by the name of Ray Blanchfield came over to introduce himself. He was a fine man, and he knew how to handle

men. He didn't seem alarmed that I just came from the criminally insane hospital for committing a violent crime.[3] He said,
"Have you ever worked around patients?" Well, I had, and he
said, "Good, you're just the man I want."

So I became his assistant, writing out the charts, giving medi-
cation, helping on tube feedings. Finally I got promoted to the
O.R. (operating room) as surgical nurse. That's where I picked
up most of my experience and training in surgery.

I enjoyed every minute at Byberry. I needed it for my health.
I became more trustful in my tendencies. I was trusted. I was
allowed the freedom of the hospital grounds, to a certain extent.
They were out of bounds, but I had a ground parole. I was even
given keys.

The story, as Earl Ward told it, is not much exaggerated
over the actual facts. During the war years, Byberry suffered
an acute help shortage. All able-bodied inmates were pressed
into service to help the inmates who could not help themselves.
Ray Blanchfield remembered Earl as a conscientious helper
who worked hard in the wards. Perhaps he kept the charts,
moved patients, helped in tube feeding, and did other odds
and ends, but Byberry officials vehemently deny he was a surgical nurse. Ray Blanchfield says he scrubbed up the operating
room and sterilized the instruments a couple of times when
the institution was shorthanded. Perhaps he was even given
the keys. He had a ground parole and was allowed to wander
at will.

Earl's record at Byberry was good except for one incident.
He stole a knife. He started an argument with another patient
and wanted to end it at knife point. The knife was taken away
and the incident forgiven and forgotten, because overcrowded,
understaffed Byberry had more pressing problems.

Ward certainly was in better shape than dozens of patients
clamoring for admission. Therefore, despite the knife problem,
the authorities decided to return him to society. Earl tells of
his return to the streets:

I started going home on week ends. It was decided that my
grandmother's house was the only house that I would be allowed

---
[3] Another reference to the nonexistent murder.

to go to. Naturally I had to keep away from my parents—my father, mother, brother, and sister—because there was so much trouble with them when I was a child, and I agreed on this. Then one day they decided, "We're going to send you back to court. We think you're fit for society." I went back to court and they turned me over to a welfare society—you know, one of those ladies who comes to see you once a month. She helped me adjust at home and stuff.

I wouldn't take the court's help in getting a job. I wanted to be independent. I forgot to mention that years before I'd worked in different butcher shops, so I got a job as a butcher. I was no real meat cutter, but I knew the different cuts and I could handle a knife. I worked myself up to assistant manager of a meat department.

No one disputes the fact that Earl can handle a knife. The job in the butcher shop was secured for him by his father, who knew several men in the meat business and prevailed on his old friends to help out. They did, to their everlasting grief. Ward blew up on the job and was finally thrown out because he not only endangered the lives of his fellow workers but threatened to cut up the customers.

His business activities, however, did not interfere with his romantic life. He was in love with a lovely, fragile child-woman, who had been committed to Byberry because she lived in a fairy-tale world. Whether Ward met her during his stay at Byberry or later, we do not know.

Easily impressed, Lily[4] adored the handsome, charming Ward. He showed her his best side, and, when Ward wants to sell himself, no one can be more engaging. She fell head over heels in love. Believing every word Ward spoke, she felt the world was only a vicious plot against a lonesome boy. Lily was lonesome, too, and her loneliness had forced her to withdraw from the world of reality. Ward brought her back to grim facts. This is his version of the romance:

> I was going around with this patient from Byberry. The court got wind of it. They started laying down the law to her and to me. They threatened to send either one of us back to the institution if we did not discontinue to see each other. Well, when you

---

[4] The name is changed.

try to drive two people apart, all you do is drive them together, especially with a disposition like I've got. If you order me to do something, I won't do it. If you ask me, that's different. You see, there's a technique. They used the wrong technique.

The court never ordered these two to stop seeing each other, but there was plenty of evidence that they had advised against it.

Ward continues with his romance:

> Well, we got to playing around real serious. She got pregnant, but she didn't tell me until she was pregnant four months. She called my grandmother and told my grandmother what the score was.
>
> Well, out of decency I just couldn't see something like this happening, but the courts wouldn't let us get married. So it began working on my mind . . . we had done something wrong. I could see my whole future being ruined by this one little incident. I went to the court and tried to make a deal with them, but they locked her up.
>
> To make the story short, I had a little influence with the doctor, but I didn't have enough money. To get money, I had to go back to pushing dope, to bribe the doctor to intercede for the girl. He got her in a home as a personal maid to him . . . and everything worked out.

Then Ward hesitated, laughed, coughed—and betrayed himself. This was a flight of fancy. The court did not have the girl locked up. Lily was working in a restaurant at the time. A devout Catholic, she insisted that before they were married he would have to become a Catholic, even though the child was on the way. Ward says:

> I went and took the catechism and instructions. Then we got married. That was in November of '46. March of '47 the baby was born. In the meantime, from all this worry I had a heart attack, and I moved to my grandmother's.

His frequently recurring "heart attacks" are psychosomatic. He makes no mention of what happened to his wife and child when he moved.

I started doing armed robberies and things, and got more deeply involved than ever in crime. Well, the girl became very nagging and sarcastic and one thing and another, and she bragged to another girl she had deliberately lured me.

This infuriated Ward and he left her flat. He brags that he gave his wife a considerable amount of money before deserting her, but the fact is that he left her without money for the baby's milk. His grandmother helped all she could, but the girl finally went on relief.

Ward looked around for something to do. He decided to become a doctor. He claims he went to Temple University and stole the necessary documents for an M.D. Whether he did or didn't isn't important, since from this time on Earl posed as a doctor. He appeared in Florida, and Ward says of his Florida trip:

> Waxy —you know, Waxy Gordon—well, I had worked for him, and he had some influence with the syndicate in Florida. They helped me set up offices, and I even got past the state board medical exams down there.

We checked. There was no Dr. Earl E. Ward licensed to practice in Florida. Ward continues:

> I was on the staff of several hospitals and started my practice of doing illegal abortions. In these hospitals, we'd hide people who were in trouble, members of the syndicate. We'd admit them as patients in private rooms without the authorities ever knowing. More or less as a hideout. I was right back in the old circle again, but this time more seriously.

This is a difficult story to corroborate or to brand false. The newspapers of the time were doing an exposé on the abortion racket in Florida. Whether Earl was part of it or not, we do not know. At one time he had a job as an orderly in a private sanitarium in Florida. But he seems to have had plenty of ready cash while he lived down there, and he lived in a hotel, where he had registered as Dr. Earl E. Ward and was evidently accepted as a legitimate doctor. Then his Florida stay came to a sudden end. He left the state. Earl explains his change of plans this way:

> The federal authorities moved in on some of the fatalities that happened to other doctors doing abortions. Not to mine. I was forced to leave Miami because of this. I was just one step ahead of the federal authorities. I skipped to Buffalo, New York, but these guys threw a girl in my way and told me to marry up with her while I was in Buffalo. That was the deal there. So I got married to this other girl in Miami just as a shield. She was syndicate. We went to her people's place in Buffalo to cool off.

The facts were that Earl had a whirlwind romance with a girl in Miami, whose name was Miriam.[5] He decided to give matrimony another try and he was married to Miriam without the benefit of a divorce from his first wife. In Buffalo, Miriam introduced her doctor-husband to her family. He entertained them with stories of his medical achievements and they took him to their hearts and paid the bills. They might as well have adopted a king cobra. After a month in Buffalo, he kissed his bride good-by and left on a business trip. He claims she was a problem.

> The syndicate wanted me to go to Detroit, and they didn't tell me what to do with this wife in Buffalo. So I left several hundred dollars in the bank for her, together with some jewelry. I thought that was enough since there was no serious fondness between us and she had benefited to some extent. I told her I was going to a medical convention and I would send for her. I never did. I didn't intend to.

Ward left Miriam as flat as he had left Lily. Later, Miriam got a divorce from him, not knowing that they had never been legally married. Now the twice-married Ward arrived in Detroit and registered at the hotel as Dr. Earl E. Ward. He says:

> Three or four days later I made a contact through a young lady with the syndicate. We went out to interview prospective places for a clinic. Some midwives had set up some drivers, which are necessary to operate an abortion clinic. Then we got under

---

[5] The name is changed.

way with our plans. At the time of my crime I heard of a large
sum of money being carried by this real-estate man. The sum was
$18,000. It was a nice lure.

Earl now puzzles why he tried to take the money since he
had bragged he was doing well in the abortion racket in Detroit. But he reconciles the discrepancy this way:

> You see, robbery wasn't exactly what I was in, but $18,000 is
> $18,000. I thought I could have it, and if I could, it was mine.
> And there was no reason why anyone would suspect me—being a
> doctor, and being set up, y'know. So I started out on the crime
> and, unfortunately, I was apprehended in the act.

Ward's activities in Detroit are a mystery. Those who should
know claim the syndicate does not hire sick men. Discipline in
organized crime is even more important than in a legitimate
business: they need men they can rely on. But he did come to
Detroit and sign the hotel register as Dr. Ward, and where his
money came from no one knows. He seemed to be pretty much
alone except for pickups in various bars and cafés. The good
doctor had few calls.

Then he started out on a heist. Armed to the teeth, he boldly
strode into an insurance office at closing time. He held up the
four men who were inside. They had $29 among them, which
Earl collected. In a fury because of their small resources, he
took one of the four men with him, thus securing a kidnapping
charge for himself. At gun point his victim entered the car.
The other three notified the police, carefully giving Ward's
license number. The streets of Detroit were treated to the sight
of a wild driver skidding around corners, followed by police
cars until a bullet zoomed too close to Ward's head for comfort,
and he was stopped.

Ward went to trial. The sentencing judge, with all the wis-
dom of Solomon, sent him to Michigan's maximum-security
penitentiary at Marquette. It is interesting to speculate whether
the judge ever saw the previous reports on Ward. Did he know
of Ward's commitments to two state hospitals? Had he seen the
psychiatrists' specific warning that Ward could not be controlled
in a penal atmosphere?

Michigan found out. At Marquette Earl put on a real show: temper tantrums, hysteria, violence, knifings, heart attacks; and soon he aligned himself with the worst element in the institution. He made one friend, an inmate called "Crazy Jack" Hyatt.[6]

While Ward was busy continually giving Marquette a hard time, Crazy Jack saved up his energy for a headline-making trick. Rumor has it that Earl Ward brain-trusted this deal, but that is only rumor.

Crazy Jack and two other inmates kidnapped Michigan's Governor "Soapy" Williams while he was inside Marquette making a routine inspection. The governor's bodyguard, George Kerr, describes it this way:

> We were in the mess hall. Suddenly the door swung open. Convict Stearns[7] grabbed Governor Williams by the arm and had a cut-down butcher knife at his throat. He said, "Soapy, come with us." I fell in right behind them. The next thing I knew, I had a knife in my back. My main purpose was to get the knife out. I saw the governor had his situation under control, so I swung around to face this inmate. He was making mad passes at my throat so I figured I had enough, so I shot him. That's when Crazy Jack Hyatt came into the picture. He started screaming like a mad man—he couldn't get in the door so he jumped right through the screen.

This incident led the warden to wonder if Earl Ward and his pal Jack Hyatt might not be wrongly placed inside Marquette. He petitioned to have Ward and Hyatt removed. Ward was to be sent to Ionia State Hospital for the criminally insane. But Ionia was overcrowded and couldn't take Earl. Marquette refused to keep him. Then the officials got an idea. They had already shipped Crazy Jack to Michigan state penitentiary at Jackson. They found a home for Earl there, too.

There were sixty-five hundred inmates at Jackson about to explode. Earl Ward joined them.

---

[6] A Canadian doing twenty-five to thirty years for armed robbery.

[7] Serving life for armed robbery. According to the warden, he had just been released from two years in solitary.

anatomy of a riot

. . . McGraw Reporting

ON SUNDAY, APRIL 20, 1952, THE STATE PRISON OF SOUTHERN Michigan at Jackson, the world's largest walled penitentiary, had not only our nation's biggest riot, but one that became to rioters in other prisons the text-book model for all prison riots. Under what has been reluctantly called Earl Ward's "brilliant leadership," it involved a greater number of rioters than any other, it went on for a longer time, and it had the most carefully worked out set of riot demands. But in the long run it accomplished less for the inmates than any other riot in the contagion.

Since Detroit is my home town, what we found in Michigan surprised me much less than it did Peg. For instance, I knew that Michigan, despite its sprawling factory area around Detroit, is politically a farm state and, while the state has gone Democratic in gubernatorial races, the legislature is usually Republican. This embarrassing split was in operation when we visited the state some eight months and one dirty election campaign after the Jackson riot.

Since Michigan was the second riot spot we covered, we were still groggy from attempting to untangle what we had come to call "Jersey logic." We were all set to receive another "spring fever" slough-off, and we did not know how we could investigate this as thoroughly as we had Bates' story. In Michigan we did not have the contacts we had around New York for reaching dependable ex-inmates. When I last lived in Michigan, I had been a college instructor. Campus life, at least in my experience, had not even involved panty raids, much less contact with what Bates considered their prison counterpart. With no inmates to talk to, "The Challenge of Our Prisons" was going to be a hard series to put on the air.

Leery of commissioners by now, we decided that the best jumping-off place would be the governor's office. Michigan's Democratic governor, G. Mennen "Soapy" Williams, is famous for leaving his doors open, literally and figuratively, to the press. In the middle of conferences newsmen can wander into his office, pull up a chair, and listen in. Williams gives the impression of being positive, bright, and aggressively unafraid. He used to be a football player. He still looks the part without the usual ex-athlete spread. We liked him as, complete with green bow tie and Republican legislature, he greeted us and proceeded to blame the whole riot on the Republicans. He said:

> The story of Jackson prison is a story of warnings disregarded. Every year I urged the Michigan legislature to provide adequate guard forces. I asked them to appropriate the necessary funds to build additional prison space and relieve the overcrowding at Jackson. But the legislature continued to crowd more and more prisoners into the prison and, at the same time, it progressively reduced the appropriations for guards and other essential prison facilities. The riots were—in part, at least—the result of this short-sighted policy.

Since we wanted both sides of every story, we immediately went to the man Williams had defeated for the governor's office election before last, Republican Kim Sigler. Kim was a character in his own right. Where Williams is known for his bow tie, Kim went all the way and was proud of being the best-dressed man in Michigan.

But he actually became famous as a flying prosecutor investigating some of the many political scandals with which Michigan has abounded. We had met him before while covering one of those scandals, which, incidentally, involved Jackson prison. Kim had been looking into the private lives of some legislators with incomes that by some strange political mathematics ended up netting more than they grossed. His investigation had been suddenly emasculated by the murder of his star witness, State Senator Hooper.

Hooper's killer has never been caught; but, according to the best police mind I met in Michigan, the late Captain Edward Cooper of the State Police, a prisoner was released from Jackson prison just long enough to do the job. This was never legally proved, but out of the investigation of Hooper's death grew scandals involving Jackson. It seemed that well-paying prisoners were being chauffeured to brothels and to drinking parties at officials' homes; big-time gambling was common inside the walls, as was more than the usual amount of prison thievery.

Out of this complex compound of scandals came diverse results. Many prison officials "resigned" under fire, and Kim was elected governor of Michigan in an overwhelming flurry of popularity. In the next election he was defeated by Soapy Williams. Up to the time of his recent death in an airplane crash, he was in private law practice. To us he seemed like a good man to present the Republican viewpoint.

"You mean there's another viewpoint?" he asked.

We observed about two minutes of utter silence while Sigler thought over what he should say, his eyes closed, his hands making church steeples in front of his gaily checked vest. Suddenly, he came to life.

"All right. How long do you want this?"

"About a minute."

Kim took a breath and fifty-eight seconds later we had Kim's point of view. Right off the bat he lit into G. Mennen by hitting out at the commissioner of the Michigan Department of Institutions and Corrections:

It seems to me that Governor Williams' appointee, Mr. Ernest Brooks, although he's a very fine gentleman and a good citizen, has not had the experience or training necessary to run a great institution like Jackson. The man who heads up such an institution should be a man of long experience and proven ability in penology. Mr. Brooks has not had that training or experience.

Now the governor has often said that the Republican legislature is to blame for the recent riot because it did not appropriate the necessary funds with which to employ additional guards and do other things that were required. I'm confident in my own mind that, if the governor were to appoint someone who knew what he was doing, there would be no trouble about getting any necessary money for the prison.

After that statement we had to bounce back to the ramshackle capitol to get more from Williams. Soapy was staunch in his defense of Brooks:

Let me say from the beginning I have had complete confidence in Ernest Brooks to do the job that had to be done. Mr. Brooks has had long experience from the legislative point of view with the problems of penology. He is not an expert penologist, it's granted, but he is a capable administrator. That's why I'm confident that he has done a good job and will continue to do a good job.

After all this, meeting Ernest Brooks was quite an experience. He looks like F.D.R. and is not far behind the late president in personal charm. If there were a pinch more aggressiveness in his personality, Brooks would probably be a political power on a national scale. As it is, he did become mayor of Holland, Michigan, where he initiated the Tulip Festival. As a legislator he had interested himself in prison problems and, when Williams came into office, Brooks became head of the corrections department.

He hastened to admit his lack of penal experience or knowledge. He told us frankly we would find that a lot of the riot was his fault; but his mistakes, he maintained, grew from a sincere effort to introduce progressive penology in Michigan. Unlike Bates, he told us to go ahead and talk to prisoners—rioters and nonrioters. His only admonition was simple: "The whole thing was and is a mess. Finding the truth will be tough, but we'll help you any way we can." Brooks may not have been a master penologist, but he certainly had his doctorate in press relations.

Brooks is an easy man to tear apart. He has been criticized, ridiculed, and castigated by newsmen, politicians, and investigators. Our own feelings were that, while he is vulnerable, this treatment is not entirely fair. His intentions were good, but it must be admitted that these good intentions paved the road to a hell of a riot. Knowing penology only on a legislative level, once in active prison work he quickly fell into the penological trap of becoming emotionally involved. Perhaps his years in politics had so ingrained into his soul the habit of doing favors that he failed to recognize the difference between practicing progressive penology and just being a pigeon for inmate sob stories.

Brooks enjoyed dashing over to Jackson from Lansing to wander around the prison without even telling the warden he was there. The latter gentleman was often surprised no end to discover some of the promises to which he had been committed by his boss.

A case in point was a two-time loser, the son of one of Brooks' political cronies. Although the boy was considered a bad security risk, Brooks liked him. Officials took a dim view of Brooks' order to transfer him from maximum security inside the walls to a minimum-security camp. But, "orders is orders." Shortly thereafter the boy was back at Jackson with three years tacked on to his sentence for attempting an escape.

But inmates were not alone in finding Brooks "a good Joe." Personnel at the prison also discovered that, while normally eloquent, Brooks seemed to have a constitutional inability to say the word *no*. They began to bypass their immediate superiors and go directly to the commissioner with requests and complaints. This was made easy for them by Brooks' setting up his department on a one-man-rule basis.

On paper, under the administrative commissioner there was supposed to be a trained penologist to run the prisons, another to handle probation and parole, and a third to act as chairman of the parole board. In actuality, as a later report[1] said, the department had "a commissioner who had no experience in institutional, probation or parole work . . . filling all four of the top positions in one of the largest and most important correctional systems in the country. This involved duties and responsibilities that would have tried the capacity of the most experienced administrators in the country."

Brooks was not that "most experienced" prison administrator. No one has ever found out why he did not hire men for the three jobs under him. Even MacCormick, while investigating the riot for the governor, could not get a satisfactory answer.

Furthermore, in Jackson itself, much the same situation held. Set up to have a warden as administrator, it was also to have a deputy warden to do the actual work of running the place. The state institution, on paper, was supposed to follow the federal plan of having two assistant deputy wardens: one in charge of custody (keeping behind bars convicts who took a dim view of being there), and one in charge of treatment (reforming these men).

But actually no deputy warden was ever hired, and the warden, General Neal Frisbie, a military man, had had no civilian prison experience. He had made himself popular with the inmates by issuing some 232 rules which, if broken, meant being sent to the hole. Under him in place of a deputy warden were two assistant deputy wardens, who alternated in running the prison for twenty-four-hour periods.

To cap the situation, the prison itself is a monstrosity. Enclosed in 57.6 walled acres, at the time of the riot, were 6,475 prisoners, too many even for this prison. New inmates were sleeping on cots in the halls because there was no place else to put them. According to the American Prison Association, twelve hundred inmates is the limit any prison should have at any one time.

---

[1] *Special Committee to Study the Michigan Department of Corrections—Report,* February, 1953, p. 28. This is also called "The MacCormick Report."

Idleness was one of the curses of Jackson, although it does have better and more industries than most prisons. There, as behind all prison walls, several men were assigned to do single jobs that would not strain the work capacities of one really unambitious two-toed sloth. Despite this doubling of workers, Jackson's *idle* population was seventeen hundred and fifty, a figure equal to the *total* population of Sing Sing.

But this was—and is—only part of Jackson's population problem. Theoretically Michigan's branch prison at Marquette, in the mosquito-ridden swamps of the northern peninsula, is supposed to take all maximum-security risks; Ionia State Hospital, the criminally insane; Michigan Reformatory at Ionia, youthful offenders; and the Detroit House of Correction, those who are considered jail cases in most states. A quick look at those institutions throws a lot of light on Jackson.

The reformatory at Ionia is crowded, so at the time of the riot there were around one hundred fifty kids in Jackson who should have been at Ionia. The Detroit House of Correction is not crowded, but the state must pay Detroit to board prisoners there.

Because Ionia State Hospital is crowded, Jackson, at the time of the riot, had one hundred mental cases in Top Six, its mental ward, and another one hundred mental cases mixed into general population. Also at Jackson were one hundred and fifty sexual psychopaths who originally had been committed to Ionia for observation because they were considered too dangerous to be loose. Never convicted of a crime and with no sentence to serve, these so-called guests theoretically were under psychiatric observation. Of course, it could be pointed out that Jackson had no psychiatrist on its staff, but Ionia had a rule that if a prisoner was sent there from Jackson for such minor infractions as developing a homicidal mania, Jackson in turn had to take one of Ionia's sex psychopaths to its steely bosom.

With these sexual psychopaths were mixed some 859 other sex offenders. The rehabilitative value of mixing sex offenders with sex psychopaths and then putting that mixture in with first offenders somehow escapes my untrained eye.

To flavor this mixture, Michigan has no death penalty. While many arguments may be advanced against capital punishment,

one disadvantage so-called lifer states have to face is boarding a greater-than-usual number of long termers. This is true in
Michigan, where the laws are especially severe to make up
for the state's lack of capital punishment. Of course, Marquette
was supposed to handle the difficult cases, but the record
shows that cases that were too tough for Marquette were sent
to Michigan's haven for the homeless convict—Jackson. And it
goes without saying that Marquette is crowded.

This then was the mixture, well stirred in Lansing, that
simmered in Jackson. It was a volatile mixture, but Michigan
seemed to keep lighting matches just to see if it would go off.

It did.

April in Jackson. The prison was quiet. Guard Thomas Elliott
was making the rounds of Fifteen Block (the hole), a dark inside block* reserved for punishment cases and some of the
overflowing mental prisoners who were even too dangerous to
mix in with first offenders. Guard Elliott was an experienced
prison man of a whole week. He had not gone to guard-training
school because guard training had been discontinued before
he got there. Although Elliott was always described to us as
a "kid," prison officials said he had been assigned to the ticklish job of guarding the top tier of Fifteen Block because "you
have to find out if a guard has the stuff or not."

They found out.

Ray Young,[2] a prison "punk," noticed the new guard in his
smart uniform patrolling the tier. Ray called Tom Elliott
over to his cell. Ray had a problem. It seems he was going to
be let out of Fifteen Block the following morning and he had
a present for a boy chum down the way. Would Tom be a good
guy, open the cell door, and let Ray take the present down the
block?

Tom would. In a segregation block reserved for the prison's
most dangerous men, Guard Elliott opened the cell door and
found out that Ray had fibbed. Ray did not have a present at
all. He had a knife. Persuaded by a knife at his neck, Elliott

---

[2] Sentenced to five to fifteen years for breaking and entering. On record as an
habitual drunk.

soon found himself inside the cell looking out at Ray, who, keys in hand, was unlocking cell doors with an efficiency that the new guard might have envied.

After Young had sprung enough of his friends to make things interesting, they all went down to the next tier and captured Guard Akins. More of the boys were let loose and further descent was made with more doors being unlocked and Guard Hinton being taken. Finally, on the ground floor, they ran into a problem. Guard Carrier was in the front office near a telephone and a window; so, to take him, the boys made Guard Hinton, at knife point, call his colleague out of the office into a more capturable position. When this worked, Ray Young and his cohorts used the same technique to capture Guard Holmes, who was patrolling the outside of Fifteen Block.

However, it was at this time that Guard Hinton did about the only fast thinking evidenced by any official that Sunday night. When Holmes opened the door of the block to come inside, Hinton dashed out and escaped. Even with this loss, by 6:30 P.M. the riot in Fifteen was well under way with four guards and some fifteen knives in the hands of the inmates.

Where the knives came from is anybody's guess. Ray Young later said he was given his by "an official." Little credence is given this statement, but somebody must have had either an extremely open mind or very closed eyes if fifteen knives could suddenly appear in a segregation block.

But at 7:00 P.M. Jackson did have its eyes opened to the grim fact that it had a riot. Outside of the hapless guards, now in durance vile, the first official to find out about it was Guard Captain "Capt" Tucker. Capt Tucker was in the main hall office when his phone rang. On the other end was Earl Ward. He informed Capt that inmates had taken over Fifteen Block, that they had hostages and that they would kill some hostages unless George Bacon, the deputy warden in charge of custody, came to Fifteen pronto. Also, said Ward, since this was not an escape attempt, would Capt Tucker come over to Fifteen Block and lock the doors so he, Ward, could keep control of the situation?

Tucker hung up, put out the proper alarms, called the state police, and hurried from the rotunda across the darkening yard to Fifteen Block where Ward, standing outside, waved a cheerful greeting and stepped inside the tool-proof steel door. With Fifteen Block locked, Tucker went back to the main-hall office. There he was met by the other principals of the strange, much-misunderstood drama about to be enacted.

Despite the fact that this was not his twenty-four-hour period to be in charge of Jackson, Assistant Deputy Warden Bacon was the first top official to arrive at the prison in answer to Tucker's alarm. Informed that the rioters wanted to talk to him, Bacon phoned Fifteen. Ward answered and curtly told Bacon that from now on all prison officials would "take their orders from me." He then hung up on the startled deputy with the comment that they had to "get organized." What that meant, Bacon could not find out. He tried to reach Ward again, but each time he telephoned Fifteen, another voice was heard and no coherent answers were forthcoming.

Although prison officials were not aware of it at the time, not all the inmates of Fifteen Block were let out of their cells. Many of the younger inmates, including the new arrivals at Jackson who were in Fifteen only because there was no place else to put them, were not allowed to leave their tiers. Many of the homosexuals, by choice, merely paired off and never participated in the actual rioting at all. Only a comparatively small group of "trusted leaders" was organized around Ward.

I asked Ward how he got to be leader.

"I was chosen as the leader," he said. "I mean, more or less for my intellectual capacity for dealing with the officials—you know—and having recently been from the streets."

Once the leader, he took command as only a man of great personal magnetism can. He combined his gift of salesmanship with his natural ability to make people like him, added a forensic logic that would make Darrow tip his hat, and proceeded to control—even to rationing cigarettes and food—179 "chronic troublemakers, persistent perverts, and aggressive psychopaths" who were in a state of anarchy.

In Frisbie, Ward was fighting a military man, so he set up a semimilitary, semiprison organization. Realizing the value of his hostages, he made Crazy Jack his "first lieutenant in charge of custody."

"Jack was in charge of the guards," Ward explained. "That was his sole duty—protect the guards at the cost of his life, if need be."

Under Crazy Jack, Ward appointed what he called "my counselors," showing his favorable disposition toward the treatment officials of the prison.

The block itself was set up with the hostages on the top tier. Ward's headquarters were in the block's front-hall office, which commanded the window facing the rotunda (the heart of the whole prison) and the block's only outside door. Weapons were distributed to the "top leaders," and barricades were set up behind the front door and on the stairs leading from the base[3] to the second tier. Armed counselors were posted to police each tier. Ward not only "got organized," he was very much in command.

Prison officials found this out at eleven o'clock, four hours and innumerable fruitless phone calls after the first alarm. But if Fifteen was organized by this time, the officials were not. A question often asked after the riot was, why was no organized riot plan put into immediate operation? The reason is simple. Jackson had no such animal. Warden Frisbie maintained he had drawn up one and submitted it to Brooks, but Brooks had lost it.

While the warden was busy not putting the lost riot plan into effect, his two assistant deputy wardens were getting along with all the camaraderie usually associated with two tomcats. These two men with equal power in the running of the prison were the victims of Brooks' indecision as to whether Jackson should emphasize a custody or a treatment philosophy.

He had tried to compromise by putting the prison in the hands of both men at once. How well they worked together can be judged by their own words. Said custody's Bacon of his relationship with treatment's assistant deputy, Vernon Fox:

I knew Mr. Fox as a clean-cut young man who didn't have too many years experience in prison. He did have a marvelous education, had his doctor's degree, but he was totally unfamiliar with

---

[3] Ground floor.

the security aspects of an institution of this size and with the
meaning of custody.

I might give you an example. Deputy Fox believed that modeling clay was all right in a prison of this type, and yet the custody
people knew that modeling clay can be used to make a simu-
lated head to place under the blankets so that a man may have
six to twelve hours in which to escape before a guard would notice the difference.[4]

Beetle-browed, heavily built George Bacon went on to in-
sist that he personally liked Fox and that we must get Fox's
side of the story. We did.

About two months after talking to Bacon in the large, damp
room that had once been Vernon Fox's office, I called Fox on
the phone in Florida where he is now teaching sociology. I
asked him questions which he answered while a tape recorder
supplied by the NBC station in Jacksonville took down our
conversation. I mentioned Bacon, and Fox answered:

The differences between custody and treatment have been over-
exaggerated, I'm afraid. There were differences, but these differences weren't as gross as the newspaper accounts have led people
to believe. That's the fault of somebody attempting to find an
answer for the riot, and that's a convenient answer. Really, the
differences were relatively minor—such things as whether inmates
would be permitted to have modeling clay with which to make
small figurines. My position, in individual treatment, was that
modeling clay could be a relatively constructive item and there
was no reason why inmates shouldn't have it.

While both men said the differences were minor, the matter
of modeling clay was, in each case, brought up by the speaker,
not by us, and there was an edge on their voices. Peg and I
could not help but speculate about the "policy discussion" on
modeling clay, which both remembered spontaneously and
vociferously at least nine months after the fact.

The resentments felt by the department heads were reflected
down the line. The low-paid guards under Bacon hated the
better-paid counselors under Fox, and the counselors looked

---

[4] Willie Sutton did this in an attempted escape from Eastern State Prison in
Philadelphia.

down on the less-educated guards. When a counselor was found in *flagrante delicto* with a prisoner, even his dismissal did little to allay the guards' intimations that all the counselors were punks.

This feeling between guards and counselors pervaded the whole handling of the riot and many of the later investigational conclusions. For instance, speculation as to why brand-new Guard Elliott was assigned to Fifteen Block placed the blame on this counselor-guard split.

On the night of the riot Fox was in charge of the prison, but Fox pointed out that, no matter who was in charge of the prison, final authority for guard assignments was Bacon's. Bacon said it was just a routine assignment made down the line —and so the buck was passed. But several times we heard the opinion expressed that an Elliott would never have been assigned to Fifteen Block during one of Bacon's periods of control.

By implication, Earl Ward backed up this theory. We asked him if he thought the prison officials expected a riot. He answered:

> Sure. They had ample warning that this thing was coming off. In fact, they were ready for us. They had even changed guards. They put big six footers in Fifteen—really muscle boys—they could really handle themselves. But this night it started, these two muscle boys—it was their day off, see? And nobody didn't want to wait until Monday when the muscle boys got back. This young screw, which was Officer Elliott, was a pushover.
>
> It was foolish starting the riot on a Sunday, because who can you grab? It's no good grabbing a guard—they sign their life away when they come into the place. What you should grab is a warden or a deputy—or a nice governor. Then you got *hostages*.

But to a less critical eye than Ward's, the general of Fifteen Block seemed to be doing all right with the four hostages he had. At eleven o'clock he was even "in" to one of Bacon's desperate phone calls. And by this time S. J. Gilman had arrived from Lansing.

Gilman, who is Commissioner Brooks' assistant, must have a first name, but we never heard it used. He is the type you call

"Gilman." He is cold, crisp, and efficient. The only display of warmth we saw came when he told us how maligned Brooks was. Exact opposites, the two men have a father-and-son relationship that even extends to Gilman's vain attempts to protect Brooks from Brooks. Although the inmates generally liked Gilman, some prison officials greeted his name with distaste.

Upon his arrival at Jackson, Gilman took command. He arranged with Ward for a face-to-face meeting at the window of Fifteen. As he left the rotunda, surrounded by the newspaper men and photographers who had by this time crowded into the prison, there was the feeling of a Hollywood opening night. Searchlights played across the yard, flash bulbs exploded, and Ward, the star of the show, permitted himself to be interviewed. As Gilman tells it:

> Ward and I conversed across the prison yard approximately fifteen or twenty feet apart. It was my aim and purpose to conclude the holdout in Fifteen Block as quickly as possible, certainly before morning, because we knew that we had to meet certain crises then, such as feeding the other inmates, who would have to be let out of their cells to march right past Fifteen Block.
>
> It was obvious that Ward and the other ringleaders were primarily interested in getting publicity for themselves, and consequently they were diverting their conversation to the newspaper men that were already in the prison. It was at approximately 1:30 A.M. that Ward thought of making a tape recording for the benefit of the general public. Accordingly, all was diverted to the making of such a recording.

From the first, Ward was press conscious. He felt that if he could place his story before the public, it would be won over to his side. So, when he noticed the tape recorder brought to the scene by Ron Milton of Jackson Station WKHM, he pressed it into use. However, he first demanded time to work out his statement. This was granted. As he said:

> I did not know what the other men wanted and, as the leader, I thought I should hear those men. Therefore, I listened to the different men's grievances against the officials' brutalities and sadisticisms, and the corruption of the parole board. I then dismissed everyone from the office and I started thinking of all the

ills in the different prisons of Michigan. And I just sat down and wrote 'em all out. . . . And then I submitted the grievances to my other leaders, and they were all approved.

When Ward reappeared at the window, he obligingly took the plug to Ron Milton's tape recorder, put it in an outlet inside the blockaded cell, and proceeded to make an incoherent statement. After he had been assured his words would be printed and broadcast, he allowed an impatient Gilman to get back into the picture. As Gilman said:

> After some persuasion, I did get the first so-called terms exchanged between Ward and the warden of the prison. The only term that we were actually concerned with was the demand of Ward and the men in Fifteen Block for food. Remember, of course, that they had not received any food since the night before at approximately 5:00 or 5:30 P.M.
>
> Ward's terms could be briefed into: "Give us food first, and then we will talk about releasing the four hostages."
>
> Our terms in turn were: "Release the hostages and we will give you food."
>
> I should interrupt the story at this time to state that it was not until approximately 1:30 or 2:00 A.M. that Assistant Deputy Warden Fox began to sidle over to the Fifteen Block window and gain the attention and confidence of Ward. Whereas, when Ward would make an accusation or make a demand which absolutely was unjustified, I answered him in the negative, he received affirmative answers from Fox, such as: "Yeah, I thought of that myself."—"I was going to take it up with the Warden."—"I think you're right there, Ward. That's a good point. I'm going to see that something is done about that."
>
> Ward saw the ready ear that he had from Fox, and consequently he began to direct all his attention, demands, explanations, and conversation to Fox, and pretty soon it was obvious to me that I was being shunted aside. I certainly didn't feel bad about the situation—it was okay with me because, by choice evidently of Ward, Assistant Deputy Warden Fox became the chief negotiator. I did not handle negotiations further.

This was Gilman's side of the story. One thing above all else typified our experience in Michigan. No two people ever agreed on the same story. In this case Deputy Fox said:

Mr. Gilman was attempting to find out some points about the grievances, and he was questioning this brutality angle. He said that he would investigate brutality. Well, you don't "investigate" brutality, because to an inmate the word *investigation* means "whitewash," when it comes to an official. I tried to get the point across that we had to assume there was brutality in order to work with these men: whatever they said, we start from there.

That seemed to work, and it wasn't long after that till they refused to deal with anybody but me.

In counterpoint to both Gilman and Fox, Ward had his own version:

I demanded to see Mr. Gilman since I had never met him. I wanted to see what kind of a man he could be who could have such sadistic tendencies, as some of the men said he did.

He approached the window, and I hit Mr. Gilman right between the eyes with the information I had. I sez, "What kind of a man are you, Gilman, that could allow such conditions to go on inside of Fifteen Block or inside of Jackson, for that matter?"

He sez, "I don't know what you mean."

I said, "Well," I said, "well, my information is this: that you were the one who brought the chains and the rubber hoses into this institution and gave them to Deputy Bacon with the directive on how to use them."

He said, "Well, that's very hypothetical."

And I sez, "Well, I happen to know what the word means," I sez. So I sez, "You're not talking over me." I said, "I don't think you're a fit man for the correction department."

He sez, "Well, I'm only what you might call an underdog. I only follow orders." And he sez, "My authority is only so much paper."

I said, "Well," I says, "Let's put it this way; *I* have authority and anything I do is not going to be done on paper—it'll be done in action!" And I said, "The first chance we have to dedicate a guard's life, I'm going to dedicate it to you!"

It was then that Mr. Gilman held a quick conference with Dr. Fox. He turned around to me again and said, "How would you like to be placed into an honor camp?"

I said, "What are the conditions?"

He said, "If you open the door and let the state troopers march into Fifteen Block." He said, "You march out ahead by yourself, we'll take you directly outside to a camp, and we'll take over Fifteen Block."

Well, there were quite a few of my men in the office at that time. Who's kiddin' who? I looked at them and they looked at me. Well, I knew my position would not be very steady if I even hesitated a moment, and there was no hesitance in my mind. I said, "Gilman, as long as this riot continues, don't you ever come back to this window."

He never did come back to that window.

This offer of a camp spot for Ward was vigorously denied by Gilman. Fox agreed with Gilman in saying no such offer was made, but there all agreement among officials seems to have ended. According to Gilman, Ward appointed Fox the official negotiator. According to Fox, Brooks gave him the job, telling him that "Custody has failed. Now treatment has to clean up this mess. After this riot, treatment will take over."

Fox claimed it was with this backing and an understanding that the governor knew about it that he proceeded. And to us, Fox pointed out another of his qualifications for the job of riot negotiator: the prisoners could associate themselves with him since, as a boy, he had been sent to reform school. There were even Jackson inmates who had been to reform school with him but who, unlike Fox, had not pulled themselves up by their boot straps. As the riot went on, this reform-school background was emphasized more and more by Fox's critics, who failed to point out the years he had spent putting himself through college to a Ph.D. in psychology. But that was to come later. On Monday morning, to officials, the situation of psychologist versus psychopath was secondary to a more immediate problem that affected the entire population.

Dawn had come, and with it the inescapable fact that the men were hungry for breakfast. Now officials faced a problem where they could not be right. And they were not.

They had several choices. Not feeding at all could, literally, only lead to bloodshed as far as they could see. So that was out. They could give the men "breakfast in bed"—keep them locked up and take the food to the cells. This is a long, tedious, and inefficient operation with thousands of mouths to feed. Only two meals a day could possibly be so served, and any

delays in feeding always mean trouble. Finally, Frisbie decided to let the cooks and mess-hall men out of their cells to
prepare breakfast as usual and see what happened.

They did and all went well.

Frisbie then ordered the usual procedure followed, feeding
first what, in that heterogeneous population, was considered
the more tractable portion of the prison. The north side was
unlocked and about half the prison's population went into
the mess hall. In due time they came out and went back to
their cells.

So far, so good.

Deputy George Bacon went on record as being against
pressing their luck any further, but Frisbie overruled him. The
riot was localized in Fifteen Block. The south side could be
brought around inside the building so that they would not pass
the Fifteen Block yard, and all would be well.

This began without incident. About half the second group
went into the mess hall and started to eat. Then someone gave
the battle cry: "There's salt in the coffee!"

Jackson had its second riot in two days.

It was the so-called yard riot of April 21 that gave the Jackson affair its bigness. One way or another every inmate of the
overcrowded bastille was involved as a rioter, or a victim of
the rioters, or as a frightened bystander trying to hide from
trouble.

Jackson's full fifty-seven acres were involved as thousands of
howling, maddened men broke out of the mess hall and released the pent-up emotions of months and years behind walls.
Fights were going on in every direction as vengeances, held
in barred check, were finally released. Looting and burning
were to be seen in the middle of the mammoth yard near the
stores and the laundry. And there were small groups of inmates
who just stood and watched in horrified stupor or grim fear.
The worst sights were the rapes.

Sex was incidental to every prison riot. In Michigan, the
Fifteen Block riot had its orgies, but the yard riot was dif-
ferent. First of all, its official handling was dictated by Ward.
Sunday night, with the windows of Fifteen Block in mind,

Ward had hoped to thwart any sharp-shooting state police by warning that, if any inmate were killed, one hostage would be "sacrificed." This statement guided the policy of the state police during the yard riot, so guards and state police, armed with machine guns, stood on Jackson's thick walls, powerless to do anything about what they saw below them.

Boyd Simmons of the Detroit *News* tells of standing with them and watching helplessly while a bunch of wolves jumped one boy. As a convict described the same incident to me:

"They had a razor. They chased the kid, but he stumbled —and where in hell could he go? They pulled off his pants, slit his ass hole and made a train, right there in the yard. Kids that had kept clean up to then really got it."

Other inhibitions were forgotten too. "Hard" guards were beaten up, many wounded, and one sergeant was "run out the gate, mother-naked."

The two main riot actions cooperated with Fifteen Block. Shortly after the first cry of "salt" went up, the prison store was raided. First one man went over the store wall close to the mess hall, then hundreds went over like locusts. Out came cigarettes, food, candy, and canned goods. These were passed around the prison with amazing speed. Whether it was planned or came as a spur-of-the-moment thought has never been determined, but one of Fifteen Block's big problems was solved when someone in the yard yelled, "Let's take this stuff to the guys in Fifteen."

Ward's control depended on keeping the hostages and was endangered by lack of food. Starving hostages could be worse than useless to him. Starving rioters could be dangerous and even fatal to his control. But blankets were let down from Fifteen Block windows and he soon had enough food to hold out for weeks. At the same time Ward's four precious hostages became less valuable individually. He got more.

A contingent of rioters from the south side, led by one James Wiley Hudson, in Jackson from Ionia in exchange for another psychopath, raided the north side where the inmates already had been locked up after breakfast.

The north side held what generally were the quieter inmates, the more "institutionalized." Part of an inmate's being institutionalized is the possessiveness he develops for his cell. We were told of men who had been perfect prisoners for years—until they were moved from the cell to which they were accustomed. It was this possessiveness that was violated that Monday morning. The south siders were on a rampage of looting. With the store empty and in shambles, the laundry and the library in flames, next came the north side. There cells were unlocked and the levers that controlled whole tiers were wrecked. Inmates were driven out of their cells, plumbing was torn out, beds burned, and the inmates' most precious possessions, books, letters, and photographs, destroyed. As one north sider said:

"We got so God damn little. It ain't right for other cons to wreck it."

Months later, when we were at the prison, north- and south-side inmates were still being kept apart because of the death vendettas that grew out of that morning's raids. Officials at Michigan insisted, as they did elsewhere, that much of the violence was racial in origin. They pointed out that Hudson, "a known psychopath," was considered in a psychiatrist's report "the most dangerous man in the institution." A Negro with a psychotic hatred of whites, Hudson led the raids on the north side.

In Jackson, with 91 per cent of its population coming from Michigan factory cities where racial violence has broken out and is almost always ready to break out again, much credence could be laid to the possibility of racial tension bringing bloodshed behind the walls. But, in Michigan, as in Illinois where we went into the matter much more thoroughly, the story of the racial aspect of the riot was only the officials'. Among the inmates of Jackson, as at Illinois, both colored and white said:

> Differences between white and colored is only what the screws make. They give one job to white and one to colored and they play them against each other to make stoolies out of them. And when there's trouble, saying it's a race riot takes a lot of heat off the warden. When a bunch of guys are miserable together, they don't care much if a guy's white or black.

But newsmen, with no reason to support the officials, say there was evidence of racial violence in the Michigan yard riot. However, it does not seem reasonable that Hudson's raids on the north side were racial in origin. He was too systematic. He led his men, about fifteen hundred of them, into a cell block, cut off the exits, and then grabbed guards.

We talked to Guard George Brown: six feet, two hundred pounds of hulk, topped by a likable, homely face. He was unkempt, fingernails and face a mess, but Ward described him as "one of the cleaner guards, physically."

Brown described his part of the yard riot:

I come in to work Monday morning at six o'clock. We were told to go to our regular posts. I went to Two Block. We took the men into the dining room to eat as usual and they were back in the block and locked up.

We stood around the desk for a while, and all at once the door between Two Block and Three Block broke open, and here was a mob of men coming with picks and sickles, knives, axes, everything they could pick up. They come up to the desk and Hudson asked me my name. I told him it was George Brown, so he told me to get an official on the telephone. I called the hall office and just lucky Warden Frisbie was there. Hudson said to Frisbie, "We're taking hostages." That's the first I knew that we were going to be taken. And while he was talking on the phone, why Frisbie must have said something to him, because he got mad, and he said to Frisbie, "Remember there's no capital punishment in Michigan," he said. "If these fellows don't walk out with us, they'll come out dead."

So Frisbie must have told the guards on the walls not to bother shooting at us, to let us walk out. There was about seven or eight of us officers in Two and Three Blocks that they gathered up and took out the door and marched to Fifteen Block.

I was never so scared in my life as I was marching from Two Block to Fifteen Block. All the inmates in the yard was yelling and whooping and wanting us to take off our hats, and some wanted us to walk on our knees, doing everything to ridicule us.

Well, we got into Fifteen Block. They made us lay on the floor with our hands above our heads while they shook us down for jackknives—any kind of weapon we could have had, which we don't have any anyway. After we were all laid down, they had the doors barricaded again. They took us up to the top gallery and locked us in cells.

I didn't think much about it. It seemed funny, you know, being locked up. So I stretched out and lay down and listened to the radio. Baseball game's on that day.

Later they took me down to a front window of Fifteen Block. I was there about an hour. Johnny Crockard [5] held me there in the window with a knife in my neck. The inmates in the yard were hollering to "cut his head off." I think I lost twenty pounds then.

Finally, one inmate stepped up to the window and told them to let me out of the window, that I was a pretty good screw. Ward asked the rest of the inmates how they felt about me, and they said, "Let him out." So Crockard let me down and they took me back up and locked me up again.

Then they come around later, give us cigarettes, sandwiches and cookies, hot milk.

Well, then I was yanked out of the cell again and taken to a top window of Fifteen Block where there were officers on the roof. And Hyatt says to me with a knife at my neck, "Holler over there and tell them damn screws to get off the roof or we'll kill you."

So I hollered over to 'em and they seemed to know who it was, 'cause one of them hollered and asked me if I was all right. And I said yes, so then they climbed off the roof and Hyatt locked me back up again.

Then I said to Hyatt—then I says, "For God's sakes, don't take me out of the cell again." I said, "I'm so nervous now I can't sleep or anything."

"Well," he says, "okay, Brown. We won't bother you any more." So just a little while later they come back up for another screw to put in the window. They started to unlock my door, but Hyatt said, "No. Leave him alone. He's had enough."

But if the guards were nervous, Ward was riding high. Whereas before, the Fifteen Block riot would have been over if he had killed four guards, he could now slaughter four and still have nine hostages to bargain with. To the officials at Jackson this was a vital point. And Ward worked it to its full

---

[5] Five to fourteen years for forgery. He owes fifty-eight years to Washington. Listed as "unstable."

advantage. Again came the chant: "For every prisoner killed,
one hostage goes."
And then a prisoner was killed.

In riots, as in any human excess, a point of general weariness
is reached and a reaction of complete letdown comes. One riot
was handled successfully on that basis.[6] After a while this letdown began to play into the hands of the Michigan guards
and state police.

As the riot started to abate, the police, under Commissioner
Don Leonard, were organized into a pincers movement, some
coming through the front gates; some, the back truck gates.
Trucks, tear gas, and the sheer weight of armed numbers
shooting over prisoners' heads, began to drive inmates back to
cells—not necessarily their own—and out of the yard.

As many as six or seven men crowded into some cells; others
were empty. Many cells could not be locked, and armed troopers stood guard on the tiers to keep prisoners inside. Many on
both sides were hurt in this cleaning-up process. It was mirac-
ulous that there was no more bloodshed than there was.

As the troopers marched down the halls with guns pointed,
missiles came flying out of cells. No direct hits were tried or
made, but many painful ricochet shots got home. Boyd Simmons said:

> Some of the guys were William Tell with a glass jar or a spoon.
> They would flip these things through the bars on their doors,
> aiming at a spot on the opposite wall. The ricochet would be a
> bull's eye. One of these shots hit Commissioner Leonard.

One of the prisoners expanded on this:

> Handles were being throwed out the windows in Eleven Block
> and one of them hit an officer. This prompted quick machine-gun
> fire. Guard Captain Tucker threw himself in front of the
> machine-gun and told them there had been enough—that they
> would shoot these men over his dead body. They stopped
> shooting.
> Tucker then come into the block with tears in his eyes and

---

[6] The riot at Chillicothe. See Chapter 7.

asked us, "What do you men want?" We said we wanted hot
water so we could take showers, we wanted the wounded taken
to the hospital, and we wanted something to eat.

Capt Tucker got these for us, and we calmed down.

But Captain Tucker was not in the yard when the trucks
moved in. There the prisoners moved back slowly, giving way
before the troopers, who were on foot and loaded on fire trucks.
One of the inmates who did not move back was a nineteen-
year-old sex offender named Darwin Millage. According to the
official report he refused to move back, became abusive, and
threatened violence. According to the cons he just yelled at
the troopers, and one of them got panicky. At any rate, a
trooper fired, Millage dropped, and shortly thereafter he was
dead.

Now both Ward and the officials were on a spot. There was
no way of keeping the news of Millage away from Fifteen.
Yard rioters were still milling over to Fifteen when the shooting
happened. But even if they were not, Ward would still have
heard of Millage. The fabulous prison grapevine is efficient.

Intermittently during the yard riot, Ward and Fox had been
conferring through the window—but, as a report states coyly,
"without conclusive results." But Fox was not at Fifteen when
Ward got the news. Fox says:

> Ward called the warden. The warden said Millage had died
> from cancer.
>
> "Ridiculous," was Ward's reply. And he later asked me what
> he died from. Actually, what he was doing was daring me to tell
> him the truth. Now, if I had not told him the truth, then he
> would have lost faith in everybody, and there wouldn't have been
> any negotiations. And so I said that I didn't know, because the
> autopsy hadn't been completed.
>
> And he said, "Yeah, I guess that's right. You need an autopsy.
> Then you let me know what the results of the autopsy were."
>
> Okay.
>
> When I contacted the hospital and eventually got the autopsy,
> I went back to Fifteen Block and said, "Well, I've got the au-
> topsy, Ward. He died of gunshot—ruptured aorta."
>
> "Okay. One inmate, one guard. Jack!" He called for Crazy
> Jack.

I said, "Just a minute, Ward. It wasn't a guard that shot him—
it was a state trooper. You should get a state trooper if you're
going to carry through an eye for an eye and a tooth for a tooth."

Ward guessed by gosh that was right, and as a result he didn't
kill the guard.

Ward's version made a hero out of Ward:

I pride myself on one thing—that's my word—and I intended
to carry out the killing myself. I demanded the autopsy report
from Dr. Fox. He got it late Monday evening, and he walked
reluctantly over to Fifteen Block window. The cause of death
was a bullet wound, singular in nature. I then told Dr. Fox to
get a stretcher ready, I was going to kill a guard and throw him
out the front door.

Dr. Fox begged me not to do it. He says we'd gain nothing and
that we'd be rushed and this and that and the other thing. I told
him we fully expected that, and, if they had any foolish ideas of
rushing us, that we would kill every guard in there.

It was then that I told Dr. Fox to go away from the window.
I hadda be alone to think, because I realized what a great responsibility I was taking on my shoulders. I figured I didn't mind
dying myself for a justified cause, but maybe others in the block
didn't feel as though it was as righteous a crusade as I did.

Then I gathered Jack Hyatt and a few others of my prominent
leaders together, and I says, "As an alternative, let's give the yard
men a chance. It happened in the yard—it did not happen to us.
They shot the man outside of Fifteen Block for something we did
not have anything to do with."

Then I called together some of the yard leaders. I said, "Now
look. If you men want to kill this guard in reprisal for the man
that was killed in the yard, you men do it out there. How's that?"

The decision made, Operation Sacrifice got under way. But
for so deadly an occasion the "sacrifice" had a great element
of comedy, which came from the accident of two guards having similar names. Ward had had trouble with Officer Carrier,
one of the four original hostages. Ward also had mental blocks
when it came to pronouncing certain words and names. *Sadism*
was always "sadistacism," *discipline* came out "dislepin," and
Carrier was pronounced "Curry." This was not a happy coin-
cidence for Guard Henry W. Curry, one of the second collec-

tion of hostages. Ward wanted to "sacrifice" his enemy Carrier, but to his lieutenants Guard Curry was a logical choice because he was known as a "holy Joe" who would ticket* men at the slightest provocation.

When we went to see him, small, tight-lipped and hard-eyed ex-guard Curry greeted us at the door of his sparsely furnished home with a drawn .32. After a long harangue selling us on the idea that prisoners should be treated tougher because they had no God in their souls and that psychiatrists were agents of the Devil who were out to wipe religion off the earth, he described the ordeal he had faced because a man he had never known condemned him to death with a slip of the tongue:

> Shortly after one o'clock, some inmates came down the corridor. They opened my cell door, then said, "The short guy with glasses?"
>
> Someone at the end of the corridor said, "Yeah."
>
> So the inmate who had my door open says, "I guess you're it." I was to be taken out to be killed.
>
> At the time I didn't know exactly how that was to be carried out. I might have been used as an example, beaten up and turned loose. Or I might have been taken out on the ball diamond and killed.
>
> I was taken downstairs. With an inmate on either side of me, we left the block. We walked about fifteen feet when two officers in the building across the road upstairs opened the window. And one of them struck the window with a steel gun barrel. The other one shouted "Halt! Not a soul move." Everything stopped right there. One of them shouted, "Get out of there!" so I took off for a sub-hall corridor where the state police were holding out.

Whether Ward really meant anyone to be killed, even outside of Fifteen, is a matter of speculation. Fox said he was convinced that Ward did not. But why, then, was Fox so convinced Ward would kill later? Fox maintained that under the "social pressure of leadership" Ward would kill if forced into a corner. Fox also pointed out that Ward had killed a guard in Pennsylvania and that Michigan's whole handling of the riot was determined by that fact. He expressed surprise when, nine months after the riot, I told him the truth: that according to record Ward had never killed a guard in Pennsylvania or elsewhere.

Nevertheless, it is hard to imagine Ward under greater social pressure than he was at that moment. He had promised to kill a guard; conceivably now was the time to prove to his men and the officials alike that he meant business. He had nothing to lose, Michigan being a lifer state. His supply of potential sacrifices had been augmented. If not now, when would he kill? Officials drew no hope from Curry's "escape." When the yard riot was again under control, Fox went on with the negotiations, and Ward made the most of having the additional hostages and more food. Negotiations dragged on until early Tuesday morning. During this time they dealt primarily with brutality in Fifteen and with hospital care.

Tuesday morning Fox and Brooks went from Jackson to Lansing to confer with Governor Williams. There has been some criticism of Williams for staying in the capital during all this, but he pointed out to us: "The man in top control shouldn't put himself in jeopardy. I learned this the hard way. After all, I was kidnapped once!"

Meanwhile, it was pretty much of a period of stalling in Fifteen Block and the hostages stewed. Said Guard Brown:

> Tuesday was just another day up there, with guys sharpening knives on your door, yelling and hollering. Some of the boys wanted to come in and whip ya. If it hadn't been for Hyatt, I think it would a been worse than it was. He really fought for us guys.

But Ward improved the shining hour in his own way:

> The newspaper came out, the Jackson *Citizen Patriot,* with the story that a man threw a kite* out the window telling the officials that he wasn't with us, what our defenses were, and that we had liquid flame throwers set up on different floors, and he gave our whole defense to the officials. The officials very graciously gave that note to the newspapers, and the newspapers gave the story to us with the inmate's *name!*
>
> Well, what else could we do? After all, if the officials didn't want to protect that inmate, why should we protect him? So we very graciously accommodated them, and we dislepined the man

and turned him loose. And we told him to thank Mr. Frisbie on the way to the hospital—if he was able to!

One of the men in Fifteen Block had a different view of the "dislepin" action:

The incident began very suddenly when Earl Ward went off in a tangent and demanded the presence of this Jerome Parmentier, who had allegedly written the letter. Parmentier was brought down by a couple of henchmen. As he stepped inside the office, Kenneth Moore took a blackjack from the maze of instruments—weapons that they had exhibited to substantiate their claims of brutality. Well, he struck Parmentier over the head about twenty times with that blackjack, and still it failed to render him unconscious.

At this point, well, that very fact angered both Moore and Ward, and they proceeded to beat him unmercifully. Finally Parmentier sank to the floor and they kicked at him. He kept protesting his innocence; he denied writing the letter, and so forth. He claimed that it was, well, a frame-up, and the more he talked, why the more severely they beat him. They kicked his face in something awful. And finally Parmentier (I don't believe he was ever unconscious) decided that if he quit talking, well, they'd leave him alone.

Well, he lay on the floor, and by that time Ward was pretty well worked up and he said that we'd better get them all. That was his words, "Get them all!" and by that he meant that the unpopular element of Fifteen Block was going to come by the same treatment. Well, immediately they sent word up to call one Elsworth Roberts down to the office.

Now I never knew what the grievance was against Roberts, but they brought him down and he complied silently. They told him to lay down on the floor and then Moore took this piece of chain, heavy links of chain, and beat him across the head about four or five times. I was sure that Roberts was dead. The chain cracked down on his head, and it just seemed like no man could survive that kind of punishment.

Parmentier and Roberts both lay on the floor, and Ward called Captain Tucker over to the window and told Tucker that they had a couple of dead men there, and what did Tucker want done with their body? Well, Captain Tucker, of course, was interested in seeing what was going on, and he leaned in the win-

dow, saw the two men laying on the floor. He probably didn't
know they were dead, but he assumed as much. He said, "Well,
they might as well be thrown out as left in there. They won't do
you any good in there." After Capt left the scene, when they discovered that Parmentier, at least, was not dead, why they thought
of cutting him with a knife, making sure that he was.

I think the most ghastly part of it was that Roberts was used almost as a limp cloth to wipe up the blood and gore all over the
place. I was certain he was dead. He just didn't move after he
fell down.

The two men were put out of the block, laid out in front of
the cell block, and stretcher bearers came and picked them up,
and that's the last I saw of it. I understand that Roberts wasn't
nearly as hurt as Parmentier, but that just by being silent he got
away with a lesser beating. I've never seen men go crazy as I did
then, at that time. It was all a big emotional outburst.

Across the yard, the beatings could be seen through the
window, and a shudder of fear went through the officials when
it was rumored that the victims were hostages. The fact that
the beaten men, although at first believed dead, were inmates
came as a relief.

Fox's reaction to newsmen was noteworthy, according to Reporter Boyd Simmons. Fox pointed out that Ward was objecting to official brutality on the one hand and committing bru-
talities like this on the other. Boyd used this remark to show
Fox's original, rather dispassionate point of view. According to
Simmons, Fox's attitude changed.

As was to happen several times, signs of violence inside
Fifteen speeded up activity outside Fifteen. It was Tuesday, after
the beatings, that Fox whipped together from his notes the
final eleven demands he had talked out with Ward. These were
read and approved by Ward. Then there was a new development.

Ray Young, whose conversation with Guard Elliott had
started the whole mess, went out of Fifteen Block and made the
first of two famous broadcasts over the prison system. He read
Ward's demands to the whole prison and then went back into
Fifteen Block. No trouble ensued.

Ward was so pleased with the whole way the broadcast was
handled that he threw a bone to the officials. Guard Elliott was

released. Then things settled back to normal. Ward had two more inmates beaten and tossed out of Fifteen.

By Wednesday morning the demands were on their way to Governor Williams in Lansing. Only Williams' personal approval and acceptance would satisfy Ward. Meanwhile, Earl passed time with lesser lights: members of the legislature made the papers by posing for news shots with him. As the prison waited for word from the governor, Ward planned his military strategy:

> I called Warden Frisbie over and that was really my Waterloo, because I became so disturbed at the statement Warden Frisbie made that he knew of no maltreatment by the prison officials. He made everything seem so ridiculous—in the face of facts! I really lost my composure, and I did revile him in his presence, and my partner, Jack Hyatt, started to throw a knife at him through the bars. I had to restrain him.
>
> That whole strain within that half hour or hour was really too much for me, and I became seriously ill about an hour later, and the men had to take me upstairs. They took me into a back corridor and they barricaded the corridor, my men did, because it was then that I called Jack to my side and asked him if he would take over until I was able to come back into power.
>
> I laid the final rules for Jack to get the demands, or else. I told him that if any shooting started to wake me up and we'd go upstairs and take care of the guards personally. First, we'd push the other men out of the block so that no reprisals would be taken against them. I then told him to give the governor six hours in which to sign the list of grievances. Nine o'clock was when we submitted our demands. Three o'clock was the deadline. I went upstairs and, very frankly, I fell into a deep sleep.

As before, action in Fifteen reacted outside. Ward slept and Jackson panicked. Telephone calls started coming out of Fifteen. As on the previous Sunday, the voices were many, but now the tone reflected Ward's contagious cockiness that had spread to the "top leaders."

Hyatt made the first call and frightened the prison phone operator out of a year's wrong numbers. As she said, "I know right away it wasn't Mr. Ward, because he was always so polite. Mr. Hyatt—well, he swore at me."

The officials were even more terrified. Hyatt told them Ward was no longer leader. He either said or intimated Ward was dead. As poor an opinion as the officials had of Ward, they had come, at least, to respect the facts that he had the rioters under control and that no hostages had been killed. Hyatt had nothing to commend him. As officials said, "Crazy Jack was not called 'crazy' for nothing."

Inside Fifteen, panic also ran rampant. The degree of isolation between sections and tiers of the block can be seen by the fact that inmates were frightened by the same rumor of Ward's death that scared the officials in the rotunda across the prison yard. And on the top tier, hostage Brown heard the same thing. Months later his voice still shook as he talked of the third day of his incarceration:

> They come up and told us to write our last letter to our family; us screws were all done for. And in the meantime, they took a couple of screws and threw their belongings out the window and that made it look worse for everybody. We wrote our last letter, which was telephoned to our wives, and they knew the situation we was in.

Also knowing the "situation they was in," the officials reacted in their own way. Fox told me that maybe the whole thing was good: it speeded things up, additional pressure was being put on the governor to sign. Fox said he only wanted to have the demands approved so the hostages would be freed. Considered in retrospect, the activity in Fifteen Block did help accomplish this.

On the other hand, state police had the opposite reaction. Throughout the entire riot they had been held in check, but Commissioner Leonard made no secret of the fact he did not agree with the handling to date. Other policemen expressed the view that a few guards killed in exchange for some 170 prisoners "executed" would not be an unfair barter.

"We should have it so good in Korea," said one cop to Fox.

Cold-blooded as this view might be, there was no in between. Either the police had to stay out of the situation or it would be a blood bath—if Ward meant what he said. Ward, proud of his defenses, had made no secret of them. The narrow stairs to the upper tiers were barricaded. Lye, gasoline, lighter fluid, and matches were in easy reach to make Molotov cocktails. The only entrance to Fifteen, outside of the huge metal outside door, was where the plumbing entered the building. This space was too small to allow passage for more than one man at a time, and it was well guarded.

The fastest plan of action the police could evolve—blowing up the front of the building and dashing in with gas, bullets, and flame throwers going full blast—would take three minutes. Should all go well and resistance from the rioters be nil, it would take one hundred and eighty seconds for the first invading policemen to reach the first hostage on the top tier. Question: How many hostages could Ward, Hyatt, and their goon squad kill in one hundred and eighty seconds?

In the minds of the policy makers, those three minutes would mean the end of all the guards. They could be wrong. But they could be right. If they went in, they had to figure the hostages would die. They made no secret of the fact that no rioters would walk out alive if it came to a forced entry.

Brooks, who was nominally in charge for the governor, did not want to come to this decision. He resisted all arguments for storming the place, but these arguments grew stronger with Hyatt's emergence to power. As the hostages' last letters were read over the phone, the police said the guards would be killed anyway; why not take a chance?

Brooks resisted police pressure long enough so that no violence broke out. The lines to Lansing were kept busy as Williams, not a man to enjoy ultimatums, considered the demands.

Then the tension broke. Ward may never have had much chance of winning a Michigan popularity contest, but at least he would have placed well above Crazy Jack. It was almost with the fondness of greeting an old friend that officials saw the now familiar, heavily bearded features of Ward at the window. But the round robin continued. A couple of hours before, action inside Fifteen had brought action outside. Now this was reversed. Ward explained:

At one o'clock my men woke me up and said the men upstairs were in a panic because over the radio there were constant rumors that I had been killed, Jack Hyatt was taking over, other inmates had been killed, several guards had been killed.

I went downstairs. And it was then that Jack confronted me on the stairs and we went into a cell, and we had a little talk. And he briefed me on what had happened since I had been asleep. That was that state troopers were all alerted, doctors were alerted, and they were ready to storm us at any minute. All they're doing was waiting for word from the governor. If he refused to sign, they were ready to storm us.

It was then that I told the men to knock off all the hinges from all the doors and start carrying them up to the fourth floor. Start bringing the guards out of the cells and tying them up. While all that preparation was going on, somebody said there was some activity in the sub-hall office, and I looked across from the second-floor window and I saw they were getting some state troopers ready to come out. It was then that we opened the skylight to the roof. We had four guards bound ready to push up on to the roof ahead of the men who were going to go up there with the iron doors.

Our plan was simply this: to place the iron doors around the corner of the buildings as a protection; put the guards in front of the shields, and then bring up the hot lye, which we had already prepared, and the lighter fluid and gasoline, which we were gonna drop in bombs and light them and keep the state troopers from forcing their way in through the two entrances, which were in front.

His defenses solidified, the general went to the window and made his appearance. Ron Milton was the first man to see him, and he broke the big news of the day. The governor had signed the demands! Fox phoned Ward and confirmed this. He added that a state policeman was rushing the signed paper to Jackson from Lansing. Fox would bring it over when it arrived.

Night had fallen by the time the governor's courier came. It was a cold spring evening, so before final ceremonies were consummated, Ward handed out a blanket, which Fox threw around his shoulders. Then came the final signing of the demands.

Of course, everything was not just as Ward had planned. The governor had not signed the demands—he had signed a paper authorizing Brooks and Frisbie to make the decision.

Brooks and Frisbie, in turn, had signed the demands. Fox persuaded Ward it was the same thing. Ward signed his acceptance.

Now the riot was over.

It was over, except that it went on. Ward was afraid of a trick. Newspapers and the radio had to confirm the acceptance. Also, Ward wanted to surrender in daylight. There seems to have been confusion as to whether this meant daylight Thursday or Friday. At any rate, according to Fox (and tacitly admitted by Ward), Earl had promised one more night of orgies to the homosexuals.

Wednesday night passed without incident. Fox, however, said that the police, despite their denials, improved the darkening hour by planting dynamite in preparation for a final storming of the battlements.

Thursday morning brought the papers, but Ward felt that one edition could be faked. He had to see the evening papers.

The riot went on. Leonard's pressure on Brooks reached a new high. The demands had been signed; leaving the guards in there might be more dangerous than trying to break through.

Then word came out of Fifteen that Officer Ackens had collapsed and they were going to let him out. With Ackens, out came inmate Moore, the "top leader" of the earlier beatings. He ran across the yard to the sub-hall office and surrendered. Ward was ready to kidnap Fox, who was standing there, but Fox talked him out of it.

Fox checked back at the hall office and discovered that Moore had "peached double cross" on Ward. Moore said Ward never planned to surrender. This added fuel to Leonard's arguments, and Brooks finally gave in. The block would be taken by storm.

The events inside the block leading up to Moore's escape showed that Ward's leadership finally was slipping. Ward did not admit this to us; he phrased it more dramatically:

> One of my top leaders[7] was plotting to overthrow me. I do not say he was plotting to kill me—I never found that out, but the thing is this: he would have had to kill me to take over.

---

[7] We found out this was Ray Young, who felt, since he had begun things, he—not Ward—should have been the leader.

My right lieutenant, which was Moore, was a homosexual. He went up to this other leader's cell and stayed there all night. They made plans, which were this: they were gonna take four guards out of their cells and tell Hyatt I wanted them downstairs. Once they got 'em out of Jack's protective custody and down on the second floor (they had set up barricades and everything else), they were gonna hold out there for their own demands and for more publicity. This one leader didn't think he got enough of a break. I didn't think he was qualified for leadership mentally, morally, or otherwise, and that's why I dismissed him when I took over.

On Thursday morning some of my lieutenants got word of this plot and they came to me and they told me that the kid was planning to overthrow me and that Moore, my right hand man, was in on it. Well, I called all the other leaders together. I decided to do some kind of dislepin. And hold court.

In the meantime, Officer Ackens had a nervous collapse. Moore (we hadn't moved in on him yet) was the one that brought the officer downstairs.

Well, I had to get the officer out of there before I could finally conduct a court, so I called Dr. Fox over and told him that we had a guard in here who was collapsing mentally and physically, and could he kindly take him off our hands immediately? Dr. Fox made the necessary arrangements so we could open the door under a safe conduct. When I opened the door, Moore somehow or other got past me and made a run for the hall office.

It was then that all my other men wanted to really start cutting. We knew there were others in on the plot, so we brought the secondary leaders in first. I passed on them that they were to be killed, and I dismissed them. It was decided that the kid also was to be killed, but it was up to me for final judgment. Then I sat the boy down and I talked to him. I tried to talk to him like a father. I told him about several character weaknesses where he was concerned, and that older men had taken advantage of these characterizations or weaknesses, and were just using him as a tool.

I wasn't weakening at this stage. I was just so disgusted at the whole thing. I knew that, once the other men had taken over, the kid would not be the leader, because they had no respect for him. They didn't want to be bossed around by a homosexual or sexual pervert. If they were gonna take orders, they were gonna take orders from men, not a so-called punk!

Finally I said to this top leader, I said, "Look, kid. I'll make a deal with you. I don't have to make no deal; all I have to do is turn my back and you'll be wiped out right in front of my eyes. I don't want that. If we start killing now it's gonna be a blood bath, because I have some enemies in here that I'd like to take care of, some of the other leaders have enemies, and I promised them that once one inmate was killed, they could get their enemies.

"The thing is over as far as I'm concerned. We've signed the surrender terms. All we have to do is walk out that front door and we're set. If I give the word, you'll never see sundown. I'll tell you what I'm gonna do. I was gonna surrender tomorrow, but if I surrender now, it'll spare your life. I'm gonna do that because I know this: I cannot guarantee your life another twenty-four hours. This thing is entirely too hot."

Right in his presence I reached over and got the phone, and I called Dr. Fox at home.

By the time Ward reached for the phone, preparations outside had progressed to the point where sharp shooters had been posted again. Fox was the lone holdout against the planned attack. He was told he was tired and should go home. He did.

He had been home only a few minutes when Ward telephoned. Now two very different men were talking: previously the leader of the country's most dramatic prison riot had talked to the spokesman for one of the largest and richest of our sovereign states; now a prison subofficial, who must have known he was almost out of a job, was talking to a man whose magic power of leadership was vanishing like water down a drain. And in each man's mind was a secret he felt he dare not reveal to the other.

As Fox said:

"I didn't dare tell Ward the police were ready to blow the place up. You know what his reaction to that would have been."

Ward, with his mutinous subject beside him, also played it cagey:

I told Dr. Fox that I think it would be best for all concerned if we did like he originally suggested, surrender today and not tomorrow—Friday being his birthday. I says, "We'll give you a birthday present ahead of time, Doctor." I never told Dr. Fox I feared more trouble would break out in Fifteen Block and that

The 1952 series of prison riots began at New Jersey State Prison at Trenton and spread to the state prison farm at Rahway where inmates used bed sheets to carry to the public their protests and demands to see a representative of the Osborne Association. (*Wide World Photos*)

The state prison at Jackson, Michigan, had the nation's biggest and most costly riot when 6,000 men went on a rampage. *Above:* A ruined organ in the auditorium. *Below:* The library, along with the laundry and the commissary, was completely ruined in the riot. (*Both photographs by United Press Photos*)

Jackson was unique in having two riots at the same time. In the "Fifteen Block Riot" Guard Thomas Elliott (*left*) allowed the riot to start by opening a cell door in the *hole*. "Crazy Jack" Hyatt (*center*) and Earl Ward (*right*) led the holdout in Fifteen Block. (*Wide World Photos*)

As convicts went completely out of control in Michigan's yard riot, many guards were injured, and nine others were captured. The yard rioters handed these over to Ward in Fifteen Block. (*United Press Photos*)

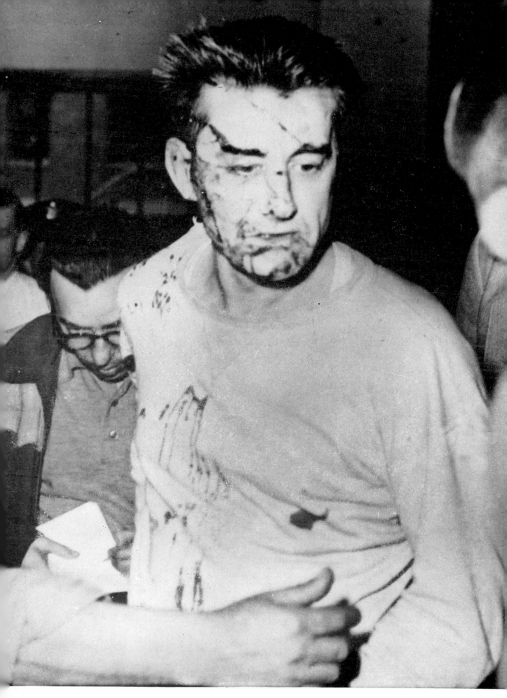

In the Fifteen Block holdout, convicts turned on convicts and Ellsworth Roberts (*above*) was one of four men beaten with chains and thrown out for dead in an orgy of brutality against "the unpopular element." Roberts was "used almost as a limp rag" to wipe up blood on the floor. (*United Press Photos*)

When the final surrender came in the Fifteen Block holdout, guards who had written their last letters were released. Both they and their families were in tears after their five days of captivity. (*Wide World Photos*)

Accusations and counteraccusations were made both during and after the Michigan riots. *Above:* Convicts show the chains they alleged were used by brutal guards in Fifteen Block. *Below:* Weapons used by rioters in the yard riot. Even months later not all of the knives stolen during this riot had been recovered by custodians. (*Both photographs by Wide World Photos*)

The climax of the holdout in Fifteen Block came when Earl Ward, called a "brilliant psychopath," signed the demands already signed by Michigan's governor and by prison officials. Ward's "top leaders" look on. (*Wide World Photos*)

consequently more men would be killed. I let him believe that it was a birthday present to him. Nothing more, nothing less.

Since all the other agreements were just a formality, there was nothing else to do but just walk out. I asked him if he could get back to the institution immediately and set up the arrangements for the final surrender.

He said, "Earl, stay where you are. I'll be back at the institution within a half hour."

It was then that I took this kid back up to the fourth floor. I took him down to the end of the block and I talked to him. I told him, "I don't have to do this, but I'm doing it because I'm who I am, that's all."

The other men didn't go for that. They thought I was a damn fool for giving in at the final moment. They didn't think I was weak—they just thought I was a damn fool, period.

There was another hasty conference at the Fifteen Block window. When it was over, Fox told officials everything was all set. The state police were to get out of sight, guards and newsmen were to be placed in accordance with Fox's specific instructions, and a steak-and-ice-cream dinner was to be prepared.

Fox disappeared into an office. He reappeared and went back to Fifteen. Then he was heard over the prison broadcasting system with a speech that made Jackson officials wonder if they had been partaking of the weed. Over the P.A. came Fox's words:

Earl Ward, Jack Hyatt, and all of the others in charge of the men, are men of their word. In accordance with their agreement the boys* from Fifteen Block are going to file into the dining room at four o'clock. No state police will be in evidence. With Ward's permission, institutional custodial personnel will take positions in the yard during the operation.

Earl Ward is a natural leader. He and the other boys are to be congratulated on the good faith with which they have bargained. Their word has been good. My word has been good. This may presage a new era of good sound inter-relationship between inmate and administration in American prisons. They have done a service. Congratulations to you men of Fifteen Block.

No one had quite recovered from the speech, which was broadcast at three-thirty, when at four the doors of Fifteen opened and there occurred what was, to Gilman, Michigan's most humiliating experience of the riot. When he described it to us months later, he still burned:

> At exactly 4:00 P.M. on Thursday afternoon, after we had posted armed guards to prevent a possible mass break and the seizing of additional hostages, we began to see the barricade being removed from inside Fifteen Block. Evidently Ward timed the release of the men exactly on the nose, and reports reached us that Ward was strutting his stuff with such remarks as, "I ought to be in Hollywood. I'm really arranging this thing right."
>
> The barricade was removed and the front door opened. Ward posted six inmates on the outside of the block, immediate henchmen and leaders of the holdout in Fifteen Block. And these inmates searched the run-of-the-mine inmates as they came out. The stipulation Ward made was that each of these released inmates would walk backwards until he was searched by several crews of two henchmen and they were satisfied that he had no weapons or possibly other contraband.
>
> Then the henchmen themselves were searched by fellow prisoners and they too relinquished the knives and other tools, hammers, etc., that they had accumulated and these men also were permitted to go to the dining room.
>
> Last, of course, to leave was Ward and Hyatt. They too threw away whatever weapons they had in their hand and were permitted to go into the dining room to partake of the so-called steak-and-ice-cream dinner.

As the inmates went in for so-called steak the guards went to their families. Big Guard Brown told us:

> At four o'clock Hyatt looked out the window and says, "They're marching out." So we marched downstairs. The inmates had already threw out their weapons, and the fellas that weren't in the riot parcipitating, come back in and gave us fellas the keys to the block and all the weapons, like the blackjacks and the stuff that they claim was in there, and everything was fine.
>
> Then we were supposed to march out and go in and have a steak dinner with them, but as we marched out, why Captain Tucker was there and separated us fellas and that's when we all broke down. I know I fell into the arms of Warden Frisbie at the time, and he told me to keep my chin up, that everything was all

right. And all over the hall there was flash cameras flashin', newspaper photographers and Commissioner Brooks was there. And he said to us fellas—"Take off as long as you want to."

When I got home, it was the same stuff over again. My wife was crying, my mother was crying . . .

Guard Brown stopped in mid-sentence, tears running down his tough, begrimed face. To him the riot was not over. Emotionally it never would be.

To the men who had handled the riot, it was not over, either. Hardly had Ward thrown down his cutting knife and picked up his eating knife than investigations started.

The first of these was the usual unofficial but deadly inquiry of the press. Probably no event of this kind had ever been as intensely covered by the press, newsmen even participating in some of the conferences outside of Fifteen. Now these newsmen gave their reactions. They consolidated into an almost solid anti-Fox block. Said Boyd Simmons:

In the early days of the riot, we talked to Dr. Fox on a number of occasions. And at that time it seemed to me he had perspective, that he was viewing the events in Fifteen with the detachment you expected of his position.

But, as time went on and the strain began showing on everybody, it seemed to me he began changing his viewpoint to a point where, towards the last (and I know this was what the other newspapermen thought), he seemed more and more to be defending the men in Fifteen and advocating their point of view. It was almost as if, in his constant dealing with them, they had somehow won him over to their way of thinking instead of him winning them over to his.

Simmons and the other newsmen jumped on the final speech and "the steak-and-ice-cream dinner" as their prime targets. To them, the latter represented prisoner coddling at its worst.

But Fox declared he had promised the dinner only because Ward had demanded it. It was little enough to give in exchange for the lives of the hostages. In part, Gilman backed up this statement by pointing out in detail that the steak was not prime meat, but way down on the list of cuts. After all, he pointed out, Jackson bought the poorest grade of meat acceptable for human consumption. Steak at Jackson was not steak to people at home.

(What inmate reaction was to this statement, after all the fine things they had heard about their food, was never put on record.)

While Gilman poo-pooed the importance of the steak dinner, Ward whiled away his time sawing off the limb on to which he had maneuvered Fox. He vowed the suggestion of "steak and all the trimmings" had been made by Fox in the next to last conference Thursday afternoon:

> Dr. Fox says, "How about a nice steak dinner?"
> And I says, "Who's kidding who? We're all hungry."
> He says, "Well, I think I can make that arrangement."
> And I said, "I want everything, not this usual affair we have here. I want all the trimmings."
> He said, "We'll have good steaks."
> I said, "We can't ask for anything more."

Ward did, however, admit to authoring the portion of the surrender that had shocked Gilman. He went on:

> I said also, "In the final surrendering, I want full charge of my men. I don't want any custodian to lay a hand on my men to search 'em. I'll search 'em, and if any of them have any weapons on 'em, I'll pass judgment on 'em right then and there.
>
> "And another thing, I do not want any state police in evidence whatsoever. This will enable the custodian officials and the prison officials to get back in the position they held before the riots. They will get their respect back, some of it, and their confidence. They will handle the prisoners—not the state police. We have to live here with the guards; therefore, they should have charge of us."

As Austin MacCormick pointed out, this thinking showed the remarkable insight Ward had, for a psychopath. But this insight did not help Fox, who was stuck with the story that the steak dinner was Ward's idea. Fox said he had brought it up again to hasten the surrender. He detailed the pressure he was under. He had sweated out the demands and got them signed. Then he was watching all his work collapse as Commissioner Leonard "held a gun at my head" by readying his state police for a bloody and deadly battle.

But all explanatory statements have been forgotten. Citizens of Michigan still cite the "steak-and-ice-cream-dinner with all the trimmings" as the main point of the riot. To them the picture of murderers, rapists, and psychopaths stuffing themselves on filet mignon shows the depths to which prisons have sunk.

To the public the steak dinner seems to have overshadowed the even deeper wound inflicted on the raw and bleeding carcass of Michigan penology by the congratulatory speech and the demands which the governor signed in all but fact. However, the first investigation of the riot by a board of inquiry [8] tore into both these.

First of all, the board sloughed off the demands by saying they were unfounded, then detailed what it felt caused the riot. Actually, what it listed as causes were really reasons why the riot *could* happen rather than why it *did* happen. The board listed the size of Jackson, the inadequate custodial facilities (too few guards, too little training, too many knives in cells), and the differences between the custodial and treatment staffs as the causes of the whole shooting match. It mentioned parole policies as a "complaint," but dismissed this on the basis that "criticism of this (parole) board is not new."

The board ended up by recommending stronger custodial measures and a suggestion that "the matter of capital punishment (in Michigan) should be re-examined." The demands themselves were slightingly mentioned in the outline of the riot's chronology.

To penologists, however, the demands were important. They constituted a unique document. They were put together at a time when prisoners could voice their thoughts without a warden staring down their throats as he would in a formal investigation. They were formulated by two brilliant men: one a psychopath with a strongly developed social sense; the other a psychologist with an education in penal theory in addition to experience, both as an official and as an inmate, in penal institutions. French penologists wired congratulations to Fox on the demands.

The final demands were, admittedly, Fox's. When Fox was

---

[8] Report of the Board of Inquiry—Southern Michigan Prison Riot, 1952. This is not the MacCormick report.

accused of writing a couple of them, he denied it: "I wrote all of the demands," he answered. "I took their (the rioters') demands, recast them so that they were right from a penological point of view and acceptable from an official point of view. Then I changed caps and accepted them."

We went over the demands carefully with Brooks, Ward, and Fox. Their viewpoints differed.

The demands were:

(1) *Cell Block Fifteen remodeled to provide for adequate lighting and proper treatment facilities.*

Said Commissioner Brooks, "There is some justification in this demand. Dr. Finch, the Chief of Staff of our Medical Department, has called to our attention a number of times the fact that Cell Block Fifteen was not as good as it should be for living conditions."

(2) *Counselors should be given free access to Block Fifteen.*

Answered Brooks, "I agree with that only in part. Fifteen is a custodial block. It is the place where the men are confined because of improper conduct within the prison. If they are to have privileges in there, they must be limited privileges."

(3) *Provide segregation procedure so that treatment personnel will have favorable representation on the Segregation Board.*

This, too, Brooks did not agree with. On the other hand, these last two demands were important to Fox. Ward had at first merely demanded "the elimination of brutality in Fifteen Block." Fox pointed out to Ward this demand defeated its own purpose since it would only mean an investigation proving that there had been no brutality in Fifteen. Why not, Fox suggested, see to it that outsiders could come into Fifteen so that any fresh and unexplained bruises could be spotted? That way, inmates could complain and be sure their complaints would be looked into. Ward bought this.

Fox's critics, however, pointed out that this put "treatment" men into a "custody" block and it gave Fox greater power.

They cited this to prove that Fox's whole motivation in handling the demands was personal ambition.

(4) *Eliminate inhuman restraint equipment and damaging hand weapons.*

Brooks said: "This is an interesting complaint. Necessarily, we have certain restraining implements in order to handle inmates when they are not behaving themselves properly. We need them in self-defense. Guards will be attacked from time to time by inmates. That happens in every prison. Nevertheless, they are in such small numbers and they are used so infrequently that there is absolutely no justification in speaking of them in terms of being 'inhuman.' "

This was the point of view maintained by all officials, but Ward had posed for newsreels and photographs with the blackjacks and chains, which he claimed were in common use inside Fifteen.

(5) *Select officers for Block Twelve (ill and infirm prisoners) who will not treat inmates brutally. Specifically at this time, Officer Lovett is to be relieved of duty.*

Brooks' answer: "As I said before, officers are not treating inmates brutally now, nor have they ever during this present administration. We naturally select officers to the best of our ability. We employ men who are available to us. We train them carefully and well. Again, there is no sadistic brutality within the prison."

I asked about Officer Lovett. Brooks looked vague.

"We were perfectly willing to give Officer Lovett another assignment," he said slowly. "In fact, we were already planning to place him on one of the posts outside of the walls where he would not come into contact with the inmates as much as he did."

"Was this a recognition of the fact that Lovett was brutal?" I asked.

Brooks looked for help from Gilman.

"Not brutal, was he? What *was* the complaint on Lovett? He was kind of a mean old bitch?"

Gilman snapped to attention. "I really don't know, commissioner. I think Lovett was removed the next day—"

Brooks nodded. "We put him outside."

Gilman went right on: "—merely to successfully complete the negotiations under way at that time, not so much an acknowledgment that the guy was brutal or inhuman or so on. Once we were into the negotiations we wanted to show that our hearts were in the right place and that we wanted to meet them halfway, and so Lovett was taken outside.

"Also for Lovett's sake. In other words, once it is over the air that Lovett was a so-and-so, he becomes hot inside the prison, and whether or not the charge is justified or not, in fairness to the man himself, to be adjusted later, we took him out, I believe, the very next day."

(6) *Place adequately trained personnel in charge of mental ward, with adequate personnel to handle it. Inmate nurses now assigned shall be screened for propensities for brutality, those under suspicion removed.*

Here Brooks was on firmer ground. "We certainly would like to do that, and we would do that if such trained personnel were available to us. It's not available to us and it's not available to our mental health institutions. All of our institutions are running short. Actually, the men that we have there are as trained and as skilled as they can be within the limitations that we have of using the inmates in the prison itself."

(7) *A letter on official stationery to the Parole Board requesting liberalization of practices.*

On this demand we interviewed A. Ross Pascoe of the parole board. After two meetings of being lectured at, we got him to condense his statement, in broad Scotch brogue, to this:

I have been asked by NBC to comment upon the inmate complaint arising out of the Jackson prison riot that the Michigan Parole Board, because of conservative practices and policies, was an inciting factor in that riot last April.

I am reminded that the wardens of this country, meeting at Atlanta during the session of the American Prison Congress there, in conclave determined there were nine reasons for rioting, but parole was not mentioned as an inciting factor; and that when

we viewed the parole rate for Michigan for the last four years
and were confronted by the fact that Michigan, for four years last
past, had and will this year have the highest parole rate comparatively in the United States; and we are also confronted with the
fact that statistically the Michigan maximum terms are not excessive (as claimed by inmates), nor is the amount of time served
by inmates prior to parole in excess of the general average for
the United States or in other sectors of the country, we can find
little reason for the inmate complaint that the Michigan Parole
Board in its practices and policies is an ultraconservative parole
board and one which properly should be charged with being an
inciting factor in the riot of last April.

For answers to the other demands, we went back to Commissioner Brooks.

(8) *Postoperative care by regular nurses more closely supervised by medical director.*
Brooks looked unhappy. This was not a demand he could,
or wanted to, deny. "We have to use inmate nurses. Professional nurses, whether trained or otherwise, are not available
to us. The doctors in the hospital give a lot of their time to
training the inmates so as to make them capable of taking
care of their fellow inmates who are being hospitalized."

(9) *Placing men up on the dental list for dental treatment
must cease. Distribute dental treatment so that persons
who work in the hospital, or who have special contacts or
cigarettes, cannot get dental treatment ahead of everyone
else.*
I asked Brooks what it meant. He chuckled: "Naturally,
you're going to find little silly, simple rackets in the prison
as much as you find them on the outside world. Just as we will
pay a little bit extra for theater tickets by going to one of those
agencies instead of standing in line at the entrance to the theater, so will the inmates pay a package of cigarettes or two if they
can get ahead in the line for dental care. This is something that
absolutely could not be coped with in the prison any more than
it can be coped with in the outside world."

Ward, on the other hand, told us men with aching teeth had to wait up to six months to see a dentist. He blamed lack of dental personnel.

(10) *Inmate council should be created, elected by the inmate body, to discuss problems regarding inmates with the administration.*

Brooks again was on uncertain ground: "This has been tried, I understand, with real success in several institutions throughout the United States. We certainly should try it, because we must be as progressive as they are. If the inmates can sit in on the council and tell us more about what is going on within the institution than we can find out by wandering around, then of course we need their advice and we need their help. I am in favor of such a council. I would like to see it established."

But there again the problem was not so clear-cut. The inmate council was one of the original demands made by Ward. But Fox pointed out that Ward wanted every prison rule, even those affecting custody, submitted to the inmate council for its approval. Further, Ward had named the members he wanted on that council. "And," concluded Fox, "that would have been some council!"

As it worked out, Ward agreed that the council would be only advisory and would work under Fox. Ward quoted Fox as saying together they would "run the prison," but Fox said he sold Ward on the amended version of the demand on the assurance that the council would have a fair hearing. Fox would see to this.

Again, this was seized by anti-Fox forces to prove that he used the riot to increase his own power.

(11) *No reprisals against any ringleaders or others.*

Again we went to Brooks for the answer: "There is absolutely no reason why we should carry out reprisals against these ringleaders. In the first place, we do not believe in nor do we practice inhuman, sadistic brutality. The only punishment we could possibly give these men is to continue their confinement in Fifteen Block. They are already there, so continuing them there would not be a reprisal. In the matter of the violation of state laws, the destruction of state property, arson, and other acts, that would be left entirely in the hands of local prosecuting attorney and the attorney general for the State of Michigan. And it would not be in the nature of reprisals at all. It would merely be punishment for offenses committed during the riot."

There was no doubt that Ward considered the due process of law a reprisal. He told us, "The attorney general prosecuted us and persecuted us for revealing the conditions in the prison."

As a result of the prosecution, Ward was sentenced to twenty to thirty years, to be served concurrently with his original sentence. He is now in Marquette. Whatever happened to the original plan to send him to a mental hospital, I do not know.

Ward also said, "We were double crossed by the governor himself." And Fox agrees with him. He claims he worked all through the riot on the basis of Brooks' promise that treatment would take charge of the prison, but that pressure from Leonard during the riot and from the public after the riot was so great that Michigan penology has retrogressed to a philosophy of pure vengeance.

And, according to Fox, it was this pressure that got him fired, the congratulatory speech merely being an excuse. He further maintained the speech meant nothing, being made simply to hasten the final surrender. Ward had demanded it in the "happy birthday" telephone call of Thursday. They had talked it over at the window. Fox wrote it out for Ward's approval and then put it over the prison radio.

Fox's story is backed up by Joseph Dellinger, a counselor who was with him at the time:

> Dr. Fox called me and said, "Where is the tape recorder?" and I replied that it was in my office and then he said, "Let's get it. I want to record a speech to Fifteen Block. I'm too tired, too uncertain of my voice, to do it over the P.A. system."
>
> We recorded that speech, took it to the parole-board room and put it on the network. We can't separate the other blocks from Fifteen Block, and so it went to all the men at the same time. We then put the speech on the P.A. system which would blast it out over the yard to make certain that everybody got it, especially Fifteen Block.

It served only one purpose and one purpose alone, and that was to congratulate Ward and Hyatt, to satisfy their ego so that they might be taken off the hook, so to speak, by the inmates in Fifteen Block who might censor Ward for allowing the guards to be released twenty-four hours earlier than planned.

We did make a mistake, however. We had been working all that week and were very tired. We neglected to inform the press or any one else around that we were intending this speech to be directed to Fifteen Block for one specific purpose.

But there Fox's support ends. Ward claims the speech was all Fox's idea, that he never asked for it.

The matter of whose word should be taken on this matter would be easier to solve were it not that Fox said the demand for the speech was made on the phone. All calls out of Fifteen were allegedly monitored by the phone operator, Virginia Dunayski. She swore to the board of inquiry that Ward made no request for the controversial speech. Fox answered:

Now here is an item that I think may have been overlooked. There are five trunk lines running into that prison. The trunk lines were busy at all times. There was one operator. I don't see how she could have monitored the calls all the way through.

Secondly, when I told the warden about that, he said, "Why, the state police have taken tapes of all of the calls that emanated from Fifteen Block!" Where's the tape?

We were told that, by accident, no tape was made of that call. Fox answered that with another question: "Why did the state police, '*by accident*,' not make a tape of *that* call? I ask you?"

Here is a place you pays your money and takes your choice. However, the report of the Board of Inquiry makes it clear that Fox was not believed. The committee found "his conduct . . . wholly inexplicable" after pointing out that they did not think Leonard had "a gun at his (Fox's) head" as he maintained, and that he should have been firmer. Fox answered by pointing out the board members read about the riot while it was happening; he, Fox, was on the spot.

The spot he was on after the riot was worse. His resignation was accepted. According to penologists, some of whom were completely on his side in theory, he went too far. However, they admit they do not know what else he could have done. They conclude that he will never hold another prison job. On the telephone from Florida, Fox spoke to me, glowingly but unconvincingly, of the advantages of academic life over the more active life he had grown used to. Whether you agree with Fox and his actions or not, there is tragedy, in the classic manner, inherent in his story.

Fox was not the only man to leave Jackson. Frisbie left, and Brooks replaced him with Warden Bannan of the Michigan Reformatory at Ionia. Bannan is considered tough but fair. When we asked him about improvements at Jackson since April, he pointed out that new gun turrets were being built and custody was being strengthened. Rehabilitation policies were not mentioned.

He blamed criminals on the breaking up of the family unit, the lack of church-going among teenagers, and the invention of the automobile. While this analysis gave Peg a guilt complex because we were away from Terry, we were struck by the fact that Bannan gave no suggestions of how his prison might help the social failures who end up in his care.

George Bacon, no longer posted inside Jackson's walls, handles camps. His place was taken by Assistant Deputy Charles Cahill. But the riots go on. Another major disturbance broke out in November, 1952. Again it was in the mess hall, where inmates made it known (despite an official report to the contrary) that they had not liked the food before the big riot and still didn't like it. Charles Cahill told us the story:

> At the time, I was the acting warden during Warden Bannan's absence. The start came shortly after four o'clock, when I was notified of trouble in the dining room. My assistant, Assistant Deputy Tucker, immediately went down to the dining room and laundry, as we heard there were fires started. As rapidly as possible, I assembled a group of men armed with shotguns, armed myself with a submachine gun and revolver, and we immediately hurried to the scene. Because the April riots were mostly on the south side, we covered it first. After everything appeared all right on that side, we went to the north side. As we got

into Two and One Blocks, there was quite a lot of destruction. The inmates tried to keep us out of the block by throwing things from the galleries, blockin' the doors. We fired a few shots into the roof, not at any individual, and ducked down into the yard and entered the block from another door. The inmates had taken the levers from the lock boxes, and the keys were not available because the officers were pulled out. So consequently most of the cells could not be locked.

We run everybody into their cells and then sent for help with keys to set the levers so that we could lock the doors after we got them in. Then we went over One and Two Block, both of them, gallery by gallery, to see that they were locked in, because it was quite evident that most of the trouble was from those men."

We asked, why the riot?

Well, as far as we've been able to discover, somebody put salt in the coffee. We have an inmate by the name of Haines in the hole for putting the salt in the coffee. Haines, by the way, has admitted that he put salt in the coffee in the previous riot, too. You know, it's not very good drinking coffee with salt in it.

This we knew. In studying the riot, we had done much speculating about the battle cry that had set off two riots. We asked several officials what was meant by "salt in the coffee." We got various answers.

"Well, somebody just put salt in the coffee."

"It was a prearranged signal by trouble makers."

"No, it wasn't salt peter."

All of these answers were the truth and nothing but the truth. But they were not the whole truth. . . .

It was several days later that we had lunch with Boyd Simmons of the Detroit *News*. To him we described our visit to the prison and some of our reactions. Boyd did the impossible —he interrupted Peg.

"Say, did I tell you not to drink the coffee at Jackson?"

"No."

"Did you drink any?"

"Yeah."

Boyd burst out laughing. "I should have warned you. At Jackson the favorite trick is to put salt in the coffee, not only to cause trouble with the inmates, but to get back at officials. And it's tradition to put salt in any coffee served the press."

Boyd was dying at this point. "During the riot the newsmen noticed our coffee was salty too," he went on, "and we couldn't understand it until a couple of us caught some trusties in the hall using our coffee pitchers as urinals. News people never drink coffee at Jackson."

Peg, and I knew to the depths of our sinking, churning tummies the meaning of the cry, "There's salt in the coffee."

After our swing around the country, back in New York we kept getting new information out of Jackson. Austin Mac-Cormick gave us a summary of his findings for the governor's "Special Committee to Study the Michigan Department of Corrections." He said:

> The main causes that lay back of the riots that have been going on more or less continually at the Jackson, Michigan, prison seem to me to be the excessive size of the institution, its excessive population, the heterogeneous inmate population that had resulted from making it a dumping ground, and the terrific turnover in the custodial force because of the low salary schedule. The guard force has been completely demoralized, and it couldn't have maintained discipline even if the size of the place were reasonable.
>
> Plus that, politics have played a part in the situation. The head of the department is a political appointee with inadequate experience, and while my chief recommendations have been that the population of Jackson prison be reduced and that specialized institutions be operated to keep it from being the dumping ground that it has been, the thing of paramount importance is that they put the department under a fully qualified career penologist.

We wondered what Brooks' reaction would be. On the phone the advocate of the soft answer said:

> Michigan is grateful to Austin MacCormick and those who worked with him in making his survey. Our attention has now been focused upon the glaring defects in our system and, what is

more important, that they are not incurable. With the help of
our legislature we will soon have the needed facilities which will
go far toward enabling us to avoid further serious trouble.

But MacCormick's report also dared to criticize Mr. Pascoe's parole board for forcing inmates to plead guilty before
considering them for parole; being cynical, sarcastic, and dic-
tatorial; not spending enough time at hearings; and poor inter-
pretive procedure.

Pascoe rose up in arms and again cited his warden's report
along with the fact that MacCormick's investigators listened
to prison complaints longer than to the board's explanations.
MacCormick withdrew none of his report and said that, all
of Mr. Pascoe's figures not withstanding, Jackson would have
more riots unless conditions, parole, and brutality were corrected.

Then Dr. Finch quit. Dr. Russell L. Finch was an old-timer
with the corrections department, having been the first full-
time medical man at Marquette in 1922. Now, in two typed
lines, he left what he called "the closest I can come to medical
missionary work." He said he would give no reason for his act
until after January 15, 1953, when his resignation became effective.

On January 16 I called him and recorded his conversation.
He told us:

On November 30, 1952,[9] there was a disturbance in Fifteen
Block at about twelve-thirty in the afternoon. Four men were
severely beaten. I was not notified of this.

At two-thirty that afternoon my inmate nurse, who looks after
the Fifteen Block, told me that there had been some beatings in
the block and asked me to see these men. I went to Fifteen Block
where I found these men and immediately admitted them to the
hospital.

One man had a broken arm, a bad blood clot in his thigh, and
a very bruised lower leg. Another man had severe lacerations of
the scalp, down to the bone, which required fourteen or fifteen
sutures. Two other men had bruises.

The report came from Commissioner Brooks and also Warden

---

[9] A few days after we were there.

Bannan that the beatings were to stop an impending riot and that the guards had to defend themselves. Yet one of these men (with the broken arm, a blood clot in his leg and another bruised leg) was a man five foot two inches tall, who weighed 123 pounds. Three guards with blackjacks and nightsticks beat him up. According to them it was in self-defense, which is just inane if you ask me.

And this is an interesting sidelight. The following morning the assistant deputy in charge of custody[10] called me and wanted to know about the beatings, because he hadn't heard of them until he came in that morning. A few minutes later the warden called and asked me about it. If there was an impending riot, it surprised me that these two did not know a thing about it until the following day.

I made a report to the warden and took it up to him on Monday afternoon. He was very indignant about the treatment of these men and stated that such things would not be tolerated by him. Now he comes out and tells the papers that there were no beatings. I told Commissioner Brooks they're just insulting the intelligence of people by giving out such information as that.

I asked Finch if he thought this was an isolated situation or was brutality a general practice at Jackson. He snapped:

Blackjacks apparently are normal equipment since Warden Bannan has taken charge. Custody has taken over. Now I believe custody is important, but we still have a legal as well as a moral obligation to try to rehabilitate men who are susceptible to rehabilitation. I feel no good can come out of brutality and, regardless of the reason for trouble, I don't believe it can be condoned under any circumstances. There are too many other ways to deal with situations besides beating a man up.

I closed by requesting a prognosis for Jackson.

If they remove some of the sadistic elements there, we may be able to do some good at Jackson. If they don't, then I'm just afraid to say what might happen.

Confirmation of Dr. Finch's pessimism came unexpectedly. Just before air time for the first of our two Jackson shows, a strange call came in. The call, following a pattern that had

[10] Charles Cahill.

become familiar, opened with the words, "You don't know me,
but I gotta see you."

These words prefaced many calls, but this one was from a
kid named Pat. His story was simple. He had been released
from Jackson the day before. Some of the boys had told him
to come to us because they did not want another riot. If on the
radio we told about the gasoline that had been stolen and hidden ready for a blowup that would make the April shindig
look like a Vassar pillow fight, the officials might finally take
constructive action.

We checked into Pat pretty thoroughly in New York, Jackson, and Lansing. His story held up. We put him on. His voice
shook, his manner was effeminate, but some of his words
might have been Fox's, MacCormick's, or Finch's:

> I'm just out of Jackson. I was there last April when eleven
> demands were made to the governor of the State of Michigan.
> The governor capitulated to these demands but these eleven de-
> mands have not been carried out. The governor has gone back
> on his word. Those eleven demands were well founded. They
> were not entirely the inmates'. They were a cooperation of the
> inmates and Dr. Fox, whom the inmates considered a friend.
>
> However, not one of these demands have been carried out. The
> explosive situation at the prison since the time of the first riot
> has been mainly due to the parole board. It will give nothing
> but three-year flops.* If you don't get a parole, you aren't con-
> sidered for three years no matter what.

We asked Pat about Dr. Finch. Pat, always close to tears
with mike fright, became impassioned:

> When the news became known to the inmates that Dr. Finch
> was resigning because of the brutality in Fifteen Block, a petition
> was immediately taken among the inmates with more than two
> thousand names affixed to it. This was confiscated by the warden
> and the men who were distributing it were put in Fifteen.
>
> The petition was not turned over to Dr. Finch as the inmates
> had wanted. The petition asked the doctor to overlook what had
> happened. We knew that if Dr. Finch left the prison, medical
> treatment there would drop. Dr. Finch built up the medical de-
> partment to what it was today. Thousands and thousands of dol-
> lars of plastic surgery has been done there free for inmates, faces

improved, scars, ears, noses, everything repaired free of charge.

Shortly after Dr. Finch resigned, in the sign shop of the prison a sign was made which read: FINCH GENERAL HOSPITAL. This sign was placed up by the hospital in remembrance and the love that the inmates had for Dr. Finch. However the sign was not there half an hour when it was taken down by officials at the order of the deputy warden.

Dr. Finch resigned January 15. The following morning a grand riot was scheduled at the prison. However, it was a foggy morning and only the working men were let out of their cells. This left almost two thousand men locked up. So the inmates did not feel that this was the time to have a demonstration and therefore the riot didn't come off.

However, the brutality that Dr. Finch resigned for is continuing at the prison. Strong-arm methods are still being used. The situation has become so explosive that the inmates have planned, carefully planned, a demonstration that will wreck the whole place.

After he had finished, Pat went over to a grand piano in the studio, sat down, and played one of the most beautiful sonatas I have ever heard. It was his own. Then he left. Despite the fact that we wanted to introduce him to our musical director, Morris Mamorsky, who could have helped him, we never saw him again. We do worry about him, however. Pat is an epileptic, but Dr. Finch, for the first time in Pat's hectic life, had given him medicine that prevented seizures. Without this he could die. For the sake of his music, if nothing else, I hope Pat is still alive.

Since our broadcasts, Jackson has been quiet; but, while it is true that Jackson now has a stronger custody setup than before, it is also true that "a guard can still be kidnapped and not found for a week." There are still too many men and too many acres.

The guards are better paid, but conditions for the prisoners have not improved. The State of Michigan is practicing vengeance penology. Vernon Fox points out this can work and brutality can be effective—only providing you never release the resultant caged animals back into public life. But prisoners at Jackson are neither securely nor permanently incarcerated. So Fox predicts more riots.

Dr. Finch predicts more riots.

Austin MacCormick predicts more riots.

Earl Ward predicts more riots. "And the next one will be bloody!"

Authors' Note: As this book goes to press, the Southern State Prison at Jackson, Michigan, is again in the headlines. In December, 1953, thirteen or more prisoners escaped through a tunnel. This brought some embarrassing questions about the new security measures.

As if this were not enough in an election year, the legislature has indicated that it might not approve Governor Williams' new bipartisan, six-man board of commissioners under Ernest Brooks, chairman. Even ex-Senator Brooks, always previously given automatic approval by the legislature under "senatorial courtesy," may not pass muster.

On the other side of the ledger, Gilman is now out of the political flurry and in charge of the state prison-camp program. This program, initiated by Brooks, has begun to relieve some of Michigan's crowding as it augments the state's conservation program. Gilman has been commended for this work by both the state legislature and Austin MacCormick, who places Michigan "very close to the top of the list, if not at the top, of the states that have developed camps."

5

meet the boys

. . . McGraw Reporting

As Peg and I progressed in our assignment, going from
Michigan into the Midwest, visiting state and federal prisons,
making forays into jails and cross-country trips late at night
to see people whom we had reason to think were important
to our story, we found our job breaking down into three definite areas of investigation: prisons (including the people who
administer them, such as Bates and Brooks), riots and their
leaders (such as Ward), and a great, literally nameless mass of
strange and varying humanity called convicts.

Besides their being the most interesting aspect of the series,
we felt it was important to know inmates. Although a small
minority of each prison's population rioted and presented demands, it seemed to us that these few inmates were the legitimate, even if sometimes psychopathic, spokesmen for the great
majority of what Bates called "the well-intentioned" inmates.
Even though some of the riot leaders were held in little per-

sonal esteem by the general population, their complaints were representative of the whole prison. For that reason, and because 97 per cent of all inmates hit the sidewalks eventually, it was important to know them.

Who and why are convicts? We asked that question of many people. The answers varied, but on one point they all agreed. Corny as it may sound, penologist, criminologist, psychiatrist, and inmate emphasized the old truism that, no matter what their record or crime, "prisoners are people," not a species apart.

This might seem obvious, but these men know that if you ask the average citizen about inmates, you will usually receive an answer born of fear and prejudice. The public, which makes heroes of gangsters, pictures any convict as a beast in stripes who must be punished. Psychologists explain this by the "scapegoat" theory, saying the public unloads its own guilt feelings on the convicts it imprisons—theoretically to rehabilitate.

Broad-minded as Peg and I like to feel we are, we were acutely uncomfortable at first as we talked to inmates. It was only after a good many of these interviews that we found we could talk to these men as people, not as a species from another world. It was with surprise, actually, that we found ourselves liking some of them and being bored with others, just as we are with our acquaintances who do not wear numbers. Only then did we feel we could start analyzing their stories for their human content and social import.

We found only one inmate who declared he was "framed," but we often met boys who were trying to solve their problems and understand them. We found, too, that the better the institution he was in, the more the inmate seemed to concentrate on what he was going to do when he got out. In poorly run prisons, our interviews were basically restricted by the inmates to the institution and its faults; in better-set-up places, the inmates could not rationalize their own mistakes so easily by pointing out the glaring errors of society as exemplified by their own institution.

A good illustration of this came out of Alcatraz. Named originally after the stately pelican,[1] "The Rock" had had a long history as a prison for wayward Indian chiefs and AWOL soldiers when J. Edgar Hoover demanded a really tough house for the specimens his boys were bringing back alive during the Dillinger—Pretty Boy Floyd era. But, ironically, management of the new bastille was put in the hands of the then recently reorganized Federal Bureau of Prisons. As the leading critics of the "hit 'em alongside the head" school of penology, they were given orders to make it the most unpleasant, harshest prison possible. In 1934, Austin MacCormick was an assistant director of the bureau, and in 1953 he was still burned up about Alcatraz. He said:

> In the Federal Bureau none of us, from the director on down, believed "The Rock" was either necessary or desirable. It's a wholly false and destructive philosophy to think we can stop crime, or even reduce it, by just creating a place that's supposed to strike terror into the hearts of criminals. We get much further by strengthening our police forces, our prosecution, our courts, our prisons in general, our probation, our parole.
>
> I consider the present proposal to abandon Alcatraz absolutely sound. It should have been done long ago, and I hope that Congress will soon appropriate the money to make it possible. The place has been terrifically extravagant; its cost is three or four times as much as any other institution to operate—per capita cost, I mean. It's never accomplished the purpose that people hoped it would, and, even more important, it's kept alive an irrational and emotional public opinion that tends to impair the effectiveness of crime control. That's the really significant thing. Even if it were located in a better place, it would still be wrong. The federal system should, and can, absorb its problem cases exactly as other prison systems treat their maximum-security risks.

With this thinking behind the running of the institution, it is not surprising that gradually, over the years, Alcatraz has turned more and more to a philosophy of rehabilitation. It is significant that in its early days Alcatraz had riots, strikes, and vio-

---

[1] It was named "Isle de Los Alcatraces" (Isle of Pelicans) by the Spanish, who first explored it.

lence out of proportion even to the vicious type of offender
being housed there.

To get the inmates' side of the Alcatraz story, we looked
up two brothers, both graduates of "The Rock," both examples
of the so-called mad-dog era of the thirties. We recorded them
in a two-by-four room in a hotel in Terre Haute, Indiana. Unfortunately, some color-blind decorator had painted it a sicken-
ing blood red. It gave a sinister quality to these two, whom we
shall call Slim and Jack. Once they had been on the FBI's list of
"most-wanted" men. The older of the two, Slim, looked the
part, with his high cheek bones, a long scar and thin lips. The
younger brother, Jack (they are both in their forties), looked
more like a Hoosier farmer turned politician. He did most of
the talking:

> My father was a Methodist preacher, and he was strict! But I
> don't s'pose he was more strict than he thought he should be. I
> don't know whether that had anything to do with my later life
> or not. I s'pose the first real trouble I ever got into, when I was
> twelve years old, I wanted a bicycle. My father said, no, it was
> too dangerous in the city we lived in, so I had a chance to steal
> some money to buy a bicycle, and I went and stole it.
>
> So I was sent to the juvenile school, and I ran away from there
> five or six times. Finally they didn't think they could hold me
> there at all, and they sent me to a reformatory. After a year there
> I was paroled.
>
> When I got out—oh, heck, I was in one thing right after an-
> other, I was always into something. We used to go out here on
> the road and we'd wait for fellows to come out of town, away
> from where they loaded whiskey[2]; and we'd run alongside of
> them and stick a shotgun out of the window and tell 'em to pull
> up. We took their load and sold it.
>
> I got caught on an auto-theft charge and was sent to Atlanta.
> When I came out of there, I fully intended to go straight—I
> didn't want any more prison. But I wasn't too convinced that
> I would go straight if something showed up that meant a little
> bit of money to me, because I wanted a farm. I wanted a farm
> more than anything, and it seemed like bank robbery offered
> what I wanted. So, when I had a chance to fall in with a gang
> that was robbing banks right and left, I fell in.

[2] This was during Prohibition.

There was four of them in the gang, and there was one that
spent money a little too lavishly. They decided to cut him out
because he was a risk, and I was cut in. I had a little pull: my
brother was head of the gang.

Slim, definitely the leader of the two, left as much of the
telling to Jack as he could. But we interrupted Jack to ask Slim
how he had become a bank robber. He answered slowly, reluctantly at first.

Well, I left home when I was thirteen, and I been pretty much
in trouble ever since. I was working in Kansas City. The police
was running a car down Fifteenth Street, and that car run into a
light post and turned over.

I come along about that time in a car, and I seen a guy get
outta that car and run through the alley, and, when he did, I went
around the block and I picked him up. And I taken him up to
my room. He was pretty well bruised up and I kept him up there
for about ten days till he recuperated.

He happened to be from Dayton, Ohio. When he left, I never
expected to see him again. Then I got a telegram from him asking if I wanted to come to Dayton and make some easy money.
So I went to Dayton. We went out on a bank robbery and we
blowed the front off a vault. I got my share of the money, but
him, I never did see him after that.

Well, after that I served time in the Indiana State Reformatory for manslaughter. I was running a——I was in partners in a
country club, which I bought into with the Dayton money. One
of the Purple Gang come in there and thought he could take the
joint. Well, when he tried to stick it up, why, I knocked one of
his partners out with a pistol, and, when I started to hit him, why
the gun accidentally went off and shot him. Instead of calling
the police in, why he was hauled outside and dumped. And then
when the story did come out, why there wasn't no way of ever
describing how it happened, so I was tried and given two to
twenty-one years.

Being technically a first offender, he was out at the end of
two years, firmly resolved that trafficking in liquor could get
you into too much trouble.

Besides, as he said, "I was always told if you wanted grocer-
ies, you go to a grocery store, and if you wanted money, go to

a bank." So he organized his own gang of bank robbers and was not at all unhappy to have some of his exploits blamed on a better-known name in the field, John Dillinger, with whom he had had some business dealings.

How many banks the boys hit is still their secret. They began to name their jobs because they felt they were safe under the statute of limitations; but, on the other hand, not all their business partners have been caught. Suffice to say, they cut a pretty wide swath through the Middle West and the Southwest, ending up in Louisiana. When it came to business details, Slim warmed up:

This particular bank in Louisiana is located on a crossroads in a little town on a highway. About fifteen miles out the east way from this town is a large city. If the alarm goes out from this bank, you've got about seven minutes to beat the squad cars coming to this little town.

They had a large payroll in this bank, and we decided we wanted it. So we went to this town, and we go to the bank, and we take a fast run. We'd run five minutes, then see where we was at. So eventually, we found a road that brought us to a small stream. So we decided that that stream would be our out.

So then we went and we cased the bank for about thirty days. Then we traveled this stream to see what it was. Then we decided we had to have a canoe, but we didn't want to buy one because it might lead suspicion on to us if the canoe was ever discovered.

Two partners of mine, I dropped 'em off at a river town. They went down to the bank; and there was a big dog tied to this canoe, and they untied the dog and took the canoe and never woke the dog up. We took that canoe to my home, put it in the garage, and give it another paint job so it wouldn't be recognized. We took the canoe over to the crick.

Then we went into the bank, which was at about two o'clock in the morning. We went in the bank from the top, disconnected their burglar-alarm system. Our other partner was to meet us in front of the bank in a car at five minutes after nine the next morning.

When people entered the bank, we stuck 'em up, made 'em open the vault, and we took the money. And there was a woman in there that had a large purse. It was about—oh, eighteen inches long and twelve inches wide and four or five inches thick. And she was frightened, plenty frightened.

And then Jack asked her, "You got anything in that purse?" She said, "No, sir. I haven't got anything in here."

He said, "Well, I'll put something in there!" So he took it to the vault and filled it up full of nickels and dimes—I bet it'd hold fifty pounds—and set it down beside her.

To rob this bank, we had overalls on over our clothes and we wore false noses and false moustaches. So at the time described, our partner was s'posed to come across the street to the bank in the car to pick us up at the side door. We left by the side door, but as he come across the street, a squad car turned the corner behind him, causing him to mosey on. And we had two sacks full of money and all this makeup on! We just walked down the middle of the street—caused such a commotion. Everybody was watchin'; they thought we was two clowns or something.

Well, anyway, our partner turned the corner. We jumped in the car and made our five-minute run. We got in our canoe, and during the night it rained most of the night, and that river was really booming. We got down that river about two mile, we run up on a brush or something in the stream, turned us over. And all of our money and guns was in these sacks. They weighted the canoe down. We had an awful time getting that canoe out of the bottom of that river with them sacks in it.

But when we got to where we was going, we tried every way in the world to sink that canoe! We finally had to chop the bottom of it out and get it up on the side of the bank and fill it full of dirt in order to get it to sink.

But this was the last of their bank robberies. Jack picked up the story:

Well, it created so much stir that I think that authorities put about everything they had into solving the case. And, well, while we were down there, we went to a fella's house, and we gave him a thousand dollars for staying at his house while we robbed this bank. And he went and bought a new car and did a little talking, one thing and another. Finally they picked him up, and he got his chance to do some real talking.

They traced us down. We were already on the farms we had bought with our money. We was married and they came along. We lost everything that we had: farms, wives, money—everything. We were sentenced to fifteen years in the federal penitentiary and twenty years in the state penitentiary, both on the same charge. Both sentences were to run concurrently with one another. But we was sent to the Louisiana State Penitentiary in Angola.

We were both put in the "red hats." [3] They haven't got the red hats down there any more; they abandoned that, but it was s'posed to be a sort of a doom squad. There was thirty men in it, and you got up at daylight and you worked all day long until at noon you stopped wherever you were in the field and ate. They brought a chuck wagon out. You went out in the morning when they could see to shoot you, and they brought you back when they could still see to shoot you. And that was every day, seven days a week—Christmas, Thanksgiving, every day. The only day that we got off was Huey P. Long's birthday.

Slim chimed in:

We was down there Thanksgiving and Christmas. We didn't know when they were. They furnished you with a stripe-ped pair of pants and a stripe-ped jacket and that's all you had. If you had the money to buy a pair of socks, you had socks. And if you could afford a stamp, you could write home. Otherwise, you couldn't even write home.

Remembering Angola, the boys began to get mad. Now they talked faster. Jack went on:

They call the man down there over you, the foreman, they call him "Massa." That's short for "Master." We were in line, lined up for dinner there in the field, and he rode up on his horse—he don't get off his horse—and he looked down and he said—they call you "fresh fish" when you first go in there, but he didn't call us fresh fish, he called us "bank robber." He said, "Ole bank robber," he said, "I bet you've got a grave yard up there where you come from. We've got a grave yard down here, too." He told us, "We've got two remedies here for you, and both of them cure all ailments. And that's buckshot and bull hide!"

All the employees down there, they make about forty-fifty dollars a month, so you know what they've got. . . .

---

[3] So-called because they wore red hats for easy spotting when they worked in the fields.

There was a long pause as both men looked into the past. Slowly, Slim went on:

Well, what makes Louisiana State Penitentiary so tough is they use convict guards. They're back there in them swamps, and they give 'em a gun guardin' other men and tell 'em, "If you see one of them try to escape, shoot 'im, and we'll give you a thirty-day furlough." And I mean that they're always looking for some way to shoot you, and they'll always *find* some way to shoot you, specially if their wife is this or that and they're wanting to go home. That's the way it sets down there.

We was there six months and five days—then the federals took us out of the state penitentiary. They said the state penitentiary'd be unable to hold us. We were very relieved when the federal authorities taken us over, and when they'd taken us to New Orleans, well, that was like Sunday School.

Jack grinned broadly:

We left Angola and went to the New Orleans jail. We got Post Toasties and milk—and say, you talk about something that tasted good! 'Cause we'd been eating grits and black coffee. And we laid on the bed and read a book! There was no books in Angola. Well, that was something—like bein' home. We really enjoyed that.

But they transferred us to Leavensworth,[4] and from Leavensworth they transferred us to Alcatraz.

Well, when we went to Alcatraz, Alcatraz was still a tough prison then. They had the silent system. They had riots, they had sit-downs, they had all kinds of strikes. They had strikes and fights and everything every week. The men went on strikes for diversion, something to break up the prison routine.

We wasn't there for two weeks when we went on a hungry strike for two weeks, and then I went in isolation. I was in isolation for two months. I come out of there, we was on another strike and it was all strikes. I guess they averaged two or three strikes a month, but finally the officials decided that the silent system wasn't any good.

They took off that pressure. They eliminated that there silent system and they made the rules more lax; and instead of a fifteen-minute music hour at night, they let the convicts play their man-

---

[4] This is how Jack pronounced *Leavenwort'.*

dolins and their guitars as much as they wanted to. The fellow in the next cell, why, he'd beef about this fellow over here playing the mandolin and he had something to beef about besides prison routines.

After the rules were relaxed, no one wanted to strike any more, no one wanted to riot, because they had something else to do.

But this was only part of the story. Thoughtfully the younger man outlined the big Alcatraz revolt of 1946:

The thing that changed me more than anything, there was a fellow there that got some guns.[5] He locked some officers in two different cells adjoining one another, and Joe walked up to one cell and emptied a .45 into that cell. I guess he thought he'd killed every officer in there. They all went down. He done some pretty good shootin'. And he went over to the other cell, put a new clip in the gun and emptied the .45 in that cell. Fortunately, none of the officers died.[6] It's a wonder. But, I don't know—I just wasn't quite cut out for that. 'Course I wanted to escape all right, I wanted to rob banks, I wanted to make money; but I didn't want to just kill everybody just for the sake of killing 'em. And I figured if prison done that to Joe, it might do that to me, too. So I decided if I ever did get out, there wouldn't be no more prison for me.

A prisoner such as I was, I didn't have any use for screws at all. After I seen what happened to Joe, I said, "From now on, every time a screw goes down this here gallery, I'm going to say 'Good morning.'" Come in there during the day, I said, "How do you do? Good day!" or "How do you do, sir," or something or other. And he, "Hello!" Every time I seen an officer, I spoke. And finally I got so I liked it, and they liked it too.

Finally, I don't know . . . I guess I just changed. They say a tiger won't change his stripes, but I guess I changed mine.

I'll tell you what happened to me then. I'd lost all my good time* on an attempt to escape. A screw told me, he said, "If you are ever going to get your good time back, you're going to

---

[5] Joseph Cretzer, murderer and bank robber. His record listed six successful escapes from different prisons.
[6] Of the nine hostage guards, six were wounded. Two other officers were killed in suppressing the revolt. A mass escape attempt was foiled by one of the murdered officers, William A. Miller, who hid his keys so that the revolt was contained in "D," Alcatraz's segregation block.

have to ask the warden for it back." I said I wasn't going to ask
for it back.

So, a year or so later, I got to thinking, "Well, maybe I could
ask for it back." So I wrote a request and asked to see the warden. I asked him, "How about gettin' some of my good time
back?"

He said, "Well, are you sorry for what you done?—for the
mistakes you've made?"

And I told him, "Well, I don't know. I hadn't really thought
about it thataway."

He said, "Well, when anyone makes a mistake, usually they're
sorry. You haven't thought about it like that yet. Maybe you're
not sorry."

Well, I didn't get any good time back that year. So the next
year I thought I better tell him I'm sorry. So I told him, "Yah, I
know that I did wrong." And I started gettin' good time back.
I guess I was kinda playing a part and finally I just fell into it—
I don't know.

Close to each other on everything else, the brothers also decided on rehabilitation together. The older brother put it
much more simply: "I was rebellious for quite a while but I
decided my way couldn't win, so I switched over to the winning side."

With their recovery of good time and a new attitude, after
more than a decade on "The Rock," they were finally paroled.
What is the first thing a released man does? Jack answered:

The first thing we did when we got out, we went into a place
and got a bottle of beer! We got a bottle of beer. . . .

In all the years we were in Alcatraz, we never saw a woman.
I mean, we *never* saw a woman! You could see ships go by, but
we never saw a woman. I mean at a distance, you couldn't a
seen one with a pair of binoculars, 'cause there's no women on
"The Rock," that is, where a convict could see a woman. Well,
when we got out, I looked at women. I mean, I *looked* at
women! After all those years . . . I don't know, I don't know
whether anyone can understand not seeing a woman for ten years
or not.

Again Slim footnoted the story:

There is no other punishment greater. Regardless of where I
was at—when I was in the red hats at Angola, the various prisons
I've been in—the only thing that tormented me more than anything else was being deprived of the opposite sex. Their dungeons, their hard work wasn't as severe as that.

Once out, they settled in Indiana. Slim got a job fairly easily
and married. Jack got married too, shortly thereafter, but he
had a problem:

Jobs weren't easy to get, and I'd previously been told by federal officials that, if I ever run into any difficulty, just drop
around to the nearest United States prison and see the warden,[7]
that he'd help me out. So I called him on the phone and got an
interview with him, and I went out there. He met me, and he
took off my overcoat, and he hung it on a hanger in a closet. He
treated me like I was the President. He told me to sit down. He
acted like he was tickled to death to see me. I told him I was out
of a job. And he told me he'd get me a job, that he knew people
about town. And the next morning he drove to my house from
the prison—that's about fifteen miles—he drove to my house himself and told me to go to work at the post office the next morning. I couldn't believe it!
But that's where I went to work, the post office, during the
Christmas rush, and I worked in the post office the same as all
the other employees. I seen the Brink's truck drive up. The man
got out with his pistol, and he stood guard at the door. They
brought in the Brink's bag, full of money, turned it in at the
window, and pushed the bag right over to the other mail—right
over to where I was working. Nobody paid it any mind, the back
doors were wide open. I was treated just like anyone else. . . .
The Brink's are a little bit careless though!
Well, then, the warden told me that by the time the Christmas
rush is over that he'd have me another job, and he had me another job. And, after a while, time went on and I broke my leg
and I had some difficulty, and my wife—I married a nurse—she
was pregnant (that is, she was havin' a baby) and I was broke.
I wondered where in the heck I could borree some money. And
I thought, "Oh, Mr. Overlade again." So I got on the phone,
and I said, "Mr. Overlade, my wife's going to have a baby and
I'm out of work now. I'd like to borree about $50."

---

[7] J. E. Overlade, warden of United States Penitentiary, Terre Haute, Indiana.

He said, "You want me to bring it to you or send it to you in a check?"

I said, "Well, either way that would be convenient for you would be all right with me."

He said, "Well, I'll mail you a check today." The next day I got a check for $50!

Then when I went to work, I went up to a store, the best store in town, and I went in and I told them I wanted the best tie they had. They trotted out some ties, but I didn't want that—I wanted a *good* tie. They finally found the best one they had, and I took that tie and that fifty bucks and I sent it to the warden. And I wrote him a nice letter and told him how much I thanked him for that $50.

About a week later he give me a reply to my letter, and all his letter was thanking me for that tie. You'd think that I gave him that tie and he didn't loan me no fifty dollars. Say, there's a swell guy. . . .

Well, after I was able to go back to work after breaking my leg, why the company called me and told me they'd give me a job for $35 a week as a night watchman. They had bought a lot of government buildings and they were going to sell them. So I went down there as a night watchman at $35 a week. That was the best I could get, because I couldn't get around very good any more. After I got down there, the superintendent told me, he said, "If you sell one of these houses, you get so much; if you sell this, you get so much; go ahead, if you can sell anything, sell it." So I sold it. And fact of the matter is, in the first five months I sold $75,000 worth of stuff. Built up a sales record there. And I got in pretty good with the company.

Slim added:

I was working for the same company. I was running a torch, cutting steel and so forth. My main reason for going to work for that company was to be in a position to obtain the steel that I wanted to do the building that I wanted to do. My dream had been to build a modern houseboat.

When we was in Alcatraz, we figured that we might be able— we had in a writ of *habeas corpus* to be taken back to our trial court—and we figured that, if we ever got back in that trial court, that on the train or in that courtroom or somewhere we was going to break loose. We were going to get out. We weren't going to do all our time. We figured how would be a good way

to stay away from the law, and we got the idea of a houseboat
on the river. And we got to liking the idea. We liked the idea
so well that when we finally realized that we might get out the
right way to get out, why that was all we thought about, was our
houseboats.

I obtained the steel and I built me a modern houseboat outta
quarter-inch plate, reinforced it with railroad rail, something I
figured would last me a lifetime. My wife and I done all the
work. My boat is 32 feet 8 inches by 12 feet, the walks around
the cabins extend it to 15 feet wide. It's modern throughout,
finished natural inside; hardwood floors; all drawers, all closets
are solid cedar, and in the construction of the boat I have about
9,000 2½-inch brass screws that cost $5.40 a gross, and about six
or seven hundred pounds brass and steel bolts. All the construction is bolted—very few nails used.

With equal pride, Jack, who had emulated his brother in
crime, told of matching his brother's dream.

My boat has three rooms and a screen deck. I gotta room for
my little girl—I call her "Snookie." And it's heated just like it
would be in a home. A flue from the stove in the kitchen is
built in and a register's in her room and she can get any amount
of heat she wants. It's finished in knotty pine, and there's not a
kid in town—I don't care where they live or how much money
they've got—that's got a nicer room than Snookie.

Oh, that boat's just like a dream, that's all—you ought to see
it. . . .

We did see it and no child does have a room anywhere in
the world better than Snookie's. Warden Overlade drove us
out to the banks of the Wabash where the two boats lay, one
behind the other, as the brothers waited for the end of their
parole and for the spring flood that would carry them out into
the main current so they could float downstream, stopping at
river ports on the way to hire out as job carpenters. They feel
that the boats will advertise their skill enough to get them
work.

The brothers listened to the "Challenge" series with mixed
reactions. Slim took exception to the closing of one program,
where we mentioned that our programs had only discouraging
endings. He wrote:

On the east bank of the river, north of the town, once was located a fort. Indians and white men died there. Why they fought is hardly remembered. Nothing now remains save a cannon pointed at the river. In flood-tide the river eats at the east bank and its rolling hills. Someday even the cannon will be gone, but the river will remain. So long as the rain comes and the sun is in the sky and the world remains, the river will live on.

Stories end, men's lives end, stories begin. This is such a story. 'Neath the cannon, near the old fort, sit two long white boats. They're sturdily built, large enough for comfort, heavy; but the rolling river will hold them in his arms, like babies. Inside one boat, a woman, her whole life before her, lies sleeping. The river has sung her to sleep. She's content with life; she's content with all life has given her: the river, her home, her man and, most of all, her baby peacefully asleep. But her man lies awake. He likes to lie awake and savor all this. He likes to know that it is all his. This is what this man has planned and dreamed. To him this is the beginning. He's heard a program on the radio, a program that has all bad endings. He full agrees, for it is so, even with him. But now the end is over—that is his story. But with the river there is no end. Around every bend is a new beginning. The river goes on and on. It takes care of its own. This story has a beginning.

Personally, Peg and I found the two brothers the most interesting of all the inmates we met. But they did little to help us find an answer to the question, who and why are convicts. They were not typical, in that they were maximum-security risks (80 per cent of our convicts are not), and they had been professionals. Criminologists told us that few convicts are professional criminals in the same sense as the brothers were. To make this point, Dr. Negley Teeters of Temple University analyzed crime in America. He said:

It is believed by most Americans that crime does not pay. Well, crime does not pay whom? Certainly it doesn't pay society. No one knows how much crime costs society but certainly it is billions of dollars a year.

So far as the criminal is concerned, obviously it doesn't pay those who get caught. But we know that the men you find in our prisons are not usually the syndicate criminals but the inept, the relatively stupid, the friendless, the sick, and those who have

no influence. It isn't really they who cause the greatest expense
to society.

Today, if a youngster wants to go into the field of crime and
he takes his training and the discipline that he might have to take
in some other business, he will probably be a successful criminal.
It's a terrible indictment against our society that crime does pay
the real professional (not the amateur) and it pays him hand-
somely, and that our convicts are not, for the most part, our real
professionals.

To understand this we had to look into the history of crime
in this country. On two distinct levels our crime has undergone
a revolution.

In frontier days and up to the beginning of this century
American crime was aimed primarily against property, and,
outside of ever present crimes of passion, violence was incidental
to the main goal of stealing somebody else's money.

Jesse James rode up to a stage coach and robbed the mail.
If someone got hurt, it was because he reached for his .45 instead of the sky. But the old days of crime are passé. Take,
for instance, the case of our most recent Jesse James, John Dillinger.

Here was the old-time professional criminal brought up to
date. Using a car instead of a horse, he cased a bank, robbed
it, and made off into the sunset. The basic pattern was that
of old, slightly streamlined by such modern gimmicks as plas-
tic surgery, the split-second use of stop watches, and the hiring
of a professional killer to make up for the fact that the great
man, Dillinger himself, could not have hit the Empire State
Building with a Howitzer at six paces.

But what happened to this man is the revealing thing. While
his exploits captured the imagination of a public who made a
hero of him, he was calling attention to crime. He put the police on the spot. Even when he was caught, he was able to
leave a local hoosegow and its lady sheriff almost at will.

Newspapers started asking embarrassing questions and the
police in the Midwest got angry as hell. They started shooting
at every character they found doing an honest job of beating
the tar out of uncooperative storekeepers who wouldn't buy

"protection." What is anachronistically called the "underworld" took stock of these Dillinger-hunting gendarmes.

Result: The madam of one of Chicago's brothels put on a red dress and went to the movies with John. After the selected short subjects, John was selected as the subject of a short burst of gunfire. Crime, by then big business, had no place for bright young free lances who mussed things up. True, Dillinger was killed by an agency of the law, but he was fingered by the nation's lawless who sighed a great sigh of relief when the public seemed to believe that crime was being cleaned up.

The Dillinger story is an example of one part of the revolution in crime, which began at the end of the last century. At that time great business trusts were growing up. The government began its antitrust actions, and a new type of crime came into existence. It is called "white-collar crime," crime committed by business and professional men and by those legal but hypothetical people known as corporations.

This new type of crime, of course, presupposes a new type of criminal, who came into existence at the same time. This criminal is in the upper socio-economic sphere, and, while many of these elite lawbreakers are prosecuted for white-collar crime and some are convicted, few are sent to prison. Yesterday's crime profiteers, who stole stock at water holes instead of watering stock, ended up on ropes or behind bars.

Therefore, the out-and-out outlaws took many tips from the white-collar criminals and also began to organize. In bigness there is strength, and with the advent of prohibition gangs grew up to develop into the syndicates of today. The men who made crime a big business merged with the men who had made big business a crime. Recently a Senate Committee—along with many local crime commissions—revealed that many dress houses are now controlled by money made in houses where dresses are of little use. White-collar and turned-up-collar crime have joined forces to run what has been called America's biggest single industry. Insull and Costello, Whitney and Adonis merge into a single untouchable class of criminal that can put up a tough legal battle before being imprisoned. Our new criminal is a businessman, and, unfortunately, the business of crime has made much more rapid strides than the clumsy machine we call the law. Jesse James rides a chauffeur-driven Cadillac over the mesa to church and country club. The law is still on horseback.

That is one side of our revolution in crime. The other side is no less important. While crime against property in high brackets has mushroomed quietly, the incidence of crime against both person and property on the amateur level has doubled and trebled. While the professional has made a business of crime, the amateur has made it a dangerous hobby. His is crime for the sake of crime.

For instance, we now have the crime-against-person called "no-reason crime." This is "mugging" or strong-arm stuff that nets little or no money. It's done just for the pleasure of beating up the victim by kids in their late teens or early twenties who like to carry knives or guns.

Each year the FBI's Uniform Crime Reports have shown an ever increasing number of youths between the ages of seventeen and twenty-five being arrested for crime-against-property. In 1952 these crimes counted for 59 per cent of our robbery arrests, 74 per cent of our burglary arrests, and 80 per cent of our auto-theft arrests. This last figure is revealing since prison men told us that few cars are stolen primarily for profit. Usually they are taken for adventure. Of all cars stolen 92 per cent are recovered, many within blocks of the scene of the crime. Taken for a joy ride, the car is quietly parked and abandoned. While this is not crime in the traditional sense, it is lawbreaking, and the culprit ends up in prison when caught. There are more auto thieves in federal prisons than any other single type of offender.

Beside the big-business criminal and the young amateurs, our increasing crime is accounted for by the sick, the drug addict, the alcoholic, the neurotic and so-called psychopathic personalities. And, of course, there are the old-fashioned traditional professionals—a few of them—still plying their trade, but cops tell us that the man who makes a business of crime is seldom in what is called "traditional crime." He is too smart. Rather, he works in the local organization and only resorts to personal or property violence when the pressure of business demands or he is faced with the gangland equivalent of firing one of the help. While the adolescent is taking over traditional crime, the smart criminal knows the pay is better, the risk less, in organized crime. He looks at prison strictly as an occupational hazard about equivalent to an Eskimo's fear of rattlesnake bite. And he is right. He seldom goes up.

Who then constitutes the ever growing prison population? Dr. Teeters answered this with statistics. He pointed out that only 13 to 18 per cent [8] of the perpetrators of what the FBI calls "offenses known" are tried and found guilty. But here is the rub: authorities estimate that only one third [9] of all crime is ever reported.

Consider that, despite the fact the number of *reported* rape cases goes up each year,[10] it is estimated that only one out of every ten rapes is reported to the police because of the unpleasant publicity that attends such a report. The same is true of cases of child molestation.

Then too, have you ever tried to report a crime to the police? There's a good chance you found the reporting of the crime tougher than just forgetting it. Tom O'Brien, one of our research men, interrupted a car thief going to work on his convertible. He was sure he could identify the thief and tried to report the attempted theft. He gave it up when a police lieutenant told him it would be "too much bother."

More painful was the experience of a director at NBC. One evening he had his nose broken, two teeth knocked out, and many assorted bruises given him by a couple of muggers on Eleventh Street in New York. He would have been more badly hurt had not a policeman come into sight, but the policeman made no attempt to chase the muggers. He helped him to a nearby hospital but insisted that there was no use reporting the incident. "After all," he said, "we can never catch those guys."

Although there was a recent scandal about New York's lack of crime recording, insiders tell us no real improvement has been made. The policeman is not writing his reports on several

[8] The figure was 18 per cent in 1951.
[9] The FBI warns that its total major-crime figures are considered conservative.
[10] The number of reported rape cases increased 2.6 per cent in 1952.

pieces of paper now instead of not writing it on only one piece
of paper as he did before.

Actual figures on this are revealing. For instance, in 1948
New York police reported about twelve thousand robberies.
However, for the same period insurance companies paid off
claims on over twenty-five thousand robberies. Since only one
in six places robbed is usually insured, it means that there
were probably over one hundred and fifty thousand robberies
for the twelve thousand reported.[11]

These are only a few of the facts that show why only one
third of all crime is reported. And, since only 13 per cent to
18 per cent of reported crime ends in conviction, at best only
about six out of every hundred lawbreakers end up in custody.

There are two sides to this coin. While it is tragic that the
professional is getting away, literally, with murder, at least
the amateur who is being caught should be more susceptible to
rehabilitation. On the other hand, we are not taking advantage
of this. As James Bennett, Director of the Federal Bureau of
Prisons, says:

> The most hopeful group that we have are the youthful of-
> fenders, and yet they provide our highest failure rate. We've got
> to develop more realistic programs for them. There must be
> better ways of getting at their problems and solving them, but we
> have not worked them out yet.

Our question, "Who and what are convicts?" received varying answers from penologists, but, ironically, the first thing
they pointed out to us was the number of men in prison who
should not be there. Prime among these are sex offenders.
Homosexuals, statutory rapists, compulsive rapists, and the psychopathic sex offender are lumped together with all other types
of offenders, and we expect them all to be cured by punishment. It has never worked.

A tragic case in point was put into the headlines by the recent Greenlease kidnap-murder. Thomas Marsh, who figured
prominently in the early days of the investigation (although he
was later cleared of any suspicion), had served two terms for

---

[11] *Terror in the Streets,* by Howard Whitman (Dial Press, 1951), covers this in
detail.

child molestation. Yet it was revealed that he was given a governor's commutation after serving only two years of his second sentence. Presumably he was considered rehabilitated because, during his two years in an adult prison, he had not molested a single child.

But the governor did have a point. More time in prison was going to do him no good. This does not mean, however, that he should be out on the street. Every time a woman or child is raped or killed by a sex offender with a record, it is one more stone in the monument to our stupidity for giving sex offenders definite sentences, then punishing them rather than curing them, and finally letting them out, ready or not, to prey on society.

From the prison officials' point of view, they already have enough of a sex problem inside the bulging prison walls without being given more. As we saw in both New Jersey and Michigan, sex is an integral part of all prison riots and of all prison troubles. Under our present prison system and our present social mores, this problem seems insolvable.

Often we heard pat answers that a good athletic program and a full-time work program would help. However, after each of these outbursts of generalities, the question, "Would that really solve the problem?" brought forth a sad negative.

Society is taking men, the majority of whom have developed natural sexual appetites, and is keeping them from any normal outlet. Under the best of conditions this has been shown to breed homosexuals. But prison is not the best of conditions.

With the lack of segregation, young men are thrown together in crowded conditions with old lags* who, as one inmate put it "don't care what they do because they aren't human no more." Mixing young first offenders with sexual deviates, perverts, and psychopaths has led to what is estimated at an 80 per cent incidence of sex perversion in some prisons. And, despite the fact that many inmates become "punks" inside only and revert to normalcy upon release, prison psychiatrists admitted to us that more confirmed perverts come out of prison than go in.

On the sly and with constant fear of exposure, some prisons have relieved their sex problems by generous week-end passes to home or brothel. And one Southern prison, tough in every

other aspect to the point of being considered worse than a
chain gang, keeps peace by what it calls the "Saturday night
curtain." In its dormitories are ropes running from wall to
wall, crisscrossing. If the boys behave all week, blankets are
thrown over the ropes on Saturday night, and prostitutes are
brought in from town.

Inevitably, prison men enviously pointed to Mexico and,
half apologetically, said that maybe they had a good idea
there in letting married men have private visiting privileges
with their wives. They always hastened to add, however, that
the American public would never stand for it because of the
feeling that part of an inmate's punishment is the deprivation
of sex. In other words, we say that if a man breaks a law, he
must become a pervert.

As long as we keep our present prison setup, however, sex
is going to plague the prison administrator. "Sex storms,"
which grow from a sudden, unnatural quiet into a tumult
of men yelling, beating on bars, breaking furniture, and engaging in mass masturbation—or worse—will continue to happen.

The drug addict and the drunkard are also problems, penologists told us, that prisons should not have but do. Some
day we will recognize that these people, as mentally sick as
T.B. patients or arthritics are physically sick, should and can
be caught before they commit crimes. Further, we will realize
that having committed a crime, they should not be sent to
prison but to treatment centers. There is no point in punishing an alcoholic for breaking and entering if nothing is done
to cure the alcoholism that drove him to it.

In this connection Alcoholics Anonymous is doing a tremendous job in many prisons. In both state and federal houses
wardens told us stories of prominent citizens—in one case a
bank president and in another the head of the local chamber
of commerce—who, as members of A.A. had worked with an
inmate, sponsored his parole, and kept him out of trouble.

A.A.'s take their job seriously. As one A.A. member, in broadcasting, told us: "We realize there is a very thin line of luck
that keeps any alcoholic out of prison. I wasn't caught break-

ing laws, but that doesn't make me any better than the ones who were."

He spends one evening a week in prison with inmates and uncounted hours out of prison with ex-inmates. But he pointed out to us that his work, while often successful, was only a stop-gap: "These guys need trained help and they aren't getting it in prison. More often than not, prison is doing them more harm than good."

Much the same is true of drug addicts. True, many of them have committed criminal offenses, but their stays in prison do them little good. In prisons with crooked guards they do not even have to go off the habit if they have money. Even if they are "cured," it usually is not permanent.

We met one boy who had had the best prison care an addict can get. Handsome, nervously controlled, the quiet-spoken Negro, once a member of a Harlem boy gang, told us his story:

> I was sentenced here for three years for forgery. Since I've been here, I had a tough time, being sick most of the time. My biggest problem is trying to get help from someone that understands the problem of the drug addict. The doctors here, they do all they possibly can, but they can't devote enough time. The best they can give me is vitamin tablets and talk to me once in a while, but that still doesn't help me much.
>
> It all started approximately in 1942. I used to live a pretty normal life. I have a wonderful family. I don't have a father—I don't know much about my father. My mother, she served the purpose of both father and mother. Well, I have a large family, seven brothers, and it really started, I imagine, from the environment I was in.
>
> I used to work and help my mother, but I wanted nice things like the other kids, nice clothes, automobiles, so I got around a bad environment, and they talked of how I could acquire those things, and naturally that started me doing wrong. And that's where the drugs started in, marijuana and different drugs.
>
> Well, I started on them, and I never realized that I would get attached to them so deep that I would suffer all these years behind it. But it happened, and after I become an addict, I wanted to stop, but I couldn't. It wasn't just like saying, "Well, I'm going to stop" and stop. You just can't do it alone. You have to have treatment.

So, in order to get drugs, it costs a lot of money. If you don't have the money, you just have to do—well, I would say you'd do most anything. I wouldn't say you'd do *anything*, but you would turn to crime to get money for drugs.

Well, I knew it had to come to an end, but I just waited for it to come to the end. Finally, I wound up in the penitentiary. A penitentiary is no place for a drug addict, simply because he can't get the help that's needed. And I feel that a drug addict should be—if he's going to be incarcerated, it should be in a narcotic hospital. He should be treated as a patient and not a convict. I feel that if he had that treatment or could get it, he would overcome all of his troubles, but as long as he's in the penitentiary and treated as an ordinary convict, there isn't any hope for him.

Authorities in the federal system agree with him. Alcoholics and drug addicts are types of offenders who most often become recidivists.* After their sentences are served they return uncured to crime in order to buy more alcohol or drugs.

This boy seemed to be no exception, despite his high resolves to find a new environment, because his physical weakness had kept him from learning a trade. As this is written, he is about to be released. Before it is in print, we wager he will be in trouble despite the full understanding he shows of his problem. The charge most likely will be forgery again; again he will be cured "cold turkey," [12] and this is where he came in.

Strangely enough, while the sick are considered poor release risks, many men who have committed worse crimes are considered good risks. Many murderers are considered minimum-security risks and are made trustees or are put in unwalled camps. The reason is simple. Many murderers are either accidental or one-time criminals. True, in the heat of passion or under the force of circumstance, they have killed, but the chances are they will never break a law again or even try to escape from prison. Once released, they are much more likely to make good than alcoholics or drug addicts.

Penologists point out that much of the money spent on keeping most murderers in prison is wasted. They are good risks

---

[12] Taken off drugs with no tapering-off process. This is a tremendous shock to the system, and that shock has to be treated if there is to be a real cure.

for probation and can only go downhill in a prison environment. The public would take a dim view of a judge who told
a murderer to go free and sin no more, but we were picked up
at our hotel and driven all over a large city by a quiet-spoken
double-murderer, who has had freedom to go out of prison
gates for some fifteen years.

Much like murderers in this respect are many embezzlers—
as contrasted to confidence men who are poor risks. It was at
Terre Haute that we met a former bank vice-president, who
had done business for a number of years with my father. Serving three and a half years, he told us his story quite freely:

> Prior to the bank crash in 1933 I had a fair position in a bank.
> Then banks were closed by the President of the United States,
> and I was out of a job along with hundreds of other bank tellers.
>
> I went to seek employment with another bank. My wife was in
> the hospital with a new baby born the day the banks were closed,
> leaving us absolutely penniless along with a lot of other people.
> I did get employment. Salary was not mentioned; banks had the
> pick of what they classed the best tellers. They needed only a
> matter of a few, and they had around five thousand to pick from.
> I was one of the fortunate or the unfortunate (I wouldn't know
> how to put that) in getting a position with the bank.
>
> We had enough money accumulated at the time for all neces-
> sary expenses, but the morning my boy was born, the banks did
> not open. Then my pay check came along and it was $45 for two
> weeks' work. My salary had been cut better than fifty per cent.
>
> We had our obligations to meet and I had to have money, so I
> borrowed a few dollars out of the cash drawer with the full in-
> tention of paying it back. It was around $300. About that time I
> was temporarily insane, and salary increases didn't come forth.
> The banks, as a matter of fact, were very happy to get good help
> for no pay, and they boasted about that.
>
> Then my position with the bank improved; I was able to bring
> in a lot of deposits, a lot of new customers. The bank kept on
> growing, and my position and advancement came along very
> fine. About four years later I was made branch manager at a
> salary of $145 a month!
>
> Holding a responsible position of millions of dollars, my salary
> still did not increase enough for me to pay back the money I had
> borrowed. I had gotten desperate and, not being a gambler, I

thought that gambling would be the easiest way for me to accumulate a little bit of money and pay the bank back. And it's the old story: I gambled and lost until my indebtedness reached a terrific height.

Then I became successful in gambling, paid back a little bit of money; but this was over a period of seventeen years, and my indebtedness reached around $150,000. I confessed to the bank on August the 21st, 1951. The bank thought an awful lot of me. I was receiving roughly $8,000 a year at the end, but it had come too late. So, rather than to live the life of Jekyll and Hyde, like I had been living in the last seventeen years, I turned myself in.

I would say definitely that it was the underpay that I received, and possibly a lot of weakness on my own part. I have been on the employment end of the banks and I've seen men at the teller's windows who couldn't afford to buy a coke for dinner. I believe that tellers should have at least $200 a month, and then only have a limited amount of cash to handle. The money is there for them, and you're just not going to see your family go hungry.

If a person wants to deliberately embezzle from the bank, I would say he is a criminal, but a lot of it is forced on to these young fellows by the banks themselves. I would say that 90 per cent of the people that work in a bank one time or other borrows money out of his till. And, if some unforeseen thing happens that he can't pay that back, he becomes an embezzler.

The amount of money that I spent on my family would be nil, except when it started. We always lived according to our income, but in order to get my small amount of embezzlement back I had to gamble. And say I had a natural cash shortage, which has happened to me. One time I was a hundred dollars short. I didn't dare to report that shortage because the auditor would have to come in to check me out, and he would discover the other shortage. So I covered it up. It is relatively simple, so long as your nerves hold out. Of course, your bookkeeping systems of today are almost infallible, but they are not—I have proven that in my seventeen years of covering up.

I can say this, the punishment that I am receiving in a penitentiary—I punished myself worse in those seventeen years. If I'd been released thirty days after I got in, I would have been just the same as I am today.

My plans are to go back to my family, my son, my wife, and go into a business with a man who offered me a position before I came to the institution. I will go into financial advice and credit when I go out.

Federal authorities do not expect to see this man again once he hits the streets.* They agree that this would be true whether he served twenty-four hours or twenty-four years. His imprisonment will not deter new embezzlers any more than he was deterred by the sentences of other embezzlers seventeen years ago. His type follows a pattern of seldom repeating. Keeping him in prison only costs money and adds to the crowding of prisons.

But what to do with him? Have him pay back his thefts? It would take him eighteen years at his maximum salary, paying out every cent he made, to restore the $150,000. Here again the experts could give us no answer that would work in present-day society.

"Why are you in prison? I don't mean, are you guilty or not. I mean, why do you think you are here?" This became a form question with us. The answers we got varied from the two hours of story that came from Earl Ward to one-line answers distilled from years of solitary thought during dark prison nights. Perhaps the most tragic came from a long termer who hesitated, then burst out as though we had wrung the answer out of him:

"I don't know, God damn. I don't know."

Perhaps he was the most honest of all we talked to—both with us and himself. But inmates tried, sometimes with painful seriousness, to analyze themselves. After we had heard enough of these stories, we came to find we could anticipate parts of each story.

Almost every story began with the words, "My mother and father couldn't get along—"; or, "My mother died when I was four—"; or, "I never knew my father—." The lectures I had heard all my life about the importance of the family unit never meant much to me until I sat across from men with numbers imprinted across the fronts of their shirts. The family unit had meant little to them too. They had never experienced it.

We mentioned this on the air and received one of those inevitable unsigned letters that plague the radio industry. Although we had never mentioned the word *divorce*, but only the lack of the family unit, it read: "How dare you go on the air and condemn divorce. The fact that I divorced a man that was a no good bum has nothing to do with my son being in reform school. He inherited badness from his father . . ." etc.

Perhaps the anonymous mother was right, but prison officials confirmed that most of their charges came from homes that, either in fact or essence, were broken. Some have even tried to build a complete explanation for crime on this fact.

But there are other theories too. One school of thought blames crime on the ever growing tensions of our world, on the fact that life today moves at a speed too great for the human capacity to comprehend it. We are experiencing jet trips that go faster than sound, the destruction of cities with atoms we cannot see in microscopes, and expenditures of money in figures that only electronic brains can calculate. Our civilization has moved beyond our ability to comprehend it, so that whole societies are breaking down. Criminals, according to this theory, are merely a by-product of that mass nervous collapse.

Perhaps either or both of these theories explain the reason we have convicts, more of them than ever before. But it still does not explain why some persons break laws under these circumstances and others do not. And this can become a nagging question, one that begins to personalize itself. You ask yourself, "Why they and not I?"

Like Earl Ward, I flunked the first grade. Like many of the boys we met who got drunk and ended up in trouble, I went through an adolescent stage where it was the thing to do to get potted to the gills every night. Like innumerable others we met, I was the only child in a home that, for a while, was broken. Why then they, not I?

This is a question for the psychiatrists, but their answers are disappointing. Psychiatry is too new, too experimental as yet, to have many answers. But worse, it seems to have to fight every step for even a chance to look for answers. Of the prisons we visited, only the federal penitentiary in Terre Haute had a full-time psychiatrist. The Federal Bureau of Prisons, in cooperation with the Public Health Service of the Federal Security Agency, is trying, but it too has problems. For instance, Terre Haute had only one psychiatrist, Dr. Melvin Heller, for eleven hundred men. As Dr. Heller pointed out, he could never consider more than the most superificial treatment for more than a handful of the inmates.

This, however, is not a situation easily corrected. Few prisons can afford to pay psychiatrists anything near the money they can make in private practice. But, if they could, there would still be a problem. As Dr. Stanley Krumbiegel, the liaison between Federal Bureau of Prisons and The Public Health Service, said:

> There's such a real shortage of psychiatrists in society itself that we can't expect to get many into prison work. Of course we can say that this could be corrected by training more people to specialize in psychiatry, but that's difficult because there's already a shortage of physicians in general, and it takes a certain type of personality to be a psychiatrist. Furthermore, it takes a certain type of personality, even if a man's a psychiatrist, to work with prisoners.

The fact that more psychiatrists are needed in prisons is not lost on the prisoners. Often we hear, "Something is wrong with me"; or, "The psychologists just spend their time making reports and studies—they don't help you with your problems like a psychiatrist would." Into prison jargon have seeped many quasi-psychiatric terms. In analyzing themselves, many inmates would begin with, "I have a tendency toward——"; or "My inversions are——."

Perhaps, when psychiatry has had time to grow, some of the answers to "Why criminals?" and "Why convicts?" will come out. The surface has hardly been scratched; the areas for study have not even been determined.

But there has been some progress toward answers. For instance, Eleanor and Sheldon Glueck, of Harvard University, have found they can predict by means of certain tests delinquency and even criminal tendencies in children as young as six. However, this is an area of study not for the prison but for the school. But school problems—overcrowding, low budgets, underpaid teachers, and political interference—are much akin to prison problems, so the prisons cannot look forward to the coming generation of lawbreakers' being stopped this side of crime by the schools. Their only hope lies in work being done in such places as Menlo Park, New Jersey.

Psychiatry has also isolated certain types of offenders. An example is the so-called delayed-maturation group. Psychologists know that many thirty-year-olds, mentally and physically mature, are emotionally immature. Myrl Alexander, assistant director of the Federal Bureau of Prisons, pointed out to us that, if watched, these physically grown-up, emotional children could be saved more efficiently than any other one group of inmates. There comes a time when they mature; when, if handled correctly, no matter what their previous record, they will never get into trouble again; when, no matter what their sentence, they should be let out of prison because a longer stay behind bars leads only to disintegration.

But this works only if the prison has adequately trained men to recognize and separate the delayed-maturation case from all the other types surrounding him. And it works only if he can be released at the psychologically right time. This would call for a much closer relationship between sentences and treatment than now exists. One of the many faults in American prisons decried by James Bennett is that, by law in some cases and by pure inertia in others, what knowledge psychiatry has been able to offer the prison man is not being put to use.

Dr. Heller, at Terre Haute, tried to overcome this by considering the whole prison as he would a single patient and analyzing it on that basis. Instead of spending all his time on inmates, he worked with the personnel in an experiment that is still continuing at Terre Haute, although Dr. Heller is no longer there. In the federal system every man, official or officer, has inmates assigned to him on a counselor plan. Heller had personnel forums where inmate problems were brought up and discussed by officials. Each official submitted to Heller reports on his assigned inmates. Heller gauges his success in this enterprise on the changed and changing quality of these reports. Though he feels he made very little progress, he feels he did make some since the reports became more intensive as the experiment continued. He feels that it is the closest he could come to solving the problem of one psychiatrist for eleven hundred men, all of whom, to some degree, need psychiatric treatment.

It was Dr. Heller, along with the associate warden in charge of treatment, Mark Richmond, who helped us find "Mac." Although we knew there was no such thing as a typical inmate any more than there are typical lawyers, doctors, or even radio producers, we felt we might be able to best interpret inmates generally if we could find one with whom the audience could identify.

Mac was good for this purpose because he had a plethora of the problems facing most of the men we talked to: he was young; although a lawbreaker with quite a record, he was not what we generally consider a criminal; he had come from a broken home; and the betting was best that prison had done him no basic good despite an exceptional amount of personal care.

He was atypical in several important respects: he was more vocal than most inmates; his intelligence was a bit higher than the average; and he had had closer psychiatric attention than 99 per cent of the inmates. These atypical qualities made him "good radio" in that they helped us present his typical qualities.

Mac had been a problem case when he came into Terre Haute. Like so many young offenders, he had not plunged into bad trouble, but, by being sullen and associating with the "tough guy" element, he had shown no desire to cooperate with officials. His ticket showed one period in isolation for fighting, but the discipline board had not been harsh because they felt, despite his sullen silence on the matter, that it had not been his fault, since his opponent was a suspected wolf.

Through the years his work record had been spotty. For a while he had been an excellent worker in the shoe-repair shop, but he had become dissatisfied with that job when he found he could make more "good pay*" in the cannery. A simple request for a transfer might have gotten him what he wanted, but he tried more devious methods with the result that he was reduced in pay and assigned to a construction gang. This meant something to him, as he showed for the first time some desire to cooperate with the prison program. He began to take a correspondence course in mechanical engineering. Because of his change in attitude, officials boosted his position and he went into the cannery as a maintenance mechanic, working his way up to top good pay.

But with added responsibilities came yet a new attitude. Formerly a paragon of cooperation, he now began to feel his oats and this climaxed in an almost physical fight with the civilian cannery foreman when Mac tried to repair a broken sealing machine he had been told to stay away from. Again, he was reduced to the lowest grade of good pay and put into the dye shop. There, after one week, he ended up in the hospital with a paralyzed right arm.

Although he had bruised his right shoulder through pure carelessness, X rays and complete medical examinations showed nothing constitutionally wrong with arm or shoulder. However, Mac was not feigning his paralysis. Dr. Heller was brought into the case.

Heller immediately decided not to make life easy for Mac. He was put on a punishment diet of tasteless but nutritious food and told his good time would be forfeited during his hospital stay. This, Heller felt, would give Mac no reason to want to stay in the hospital. Then Heller began talking to Mac for an hour or so a day. At first there were no results; then slowly Mac came around, and finally the dam burst. Out flowed Mac's story, much as he later told it to us.

Mac is tall, slim, blond, with a thick Texas drawl. He smiles uneasily and seldom, but when he does, it lights up his face. Although to Heller his story had come slowly, to us, having gone through it before, he told it quite glibly, reflecting the new understanding Heller had given him over the months. At our request, he began with his childhood:

Well, I think my trouble started back when I was a kid. My father—well, my mother and he separated when I was really too young to realize what was happening. And after they had been separated, say about two years, well, my father decides, well, he wants me.

So one day my dad come and took me down to my grandmother's. At the time I wasn't really old enough to remember. All I can remember is the washing machine in the basement, but all I know about the happenings is what I been told afterwards.

So it was, I imagine, three or four months later that they found me down in Texas. My dad's brother and me. And where my dad was, I don't know—I just turned up with my dad's brother. So he turned me back over to my mother.

Well, I stayed with my mother about four years, and I wound up with my dad again. How I got there, I don't know. So my mother married in between times, and my dad had married two or three other times; and one day I had one mother, and the next day I had another dad, or something like that.

Well, my stepfather and I, we just didn't get along. We didn't see eye to eye on anything. A lot of the time it was my own fault. I mean, maybe I was a little bull-headed about the matter, I mean —of course, I mean, I can't remember that far back, but the more I think of it, the more I think that's probably what the case was. So I guess, the way I felt, I felt I was unwanted, that nobody loved me. I mean, I was just something to beat around the house. That's the way I felt about it. Sometimes I still feel the same way.

So things went on that way until I was about, oh, I'd say about, well, fourteen, I guess. About then I decided I needed some money—I'd started smoking—so I started stealing. I stole from my mother to start with. She was saving dimes—she had a big cookie jar she saved dimes in. I knew she was putting them in the cookie jar, and she knew I knew she was putting them there, but she didn't think I'd take them. Well, I took them.

So, one thing led to another, and she caught me and she whipped me and she thought that was all there was to it. But I'd already got a sample of having money in my pocket. So when I couldn't get it out of the cookie jar—she hid the cookie jar from me—well, I found some place else to get it.

So, gas rations started. So one day I went into a service station and bought a coke. I'd been in the service station many times before that. So the man just says, "Well," he said, "put the nickel up on the counter." So I put the nickel up on the counter and the cash register drawer was open. I don't remember what it was —I took ten, maybe fifteen, dollars and a handful of gas stamps. Well, you could get good money for gas stamps, so I started selling gas stamps. And when those ran out, well, I went and stole some more. And eventually I got caught.

They gave me a break. They gave me six months' probation, but my stepdad, he said, "Oh, that was terrible," yet he didn't stop to realize that half the gas he was using in his car come from the gas stamps that I'd stole and was selling. I'd borrow his car, I'd fill it full of gas, and he wouldn't ask questions where I got it.

So finally I didn't keep probation, and they sent me to a

school. My mother paid half and the county paid half. I made good there. I stayed there from '44 till about the latter part of '46. I come home for summer vacation, got me a job working in a packing house, and all of a sudden I decided I didn't want to go back to school. I was tired of having people tell me what to do. So I up and quit my job, drove down to school, picked up my clothes, and left.

Two months later I found myself in northern California, married. How I got married—I mean, everything happened so fast I didn't, you know, just didn't stop to think. I met her on the first of September and I married her on the seventh. At the time I was only sixteen. She was nineteen. Of course, she thought I was about twenty-one. Everything happened so fast; in fact, she didn't even know my last name until the day we got the license. So that didn't last too long!

In fact, it lasted less than a month. Mac quit his service station job in California and went to work for his wife's uncle in Arizona. This led to a fight and, as Mac put it:

I proceeded to get drunk that night. And a boy sixteen years old, whiskey don't agree with him. But I looked over my age— I mean, I looked old enough to drink; the bartenders never asked no questions.

So the next thing I know, it's the next afternoon, I've already signed up for the army. I lied about my age and went in the army. It was too late then—I mean, I'd been swore in and everything. So I went up to camp and one thing led to another, and they should a sent me to a basic training, but they kept me there as a more or less stenographer, and I was discharging the other GI's when they was coming home. And it got tiresome. I mean, when I went in the army, I went in the army to fight. I mean, I thought that was a big glory. 'Course, the war was over then, see, but I didn't stop to think of that. I could see everybody else come home with medals on 'em. Well, I wanted medals too, and I couldn't get them there discharging other boys. So one day one of the boys that I discharge was my own cousin. I had him half-discharged before I found out who he was.

So he and I went into town that night. We proceeded to get drunk. One thing led to another. One of the guys we met up with had a car. We had a wreck in the car, and I got my head messed up a little bit, went to the hospital. Well, they discharged me out of the army for medical reasons.

I went home. In the meantime, the wife, she decided, "All is forgiven." So we went back to Arizona.

Although Mac did not work for the family again, proximity brought discord. Mac slugged another of his wife's uncles, his wife left him again, and the pattern reappeared:

I got drunk. I quit my job and I went out and hit the hot spots. And pretty soon my money was gone. I had about eight bucks in my pocket, and I decided, well, I'm going back to California. Well, I couldn't buy much whiskey and buy a bus ticket both, so, well, after I bought the whiskey, I stole a car. Well, I just figured I was joy riding—which, actually, it turned out I was, because I got caught before I got to California. Whiskey kind of caught up with me. I was a little sleepy, so I pulled off the side of the road and went to sleep. The next thing I know, somebody's shaking me awake, and it's the law.

About ten o'clock that morning they've already taken me back and give me six months in the county jail. It all happened in a matter of, oh, three, four hours, and well, I found myself with six months in jail.

Well, my wife came to see me after I'd been in jail for about a month. And she apologized. She says she'll be glad when I get out, she'll wait for me, that when I get out, well, we'll go some place where nobody knows us and start all over again. She don't like her family no more.

So she left, and the same day that she left, they made me trusty in the jail. So I worked in the jail during the daytime and at night from nine o'clock to ten o'clock the trusties can go downstairs and wander around town, you know, just so's they're back by ten o'clock.

Well, I stayed trusty for about three months. Then I was getting pretty short.* I had, oh, I'd say sixty-three, sixty-four days before my sentence was up. And the wife, she'd been writing maybe every other day, maybe four letters a week, maybe not that many. But, I mean, they were nice letters and everything was just fine.

Well, I quit getting letters from her, all at once. So, well, in a place like this—letters—letters—they're what a man lives for from day to day. If you don't get letters, why you don't know what's happening. You don't know what's happening, you start worrying. And you start worrying, the first thing you want to do is go home and find out what's the matter.

So I let it ride for about two weeks and I didn't hear from her. So I proceeded to go home and find out what happened.

At home, Mac found the wife once more in the bosom of her family. Words led to one bruised stepfather-in-law and Mac was on his way again, not back to the Phoenix jail, but to California. Sober this time, he made it by hitchhiking.

Well, in the meantime, my dad had opened up a shoe repair shop, so I went to work for him. I didn't tell him a word about being escaped from prison—well, county jail. I didn't tell 'im a word. He asked me where the wife was, and I said, "Well, as far as I know, she's in Arizona." He never asked me no more questions about it.

So I worked there for a while, and he got sick and had to have an operation. So I went and took him to the hospital, and I run the shop for him while he was in the hospital, used his car, used his apartment that he was living in at the time. And I'd go down to see him maybe every other day in the evening time after I'd closed the shop.

Well, my grandmother had come up to visit him. So she came up there, and that was the first time she'd seen me since I was a little tot when he'd kidnapped me and taken me down to her place. So her and I, we hit it off great. So I thought, anyway. But I come to find out that she was very possessive. In other words, she came up to visit her son, and she wanted him to only herself—nobody else. She didn't stop to think he was her son but he was also my dad. And I'd been taking care of him before she came on the picture, anyway.

So she said to me—she just come right out and tole me one day—she says, "Well, you don't need to go to the hospital today."

I says, "Well, why not?" I said, "I told Dad I was coming down."

She says, "Well, he told me last night he didn't want to see you any more."

So I couldn't figure it out, you know? So I go right up the hospital, right then. And the nurse told me, says, "Well, your dad's sleeping, I don't think you want to disturb him, then."

Well, at the time I'm hot because my grandmother told me this, and then the nurse tell me I couldn't see him—I mean, I didn't stop to think maybe he *was* asleep, you know. So I figured, well, he didn't actually want to see me.

There was a woman friend there that I'd met, and she was quite a—quite a bit older than I was at the time, and she owned a bar there in town, so I went down to cry on her shoulder.

So, one drink led to another, and the next thing I know, I went over to the bank. I cashed about $70 worth of checks. That wasn't enough, so I went down to another bank and I cashed about $150 worth of checks, all on my old man, signed his name on them, forged 'em, bought me a suitcase, went home, packed all my clothes and started hitchhiking.

Well, I kept on hitchhiking. In about six hours I'd made the whole sum of about twelve miles. So I just proceeded to steal me a car. I went on to Salt Lake and I joined the army. I joined the air corps, actually. Well, they started checking my fingerprints and they found out that I'd already been in the service once.

So they got to inquiring around and one thing led to another— I was still driving the car, that's how stupid I was. So they found out the car was stolen. Well, they gave me a year and a day. Actually, a year and a day, I mean, that's not time at all. So they sent me to El Reno.[13]

I stayed at El Reno. I made parole. I went back home, everything was forgiven. I went back to my mother's. Well, she got me a job—I had to have a job before I could make parole. She got me a job, all right. I was working, eight, nine, ten hours a day at $.60 an hour. I was trucking lemons in a lemon house, and that's pretty hard work.

I was paying my mother $20 a week for room and board, where I could have got it cheaper if I'd went uptown and went to a regular boarding house. And she wasn't doing my laundry, she wasn't doing anything. Maybe I'd eat maybe breakfast there, and she'd pack my lunch, and well, suppertime I was usually uptown. I'd eat it uptown. Yet she'd charged me for supper. At the time my dad is kicking in about $60 a month for my support, and at the time I'm paying her eighty bucks a month, so she's making pretty good out of the deal.

So one night, I was broke and I asked her for $5. She says, "I haven't got it. Go ask Stepdad."

So I went and asked him, and he made a remark I didn't like. I can't very well repeat it, but anyway, I didn't like it. So, when I didn't like something in those days, I just proceeded to do the first thing I could think about and that was to hit 'im. But that was one time I hit the wrong man. 'Cause he was smaller than I

---

[13] Federal reformatory.

was, I thought I had the best go, but I found out different. Well, he whipped me up one side of the house and down the other. So that made me all the madder, so I left.

So what entered my mind again? I joined the army.

I didn't want to join the army there, because they knew me, so I went to San Jose and I joined the army. I was taking my basic there, and I borrowed one of the boys' cars there and went into the town and threw me a wingding.

Well, I run a road block. I mean, I was doing, oh, about eighty, eighty-five down the highway on a rainy night, which I shouldn't of been doing. I shouldn't of been drinking in the first place. But you do one wrong, well, you usually end up doing two. So they stopped me and I gave 'em a big ole story about my wife was sick, she was up in the hotel, and I was going back to see her and all that. I thought maybe I was going to get away with it.

But instead, one of 'em got in the car, and they drove me down to the hotel. Well, I mean, I'd never been in the hotel in my life, so the story didn't work. So they threw me in jail that night, and the next day they said, "We'll take you to court."

So they fined me $50 or fifty days in jail. Well, I didn't have $50 on me and I didn't want to go fifty days in jail. So there was a bartender in town I knew pretty well. I told 'im, I says, "Well, you put up my bail, and," I says, "I'll go back out to the base and pick it up."

Well, this is about a week before payday and there's not fifty dollars in the whole barracks, I don't think. So I drove the car—the same car now I'd borrowed—I drove back out there, and along with me went his brother-in-law, the bartender's. He was going along to make sure he got his fifty bucks.

But Mac had a plan. He left the brother-in-law in a day room, went to his own barracks and . . .

I packed all my civilian clothes. I let the army keep their clothes, and I walked around past the brother-in-law where he couldn't see me, got in the car I'd borrowed, and drove out the side gate of the camp and just kept going.

At the time I didn't think that I was stealing the car because I'd borrowed the car from the boy maybe a dozen times before that. And I fully intended to come back in maybe—oh, maybe a week. I figured I was AWOL now, I mean, I might as well have a spree and, by the time I come back, well maybe I'll have the fifty bucks to pay the old boy back. I knew that they couldn't take me to jail now, because they already had their bail, and the only one I was worried about was the bartender. I kind of felt sorry for his brother-in-law. I don't know if he's still sitting in the day room or not, but I sure left him there.

I went on down to southern California, messed around there. I run into a couple of boys I knew, and one thing led to another. And one of them decided he wanted to go to Florida.

I said, "Well, you put up the money, and we'll go to Florida." He says, "Well, I got the money."

I said, "Well, let's go." I says, "Let's buy some gas. Let's hit it." I had my clothes in the car. I wouldn't wait for nobody.

So we went down, we filled up the tank with gas and oil, and went to Florida for a vacation. I lost him some place in Texas. I don't know where I lost him, but he disappeared some place one night. In the meantime, I had cashed a few checks. And I got down to Florida. I messed around, and one thing led to another and I ended up in New Orleans. I went to Rhode Island, I went up to New York, New Jersey . . . well, I hit thirty-seven states in a stolen car—I mean the borrowed car that I thought was borrowed.

I got flush one day. I had about, oh, about eight hundred bucks. I had about $40 when I started shooting crap, and when I walked out I had about $800. Dominoes were working that night. I just hit me a streak, and I started thinking about that brother-in-law sitting out in the day room waiting for that $50. I wired the bartender his $50, and I sent the boy that I had the car from, I sent him a wire and told him where I was at. Told him, I says, "When I get around that way," I says, "I'll drop your car off." And I says "There's a letter following."

Then I sat down and I wrote him a letter and I told him, I says, "Your clutch had burnt out." I says, "I bought you a new clutch, botcha two new tires." I says, "It'll be in good shape when I bring it back to you." Wrote him a letter, and I forgot about it.

So I got up to Memphis, Tennessee, and that $800, well, I meant I musta hit the wrong dice table, because I lost it. So I started looking for a job. See, I don't think that I'm hot, except for a parole violation from El Reno.

I read in the paper where this tank and bridge company needed some workers. So I hired out for them. And I couldn't take my car with me, they furnished the transportation in a truck. So I just put the car in storage and we left. Went up to Nebraska and was working on a water tank behind the high school there. One Sunday we had the afternoon off. There wasn't

much doing that day, so I met a couple of fellas in town and they
wanted to take me horseback riding. So we went horseback riding, had a good time. So first thing we know, we found ourselves
back in town riding the horses. One of the boys was working
that afternoon up on the tank, just finishing off the lettering job
on the side of the tank. So we went up there to see him—you
know, just more or less to signify the fact that he's working and
I'm riding a horse, see?

So I went up there, and that was the last horse I rode in a long
time, because a man from the FBI was waiting for me. He asked
me what my name was, and I says, "Yeah, that's me."

And he says, "Well," he says, "we want you."

He served a warrant on me for parole violation. I said, "Well,
parole violation . . . let's go."

So we got to jail, and I laid there about three days and he
come in and served another warrant on me for Dyer Act.[14]

I says, "No," I says, "You can't serve a warrant on me for
Dyer Act."

He says, "I most certainly can." He says, "You took a '39
Mercury." He says, "You took it all over the States. I been following you." He says, "Not just me," he says, "there have been a
lot of others following you." He says, "We know where you been
and what you've done." He says, "You've got Dyer Act."

I says, "No, man," I says, "I borrowed that car, no way I stole
it."

So one thing led to another, and they gave me two years for
Dyer Act. So I figured, well, two years, that's not bad. So I went
down to El Reno again, and the next day some detainers started
coming in from California. They finally caught on those checks.

So I figured, "Well, lookee here. I got two years here," I says,
"they can give me one to fourteen out there on each check," I
says. "That's not too good. I'm gonna leave 'em."

So I come out in general* at El Reno on the eleventh of
September. On the eighteenth of September I went over the
fence. I come out of the show. There was a lieutenant standing
there, and I just looked him in the eye, lit me a cigarette,
pushed him over a flower pot, and started running. And it was six
of us went. One of the boys got shot in the shoulder, and they
caught five of us then and caught the next one in the morning.

---

[14] The usual name for the federal law against the interstate transportation of
stolen vehicles. In "Federal," those sentenced under this law are called "Dyer
Act Kids," a term usually indicating a behavior problem rather than a criminal.

They threw us all in the hole. We laid in the hole for about six, seven days, and then they took us from there, took us to Okla·homa City, and tried us; and we got three years more.

So we went back and they put us in close-custody building and they kept us there till they transferred me here to Terre Haute. That was in '49, and I've been here ever since.

In 1952, that was the story Mac told us. Earlier, and in more detail, that had been the story he told Dr. Heller. Now the psychiatrist's problem was to weed out the clue to why Mac's arm was paralyzed. Heller knew the reason must be there, because, despite the accident in the dye shop, there was nothing organically wrong with the arm.

Heller decided the answer lay in Mac's frequent bouts with whisky and the fact that joining the army had, to Mac, become habit-forming. These two facts seem to best show Mac's feelings of insecurity. Also, Mac hated authority, as personified by his father, because he distrusted it. Unable to overcome authority by reasoning, he had always turned to violence. While he seldom fought with men his own age, stepfathers and in-laws had been his meat.

Heller tried to make Mac understand this, to give him an understanding of why he hated and loved his father and all authority. He explained that Mac liked the army for its security, but hating authority, he rebelled. Actually, Mac liked prison because here was a security against which he could not rebel successfully. When he stole cars, he wanted to be caught. Actually this is not an unusual phenomenon. Every prison man can point out inmates who committed the most stupid crimes for little or no profit, knowing they would be caught. These men come into prison happy to be back. The most definite case of this was the paroled lad who broke into the same hardware store twenty-three nights in a row, taking little, until alert authorities finally trapped him in the act.

All of these psychological problems added up in Mac to a fear of literally hitting out against authority in prison. Over-confident because he had twice succeeded in prison jobs, he was afraid of lashing out and hitting the officer who had put him back at menial work. Hence his arm was paralyzed.

That Mac understood some of this was seen by the fact that

he recovered the use of his arm. By the time we saw him, he had worked up to a top good pay job again; and, even before Heller told us about his prison problems, we were struck by his cockiness and his obvious enjoyment in telling us about outwitting the bartender's brother-in-law.

Mac was released flat, and, his father having taken care of the California check charges, he had no detainers. But Heller and other federal authorities expect him to get into trouble. Psychiatry did take care of his immediate problem, but Heller did not have the time to follow through.

Going back to work for his father will put him in the same environment that got him into trouble before. Mac's intentions, as he goes out, are good. But what will happen when the normal frustrations everybody faces begin to bother him? Probably he will go right back to the personal security of a maximum-security prison.

To most people such an attitude is hard to comprehend, but prisons have found it impossible to combat. The Macs of the world will go on getting into trouble as long as a big house is to them a home.

6

doing it the hard way

. . . Peg Reporting

I WAS IMPRESSED BY MANY OF THE INMATES WE MET—NOT those who can be tagged "professional criminals," but the Macs of the world. Prison was doing them no good. That was certain. Why do they behave as they do? We never received a satisfactory answer. But we were told by both inmates and officials, "The only way to understand these boys is to live with them day after day."

We had no time to live in a prison world, so we brought the prison world home. It all came about because of our household problems. We have an old rambling house on the Connecticut water front. Though all old houses are beset with emergencies, ours has always come in for more than its share. McGraw and I are always desperate for trustworthy help to care for our baby. In an attempt to have a constant family unit around our Terry Olga, we thought we could solve the problem by hiring a young married couple who could take over. This was a great

idea, but we couldn't find the couple. Elsa, the Belgian nurse
and her three year old son, Danny, had been our solution,
with a parade of unwieldy housemen who cleaned and took
care of the heavy work.

Midway in our penal research I got the idea of hiring an ex-
convict. Elsa and I discussed the problem thoroughly.

"A nice young boy," she suggested, "clean, and he must like
children. I would take him."

So it was that we started to look for a helper in ex-convict
circles. Bob Hannum of the Osborne Association was casing the
situation for what he thought would be ideal, but he couldn't
find what we needed. We gave up the idea of an ex-convict,
and in desperation I called an employment bureau and set up
a howl for help. That's how Peter arrived. We weren't in the
office when he came, so Joan interviewed him. The employment
office had given Peter a marvelous build-up: "He's a good all-
round handy man."

Besides the employment office's recommendation, Peter had
references, three letters that praised his work in glowing terms.
He was thirty-two years old, tall, slender, with deep dimples;
a really handsome, charming, educated Negro. Joan noticed
that he had a weakness for jewelry. He was wearing an ex-
quisite solitaire diamond ring and a diamond wrist watch, but
she liked him anyway and sent Peter to Connecticut to meet
Elsa who would make the final decision.

Later Elsa called us in the studio where we were editing
tapes. "This Peter," she said happily, in her best Belgian accent, "he is respectful and perfect. I hire him. He start work
today."

That evening, I came home alone. McGraw was working
late in the editing room. I found a happy household and a
clean house. Elsa was beaming; little Danny was following Peter from room to room with blind devotion, and Terry Olga
was clapping her little hands together, playing patty cake and
throwing kisses to him. Peter was the man of the hour.

He insisted he was more than a handy man. He wanted to
be a butler, and, although the McGraws don't specialize in
butlers, we had one. Peter served me dinner in the grand manner and then my coffee in the living room. He stood in the

corner of the room, smiling as he told me of all his accomplishments, with little show of modesty. He was a cleaning man, a
carpenter, a butler, a houseman, a gentleman's gentleman, and,
to crown all these achievements, Peter admitted he was also the
world's finest barber.

Late that night, I gave McGraw the rosy details.

"A barber, huh? Peg, you have your wish. Your Peter, so
help me, is an ex-con."

I ignored McGraw and went calmly about my daily routine.
The office was particularly busy at that time, With the parade
of ex-convicts still wending their way to our office with ever
new information which had to be checked, and a second parade
of out-of-work prison guards seeking advice and solace, we had
little time for ourselves. Then a call came in from the woman
in charge of the employment office.

"Oh, my God," she wailed, "what have I done to you, Mrs.
McGraw. That man Peter I sent you. His references don't
check." She was half hysterical on the phone. "We even called
California and tried to locate his last employer out there.
There is no such person. *He* wrote those references he gave
you. Get rid of him. We'll do anything to make this up to you,
my dear. He may be a murderer, a rapist, or what's worse . . .
an ex-convict!"

I placed the receiver quietly on the hook. Hiring an ex-
convict purposely, well aware of his problems, was one thing,
but Peter was something else. And the newspapers of the day
were headlining a ring of jewel thieves who took jobs in
households for the purpose of literally cleaning the house out.
I picked up the receiver and called McGraw, blurting out the
story.

McGraw listened and then, "He's no murderer, Peg, or rapist or infant strangler. He's a con man. You know enough
about crime to know a con man is not violent."

Logically, I knew McGraw was right. But logic isn't my
forte, especially when Terry is involved. McGraw chuckled.
"After all, Peg," he reminded me, "we haven't any jewels, and,
if he's a jewel thief, he's gonna be mighty frustrated. Sit tight
and wait until I return to the office. I'll be right over." He
hung up and I sat tight for maybe two or three seconds and

then I panicked again. One telephone call home just to check that Baby was all right, could surely do no harm. I called.

"Hi," Elsa greeted me cheerily.

"How are things?" I said in a voice that fooled nobody.

"Wonderful. Terry-O has slept all morning. Danny has behaved miraculously, and Peter is great."

The word *Peter* sent my heart skipping about like a jumping bean. "I—I want to talk to Peter, Elsa. . . . Put him on."

Peter greeted me, "Hi, Mrs. Mac. We're doin' fine here, so don't you worry none." At the sound of his voice I forgot all about my resolutions, and the sentences came rushing out, "Peter, your references don't check!"

There was a pause and then, very smoothly, Peter said, "Who, mine, Mrs. Mac?" Another long pause was followed by, "That's impossible." He started on a long, complicated story of how the employment office must have made a mistake. One thing I always said for Peter, his stories never lacked imagination.

I listened and then, quietly, "Peter, where are you out of?"

He said he didn't know what I was talking about. However, if I meant jail by any chance, he was once in jail down South for speeding, but that was only over night.

I fought for control. "Peter, I know you're lying. I want the truth. If you tell me the truth by eleven-thirty tonight when I come home, that job is still yours. If you don't tell me, you'd better not be there when I return."

I hung up. I sounded braver than I felt.

No sooner had I hung up than McGraw returned to the office. I told him about the call.

He shook his head sadly. "Peg, when are you going to learn to shut up?"

McGraw is always so logical. The first thing to do, he said, was to get a rundown on Peter from the New York police.

I called Captain W. A. Lawrence at headquarters and told him the story. He was sympathetic and promised to get right on the job. I supplemented my call to the New York police with calls to the parole authorities, to Bob Hannum, and to Washington for a rundown.

Then results began coming back fast. There was no federal flyer on Peter Benson. Hannum had no record, either. But

Captain Lawrence, of New York's finest, called back, "We know your boy, Peg. He's a con man with quite a record. He's wanted by our department for parole violation. He skipped his parole ten years ago."

All of the wind went out of my fury. A ten-year-old parole violation! I started to smile with relief. "Not a murder, or a robbery?"

"He's a con man," Captain Lawrence assured me.

"Thank God." Then another thought occurred to me. "What does a parole violation mean in terms of Peter's future?"

"In the first place, he'll have to finish his sentence. He owes the state three years." Captain Lawrence quietly added, "We'll have the Connecticut police pick him up at your house."

My emotions were mixed. I thought of Peter, charming, kind, likable, who for the past twenty-four hours had proved to be a darn good houseman. Then another thought flashed— perhaps his charm was a professional front. How would he feel being picked up? What would he do?

"No, Captain, I'll bring Peter into New York myself. You can have him here."

Captain Lawrence compromised by agreeing to have two detectives in our office to meet Peter when he arrived. "You bring your boy in and we'll take over from there."

The big problem was how to get Peter into town without arousing his suspicion.

"If you hadn't made the first call—" McGraw started. I clenched my teeth at him and cut him short. Then Elsa called from Connecticut.

"Mrs. McGraw," she started, "Peter and I have just had a long talk. He's already told me the same thing he's going to tell you. I still like Peter and, as far as I'm concerned, this doesn't make any difference."

She put Peter on the phone. McGraw hit one extension, I, the other.

"Mr. Mac, Mrs. Mac . . . I'm sure a no good, stupid kind of a s.o.b. Maybe someday I'll learn leveling with people will keep me out of trouble. I have quite a record. I was a kid in New York and I was picked up for breaking and entering. I've been in trouble in a couple of other states, too. I just finished a term at the Army Prison Camp at Leavenworth. I came out flat this last time. I'll give you all the details any time you want them. When I took this job I was on the level. I want to keep it. I'll be the best goddam houseman you ever had, and I *can* give haircuts." He started to chuckle. "I've been the prison barber in every pen I've ever been in."

"Peter," McGraw began, "good boy. I'd like you to come into the office where we can have a talk."

Peter readily agreed. He was to drive the car to the station, leave it parked there, and catch the 3:30 into New York.

We hung up. "Now what?" I stormed about the office. "What do we do with the two detectives?"

Detectives Levy and O'Neil [1] arrived at four that afternoon. Levy is hard and sardonic, with a hit-and-run sense of humor; O'Neil is tough and cold.

"You want to make a bet he don't show?" Detective Levy remarked. "I'll lay ten," he added, searching his pockets for a nonexistent ten.

"He'll show," McGraw murmured contentedly.

We watched the clock. I was rooting silently. Oh, how I wanted our smug detective friends to be wrong! Then, at four-thirty we saw the office door open slowly. And Peter breezed in, full of smiles and self-confidence until he saw the cops.[2] McGraw blocked the doorway and put a hand on Peter's shoulder.

"You're in trouble, Peter. You've got an old rap hanging over you. Let's try to clean that up."

Peter reluctantly came in and sat down, but he claimed innocence of his parole violation. He swore up and down that New York State had nothing on him. He had a long story about a payoff to some woman in the parole department, who had told him not to worry about the parole, and that everything would be taken care of. That's why he had taken off.

O'Neil and Levy began to throw questions at Peter faster than machine-gun bullets. Did he know X in Harlem? What about Y? Did he ever hear of the Z café? What happened to A?

---

[1] The names are changed.

[2] Former convicts can spot a policeman every time. They have a highly developed instinct for the men they term "the enemy."

Had he seen B recently? Peter was answering straight. He knew
A, and he knew B. He saw X just last week and borrowed a
tenner. He paid it back. He had gone to the café many times.
He had lots of friends in that section; after all, he was brought
up down there, right next door to Sugar Ray Robinson. Peter
and the detective began cutting up old touches, the good old
times of the numbers and lottery rackets.

They had talked for about an hour when Detective Levy got
up and said, "Come on, kid, we gotta take you down and book
you. We'll get the real story downtown." Levy's fist gently
poked Peter in the ribs. He winked. "We'll work you over like
old times—know what I mean?"

Peter knew what he meant. He looked at me. His eyes
clouded over, he was trying to swallow.

"This means I'm going back, doesn't it? I'll have to spend
another stinkin' three years in the damn ole pen. Come out and
interview me, Mrs. Mac, when I'm out there. I'll give you a
helluva story about that rat hole." He started to get up. He
took off his diamond wrist watch and his diamond ring. "Keep
this for me, Mr. Mac." He handed them over to McGraw. "I
sure as hell would like to have them when I get out."

I motioned to Detective Levy. I wanted to talk to him alone.
He followed me out of the room.

"Does he have to be sent back?"

"Maybe."

"Could I get him out of this mess?"

"Do you want to?"

"I think he might make good."

Levy was thoughtful. "There's nothing vicious about him.
But he's got itchy feet. He won't stay put, that's the danger. I
don't even know, of course, if I can work it. I'll try. I'll make a
telephone call."

Detective Levy made several calls while Peter and McGraw
talked in the other room. Peter kept urging McGraw to give
the detectives $100, which he felt would insure his liberty. "I'll
pay you back. So help me, I will, Mr. Mac."

McGraw discussed it with me. As we talked, we realized this
was what we had been looking for—the inmate's point of view.
The watch. The money. The distrust. The angle. Play the

angle. Perhaps Peter and the inmates knew what they were talking about. Then again, perhaps they didn't.

Detective Levy returned; he had had fair luck with his call. He thumbed at Peter. "I'll be able to get your boy off if you are prepared to give him a job."

The decision was ours. It was that simple. Three years in a penitentiary or a job in our home. I looked at McGraw for counsel.

"It's your household, Peg. You always tell me the woman is in charge of the home."

Peter was serious. "It's up to you, Mrs. Mac."

And it was up to me. Here we were, preaching to others to give deserving men a chance. Us and our big mouths. Were we just talking? Could we dare follow our own advice?

"If you're worried about Terry Olga," Peter looked at me . . . "I'd give my own life for that child. You know that, Mrs. Mac."

"This bum's a bum," interjected Levy, "a real-honest-to-God no-good bum—but I wouldn't worry about the baby. He's a sensitive bum."

I nodded my head and the words came out.

"We'll keep Peter on."

Peter smiled at me but couldn't talk.

"I'll break your goddam neck if you let Mrs. McGraw down," Levy said. "I'll have to take you downtown to the Tombs and book you for the night. We'll have him back for you tomorrow." He paused, looked at McGraw and then at Peter. "You can wear your jewelry, Peter. That was a nice-looking watch."

Peter smiled slyly, "I'd feel just as good if Mr. Mac kept it." He took his hat and coat. "In fact, fellas, I'd feel one helluva lot better."

We were told the State of Connecticut has a fine liberal parole policy.

Once a month, always at lunch time, the parole officer assigned to this case came to visit. Once he missed lunch, but he managed to make it in time for dinner.

The officer, a young college graduate, was a walking oral exam.

"Funny thing, these parole officers. They assume such a know-it-all air," Peter complained. "Holier than thou. If only they wouldn't interfere. Seems to me it's their job to help a man make a go of it, instead of tryin' to find out what he does that's wrong all the time. I don't like havin' a guy's foot in my tail all the time. Never did. None of the boys do. That's why they skip parole even when they mean good."

McGraw and I jotted that reaction down. Peter was right about the parole officer. His attitude was superior.

As a houseman, Peter found daily routine a drudgery. If he could con me into not looking into corners for dust, he'd won a moral victory. But Elsa took care of discipline. She'd "chew him out."

"Boy, the way that woman talks to me," Peter said, "she'd make my old army top sergeant blush. But I take it. Mrs. Mac, I sure as hell take it."

Elsa would flip her golden locks at him, waggle a broom over his head, and march off, leaving Peter glumly staring into the distance. "If I'd listen to her, you sure would have a clean house. But I don't listen."

It was interesting watching Peter, seeing him resist discipline, even the kind daily life imposes on all of us. We talked to Peter about it. At first, he didn't know what we were talking about. Then, one evening, he came in to join us.

"I think I know what you mean, Mrs. Mac," Peter said, "I never did like to HAVE to do anything. I get a kick out of puttin' something over. I wonder why?"

Peter wondered why, and that was healthy. Children hate having to do things, too. They resist discipline just as strongly as Peter resisted it. We suggested that Peter watch Danny when Danny was given an order. Maybe that might give Peter some of the answers he was looking for. A week passed before Peter brought the subject up again. It was during the dinner, as he passed some spinach. (He still insisted on butling.) "I got it, Mr. Mac, I got it. You know, Danny and I, we got somethin' in common. I never grew up. Man, it's sure time I did."

The textbooks call this "delayed maturation." Peter was bright enough to find it out for himself, and then he and his housework started to improve.

Despite the uneven household, Terry was thriving and Danny was behaving miraculously. Deadlines began pressing harder than ever. Now we not only spent days either recording or editing material, but at night we'd set up the recording machine and play the material back. Peter would watch us at work. Finally, he volunteered to help. He was interested in the recording equipment. He picked up the knack of handling not only the machinery, but of splicing the tape when it broke. Peter would listen with us, and we found that his opinions many times were valuable.

Taped testimony of an inmate giving a picture of prison life would elicit a "You tell 'em, boy." An official's explanation of prison regulation would call forth a "Well, I'll be damned. I never knew that's why they had that silly rule. Why don't they explain it to the men?" A neo-penologist's evaluation of a criminal's mentality inevitably caused Peter to burst forth, "Bull . . . , pardon me, Mrs. Mac."

McGraw and I felt that Peter was coming along. But he still had many problems. One was an over-active imagination. Sometimes his stories were harmless and amusing; other times, they gave us deep insight into the issues that bothered him.

One of the real problems Peter faced was the racial problem. He resented his second-class citizenship. He took this out in fantasy, but while resenting the racial situation, he was perfectly happy to indulge in any money-making scheme that would victimize Negroes.

He would come to us constantly with a plan to make a million. He had an idea that he could buy some boarding houses in Harlem and set up hotels. He wanted us to help him find backers. He had it figured out so that he could charge astronomical rents in these poor districts to whole families, who would occupy one room. These same rooms could be used as bordellos for one-night stands.

We began talking of morality. Peter said, "Look, Mrs. Mac, save it. Maybe it ain't moral, but I know a fella in Harlem that made better than a million dollars at this racket. He didn't slop away at the petty rackets, like me; he paid off the politicians. He never went to jail, and never will. Don't give me that morality guff."

McGraw and I had a tough time answering this one. Peter, as well as literally thousands of ex-cons and inmates, look around at our workaday world. They see politicians growing fat on crooked payoffs. They see the police taking money under the table. They see the racketeer gorging himself at the expense of the little man. They see big business buttering itself with white-collar crime. And then we talk morality to them.

"It don't add up, Mrs. Mac," Peter would say. "Me, I went in for the short con." Then he would add thoughtfully, "Them bastards have a long con. That's what I need."

We talked theory to Peter, and he gave us facts. We talked God, morality, religion, self-satisfaction. Peter talked the almighty buck. We tried to incorporate some of Peter's arguments in our series. They were thought-provoking. To the crooked politician, the crooked cop, the white-collar criminal, we pointed out they had a stake in the time these men served.

Peter had been with us about a month when a boy named Jack appeared, sent by Bob Hannum. We were gathering information about the riot in the federal reformatory at Chillicothe, and Jack had been the head of the inmate council there.

When Jack walked in he was bristling with information. He is a tall, skinny kid with a carrot top of impossibly wavy hair and a rolling sailor gait. He is twenty-five years old but looks a great deal younger, since he has not yet begun to shave. He was wearing a black trench coat with a turned-up collar. It was tightly belted to show off a small waist and slim hips. He has an almost female vanity about his waistline, although his other reactions were hard and cold. He talked out of the corner of his mouth, trying to be a "tough guy." It didn't quite come off. His eyes were arresting: almond-shaped, the pupils small and ice blue.

"I'm Durelle," Jack said, as if he expected a fight.

I invited him to sit down, but he answered, "I never sit down." He wanted to get right down to business. He paced nervously back and forth as he told us he didn't want the federal officials to pull the wool over our eyes. He didn't know what kind of a cock-and-bull story they had told us, but he was sure it was a phony.

I found out a lot about Jack. He enjoyed discussing his past.

Born and brought up on Amboy Street,[3] a pretty tough section of Brooklyn, he was the eldest of five children and the only redhead in a family of olive-skinned brunettes. It was his opinion that he was illegitimate, and, as the bastard child, he felt he had been grossly discriminated against. As proof of his illegitimacy, he cited the fact that his younger brother was also named Jack, after their paternal grandfather. Whenever the father was faced with the problem of introducing his family, he would say, "This is Jack, and this is my wife and," pointing to the other children, "*my* family."

Jack had a long delinquent record. "Kid stuff," he explained. He carried a knife when he was thirteen; it made him feel like a big shot. He carried a gun at fifteen. The police took it away from him, and, as a lesson, he was sent to reform school. He never committed a crime with a true money motive.

"In other words, I've been a jerk." Jack smiled up at me with a choir-boy look. He had plans for the future. He wanted to write a book. Of course, he couldn't afford to take time off and do nothing but write. He was hoping that he could find some kind of a part-time carpentry job that would pay him room, board, and spending money.

We had recently inherited a broken-down, beaten-up, ancient inn. The inn needed repairs, and they cost cash, which we don't have. Unless it got immediate attention, it would simply rot away. For years it had been a rooming house; then it had been converted into a triplex. Now it stood empty, eating up taxes.

According to Bob Hannum, Jack was a good carpenter. Instead of getting an outside contractor in to handle the assignment, Jack could hire day-by-day helpers and do the job himself. He could live in the basement apartment, eat with Elsa and Peter at our house, which was only a block away, and spend his free time writing his book. He could meet nice young people and gradually make a life for himself away from Amboy Street. I mentioned my plan to McGraw.

"This is a real bad idea, Peg," McGraw said.

---

[3] Amboy Street has become notorious since the publication of a book by Irving Shulman titled *The Amboy Dukes* (Doubleday, 1947).

I was deflated. Peter had been a successful experiment—why not Jack?

"Because Jack is an ex-convict," McGraw answered.

I pointed out hotly that McGraw was guilty of the worst kind of discrimination.

"Not only an ex-convict, but an ex-forger," McGraw answered.

"That has nothing to do with it."

"It has everything to do with it, Peg. You can't have two ex-cons in the same house—and forgers are the worst risks."

There is nothing that annoys me half as much as McGraw's impeccable logic. It gets my fighting spirit up. I had a million arguments to offer and I offered all of them. Peter and Jack would have much in common. Peter would be a good influence on Jack, and Jack would respect Peter and follow his lead. Besides, Jack was a typical "Dyer Act kid." His forgery was only incidental to car theft.

"McGraw," I pointed out, "ever since I met Mac at Terre Haute I've wanted a chance to work with one of these boys. This is our opportunity."

McGraw couldn't argue with me about that. Jack and Terre Haute's Mac had almost identical prison records. They were almost the same age. They had the same attitude.

McGraw said, "It's risky, Peg—but interesting." Then, after thinking it out, "Put it up to Peter. If Peter is willing to take on the responsibility, then I'll go along."

Jack arrived in Connecticut on the coldest day ever recorded. Some days before Peter had interviewed Jack in our office downtown. We had literally locked them together to hash matters out. When they emerged, Peter told us, "I wouldn't stand in any guy's way of getting a square break."

"What do you think of him?" McGraw asked.

"He's a kid, Mr. Mac. He's awful worried because he doesn't shave. But he'll grow a beard." Peter looked thoughtful. "Don't worry about him. I set him straight. I told him there was nothin' shakin'* in Connecticut."

Supplementing Peter's opinion, McGraw had written to Myrl Alexander for information about the boy. By return mail, Myrl pointed out that Jack was possibly a typical delinquent with a delayed maturation rate, who might respond. "However," Myrl warned, "be careful of loose cash, unendorsed checks, and similar temptations."

Warned and aware, we brought Jack over to the ancient inn around five on a Saturday afternoon. The inn was pretty well torn apart by workmen who had already ripped out much of the old heating equipment. But the basement apartment was intact, if undecorated.

The electricity was connected and we had an electric heater down there to provide warmth. We started to help Jack get settled. His entire wardrobe, consisting of one clean shirt, two pairs of socks, and a pair of work pants, was contained in a paper bag. Most former convicts return to society with little more than the prison-made suit they are given. They are desperate for clothes.

Jack stood uneasily in the middle of the room, listening as McGraw detailed the responsibilities and the opportunities of the job, and the ancient inn creaked with the oncoming night. Jack looked more like a fifteen-year-old child than a man with a record, sitting there in the harsh unshaded glare of the one large electric light. Suddenly a gust of wind moved the shutters. Jack moved nervously.

"Do you believe in ghosts?" His voice dropped until it was almost inaudible.

We laughed.

"It's not that I believe in ghosts," he hastened. He gave us a one-sided grin. "But I've been used to sleeping with a thousand other men. There's something comforting about the guy next door snoring—you know."

McGraw rose and patted Jack on the back. "Jack, since this is your first night in a whole new world, why don't you spend the night at our house?"

It was dinner time when we arrived home with Jack firmly in tow. We told him that in the house Elsa was boss.

"She's a tough cookie," Peter warned him and took Jack into the kitchen. After dinner Peter helped Jack make his bed. He conducted him on a tour of our home from the attic to the cellar.

Jack was edgy and nervous, and, when the tour was over, he headed toward the kitchen. Peter followed. "What are you after, man?"

"I thought I'd get a beer."

Peter faced him. "You don't just help yourself. You get a beer if you're invited to have one. I didn't hear nobody invite you."

Jack's cheek muscles twitched. "Sorry; I didn't know I was out of line."

McGraw was about to invite Jack to have a beer, but Peter shook his head. Later he took McGraw aside. "I got a hunch, Mr. Mac, this kid'll be better if he don't do no drinkin'." He paused thoughtfully, "You know, he ain't a man."

McGraw looked at Peter.

"O.K. You want to know—the kid's a punk. I can spot 'em. That doesn't mean anything outside, but he's got a lot of readjustments to do."

We wrote the incident off and forgot about it.

Late that night, while the household slept, we went through our ritual of stealing into Baby's room just to be sure she was safe for the night. We stood and just looked and then crept out into the hall. We could hear the soft sounds of a sleeping household. Then the silence was punctuated by the rumble of a snore. We knew Jack felt at home.

Our next-door neighbors, the Bill Shinniks, began eyeing us curiously. But, despite outward appearances, our potpourri of people was working out fine. Jack seemed to slip into our routine without even causing a ripple. He started work at the inn with a vehemence that caused even McGraw to comment, "He'll be O.K."

We took great pains with both boys to compliment them whenever they did anything well. When something went wrong, we would listen carefully to their side of the story and pass it off.

Jack wanted to make a big impression, not just by doing his job, but by interfering in the job others did. This was the first problem. The heating company wanted to install two thermostats that they had ordered. Jack decided, through his contacts with a former inmate of Riker's Island who had gone straight and was in the heating business, that he could procure for us two thermostats at half-price. We pointed out that this economy could only lead to trouble since our heating company would not guarantee thermostats that they didn't install. Jack took our refusal as a personal affront.

From the start, Jack didn't take kindly to criticism. He had two moods. One was a hyperexcited frenzy, the other a brooding, gloomy melancholia. The fluctuation in mood occurred daily, with sharp ups and downs.

Peter and Jack seemed to hit it off all right. But they went into a friendly competition over little things. Peter had been in the habit of taking Danny to the zoo on Sundays. Jack horned in on this deal and added to it by supplying ice cream. Jack tried to woo Terry Olga away from Peter, who was now her joy supreme, by buying her little gifts.

Terry and Danny however were thriving on the love and affection that were honestly displayed. Terry could only coo and throw kisses. Danny responded by deciding he had two uncles, Uncle Jack and Uncle Peter.

Bill Shinnick dropped over one evening and remarked, with admirable calm, "Uncle Jack is one lousy driver. He might try driving a little slower when he leaves and enters the driveway."

This led to an immediate family conference. Peter spoke up, "As long as we're talking about Jack's driving, I don't think he ought to drive a car."

Jack readily admitted he was a hot rodder. He liked driving fast, but he would slow down if we insisted. He was hurt at the thought that anyone considered him a bad driver. He was in his own words, "a damn good driver. I learned all there was to learn about cars at Chillicothe, in the automobile workshop."

"You learned everything but how to put on a brake," Peter complained.

Threatened with losing his right to drive, Jack slowed down, and the neighborhood dogs and cats returned cautiously to the driveway, now that it was safe again.

At this time, as a problem solver, we innovated a family round-table conference, which was supposedly for airing "beefs." Anybody who had a complaint could register it, and adjustments would be made. Jack hated the conferences, Peter approved. Jack insisted he had no problems; Peter's life had daily crises.

It was at a family conference that Elsa took the floor. She had an important subject for discussion, and, "You'd better listen, you two," she threatened. "I had a call from Danny's kindergarten teacher today. She is very angree because of the langwiche Danny, he is using." It seems that Daniel was mixing his usual Belgian flavor with such stunning remarks as, "Man, don't bum rap* me," or, "Get out of my face,* son." Not only did the local kindergarten disapprove, they weren't quite sure of what he meant.

We took a vote on a new parliamentary rule of household conduct. Convictese was out; the king's English in. But this rule almost kicked off another row, since Jack was sure Peter didn't know what the king's English was, and Peter called Jack a "goddam college boy."

As the days went on these flare-ups became routine. Peter's work was getting spotty, and, instead of washing the car himself, we found he had charged the job to our filling-station account.

As for Jack, we checked his progress with the work crew at the inn and they reported he was doing admirably. They did have one complaint, however. Jack was accident prone. He was constantly falling off ladders. He had broken a window, smashed a door, and cracked up some plaster. They hoped we were carrying indemnity insurance.

The fact that Jack was accident prone was no news to us. Frequently, we had sent him on little errands around the house. On a trip upstairs to get a package of cigarettes, he had fallen down the whole flight. On a trip to the terrace to help Peter fix a pipe, he had fallen in the sound. He had cut his hands innumerable times, bumped his head, and bruised himself. We had talked to Peter about Jack's problem.

"He's drinkin', Mrs. Mac," Peter warned.

"I've never smelled alcohol on his breath, Peter," I argued.

"Don't say I never warned you. That crazy kid is drinking, and he's not a man."

"Although we had never caught Jack drinking, McGraw noticed a gradual diminishing of a bottle of chlorophyll tablets.

We faced Jack. Jack denied drinking, vehemently at first and
then, "O.K. So I drink a little beer. And I can't hold it."
"Do you like beer?" McGraw asked.
"Yeah."
"A lot?"
"No, sir."
"Do you feel you have to drink it?"
"No!"

McGraw now treated Jack as if he were a very young adolescent and suggested that any time Jack wanted a beer, he was
welcome to it. But we would prefer that Jack waited for his
beer until we were home. Jack looked downcast.

"Sometimes, I think I need a psychiatrist, Mr. Mac."

"Want me to make arrangements for you to see one?"

Suddenly Jack turned around, tense, tight, ready to argue.
"Who said I'm sick?"

"You did, Jack," I smiled.

Jack relaxed and grinned like a big, overgrown child. He
shook his head and then, "You know the real reason I take a
beer now and then? I'm scared. O.K. now you know. I'm scared.
It makes me feel big." He slammed out of the room.

Late February, early March, is a lovely time of the year on
Connecticut's water front. The ocean is a constantly shifting
green-blue, and the trees suddenly begin to find their first
buds. Spring is in the salt-washed air, and romance hit our
home. Peter fell in love.

Her name was Suzanne, and she was a lovely, well-educated
daughter of a well-known Harlem hot drummer. Peter now
looked forward vigorously to his days off when he and Suzanne
would wander over the Connecticut countryside, holding hands
and sighing sighs. Peter was so proud of Suzanne he brought
her home for us to meet.

"She knows all about me, Mrs. Mac. She's for me!" Then
his face crumpled, "Only we can't get married. Parole."

Suzanne was all for asking the parole board's permission and
wanted us to go down and work it out for them.

"I'll be damned if I'll have any damn snoopy so and so
tell me whether I can get married or not. They'll say no—you

don't know them, Suzanne, honest to God." He walked around and tried to cool off, "If it's all the same to you, honey, I've five more months on parole; we can just stay engaged."

Much of their romance was conducted on the telephone. Peter had told us he was making his long-distance calls from the drugstore. But Jack came to us with the intelligence that our telephone bill was apt to look like the national debt.

"When you're not here, Peter spends all his time on the phone."

This called for a family round table. Peter, with his own wonderful brand of charm, readily confessed that he had over spent his monthly salary, that's why he was borrowing our phone. "Just deduct what I spent from my next month's salary, Mrs. Mac."

Peter's romance was getting a huge share of attention and Jack started getting jealous. Almost overnight, Jack informed us that he was in love. Her name was Marilyn.

Naturally we were as interested in meeting Jack's Marilyn as in meeting Peter's Suzanne.

"She lives in Long Island. I have been borrowing your car to drive there in the evening," Jack confessed. Since we had overlooked Peter's transgression on the telephone, Jack's transgression in borrowing an automobile obviously deserved the same treatment. He expected it and got it.

It was barely one night later, when McGraw was busy downtown in the editing room that I came home alone. A drawn, weary-looking Peter met me at the station. He drove slowly on the way home. I knew something was bothering him deeply. He started, "Y'know, Mrs. Mac, fate's a funny thing. If I cross Jack here, he could plant a knife in my back later on."

I waited for Peter to continue.

"If I tell you something, you got to promise you'll never tell Jack I told you."

I temporized—I couldn't promise till I knew what it was.

Peter took a long indrawn breath. "Jack's got a gun in his room. It's hidden behind the radiator. I found it when I cleaned up."

One look at his face and I knew there was no possibility of Peter's kidding.

"Where did he get it?"

Peter stopped the car. "From the attic."

"But Peter, we don't have any guns," I protested.

"You had two of them," Peter replied.

Then I remembered. They had belonged to Mother and Dad McGraw, and we had them locked away in an old trunk.

"How come you know about them?"

"When I cleaned the attic," Peter answered, "I found them in a locked trunk. I opened the trunk. I wanted to find out what was inside so's I could do a thorough cleaning job."

I shook my head. Peter's story sounded so palpably wrong. The rest of the drive home was in silence. As we entered the house, the tension choked me. It was alive and you could smell it. Jack was furious and Elsa, irritable. I could barely eat dinner. After dinner, I went up alone to Baby's room and sat on the sofa near her bed, half on guard, half thinking.

The house was silent except for the crackling sound of Elsa's radio. Then at one o'clock McGraw came home and I told him the story. McGraw suggested we sleep on it before taking any action. I refused to leave Baby's room and spent the night on the daybed there, watchdog fashion.

The morning dawned warm and clear, and some of the horror of the night before had dissipated. Peter and McGraw were talking when I entered the dining room for breakfast. Jack was nowhere in sight. Peter explained Jack had gone out to take an early morning drive. "He's drinkin' again, Mr. Mac. That's why he does these things. And it isn't beer."

"Where are the guns now?" McGraw asked.

"I got them both hidden. Mr. Mac. I'll get them for you." He dashed upstairs and returned in a few minutes with the weapons. McGraw examined them. They had not been fired.

"Goddam good thing," Peter said. "They're so old and rusty they'd kill anyone trying to use them."

McGraw and I decided to stay home until we solved the problem.

"I'm going to face Jack with the facts, Peter," McGraw finally said.

Peter blanched. "Don't do that, Mr. Mac. If you tell him, I'm

leavin'. There'll be trouble." Peter glanced at the clock on the
wall. It was his day off, and it was getting late. He barely had
time to take a shower and get dressed for his date. "You got the
facts, Mr. Mac. Whatever you do is up to you, but leave me
out of it." He left the room.

Then we heard Jack. The loud screech of the brakes echoed
in the driveway as he brought the car to his usual stop. The two
met outside. We heard their voices.

"Goddam fool," Peter fumed, "the way you drive a car."

"Aw, go jump in the lake!" from Jack. They traded keys with
bad grace and Peter drove off. McGraw directed Elsa to keep
Danny and Baby upstairs while we had a long talk with Jack.
McGraw called him into the living room.

Jack came in promptly and sat down on the floor, his legs
curled up under him like a fifteen-year-old. "What's on your
mind, sir?"

McGraw seldom wastes time with chitchat. He said, "I found
a gun in your room, Jack."

Elsa, despite orders, was standing in the doorway. Now she
moved quickly across the room to join us on the sofa.

Jack returned McGraw's look. "I know, I was gonna give it to
you today. I was cleaning up after Peter yesterday and I found
it wrapped in a towel in his room. I didn't want to scare Mrs.
Mac last night by telling her about it. I thought it was safe with
me. Look, Mr. Mac, guns are dangerous. A guy can have one
and never intend to use it, but they can go off." He shook his
head sadly. "Terry Olga is in this house, so's little Danny. This
house is no place for a gun, even if a guy has it for fun. I don't
know where Peter got it, but I was gonna make damn sure you
had it before the day was over."

"Did you know there's another gun in this house?" McGraw
asked.

"No," Jack started to get up. "Where is it? Gee, Mr. Mac, you
have no right to have guns here. Don't you realize what trouble
they might mean?"

He got up and began to pace. "Just because Peter has gone
and fallen in love with some dame and wants to buy her a lot
of damn fool presents he can't afford—well, this is no place for

that kind of stuff." Jack hung his head. "Don't tell him I told you. I'm no squealer. That's not the code. But where you're concerned, you come first."

"How do you know he wants to buy presents he can't afford?" McGraw asked.

"He hocked his watch last week."

"That's right," Elsa chimed in. "I told him not to. He wanted me to lend him some money but I wouldn't."

"I lent him part of my salary," Jack added, "but he wants a lot of dough."

We now began to question Jack closely. Then, suddenly, he burst out, "This is the first time I've ever had a home, a real home with folks that cared. I belong. I feel like part of the family. I was hoping when I finished up my job at the inn you could help me get another nearby so I could drop in and talk. I need those talks." He turned his back on us. "I got roots here." He walked slowly from the room, unable to say more.

Elsa smiled, but her eyes were full of tears. "He's a swell kid. That's what he is. I like Peter, too. I won't say I don't. But Jack's a swell kid."

McGraw began to question Elsa about Peter's claim that Jack was drinking.

"I've never seen him touch a drop," Elsa returned. "Never. Once in a while he does take a beer, but only if I allow it."

McGraw was silent for a while and then he said, "I like Peter. As a matter of fact, I'm damn fond of that boy. I'm not as fond of Jack. He's too tense for me. If we let Peter go, we'll have to stand by him in order that he doesn't get sent back."

I nodded my head in agreement.

"If we let Jack go," he said, "if he's on the level, he'll decide that being honest just doesn't pay."

I added that the same holds for Peter.

"Not quite. Peter is older and steadier. He's also able to take it. If we're wrong, Peter will feel strongly and be bitter, but Jack might take it out on society as a whole."

McGraw and I spent the day debating the situation. Obviously, both boys could not remain with us together. One had to go. Then we decided: Peter must leave.

We waited up for Peter that night, intending to have a long, full talk. But Peter didn't come home. We sat smoking and drinking black coffee until the dawn. Peter still didn't show. It was 7:00 A.M. when the front door cracked and Peter crept in. He was full of apologies; he had a long story. He and Suzanne had spent a big night dancing, and on the way home he had become tired. Afraid to continue the drive on the Merrit Parkway, he had pulled to the side and gone to sleep.

As he talked, we noticed the absent wrist watch. When he finished, McGraw said, very quietly, "We're awful sorry, Peter, that we have to do this, but we have to let you go."

Peter was stunned, "Why?"

"Don't you know?"

Peter shook his head. He didn't. But if that's the way we felt —only, "You're not going to keep Jack here?"

We didn't answer, and Peter went up the stairs disconsolately to pack his clothes.

It took the better part of the week for us to rearrange Peter's parole. First in the line of business was to get him another job. We gave him references, and the rest was easy. Since he had a job, New York was glad to handle his parole; and Peter, in a way, felt a sense of relief.

But he came to see us in the office every Thursday to give McGraw a haircut. He never mentioned Jack or the gun incident, Elsa or Danny, again. But he asked after the Baby, hungry for news of her.

Now that Peter was gone, Jack seemed to lose his old tension and once again started his work with vehemence. The very first day he remained in our home to do a thorough job of cleaning, "something Peter didn't do the whole time he was here," Jack pointed out. The second day he left the house after breakfast and worked at the inn until evening. He bought himself a mess jacket so that he, too, could play butler. We assured Jack we didn't need one, but he enjoyed the game. He'd help out in the house after dinner, always busy, always with something to do. The only thing he didn't do was work on his book, and whenever I asked him about it, he'd evade the subject.

McGraw was held up in town five nights a week, but I came home almost every night and spent at least an hour discussing

Jack's future, his plans and his dreams. His plans changed day by day. He was always playing a part. He'd talk of a group he found in Stamford. They held dancing classes. He wanted to join them. I encouraged him, but by the next night he would have forgotten the dance classes and be seriously discussing joining a youth group. Jack felt, acted and lived on a sixteen-year-old level. Many times I'd see him with the neighborhood teen-agers and he'd apologize, by saying, "I'm giving them good advice. They're crazy kids, y'know. Boy, they're doing a lot of things I used to do when I was their age, and look what happened to me."

It was the fact that Jack was functioning on a juvenile level that interested us. One night, when McGraw didn't come home until midnight, Jack decided to wait up with me. We talked a while and then the conversation lagged. Jack started to doodle. I watched him curiously.

"What are you doing?"

"Practicing handwriting."

"What kind?"

Jack shrugged his shoulders. "Signatures." He laughed. "I used to do this a lot, but THEY didn't like it."

I looked at his signatures. He was trying mine. His penmanship was bad, but I didn't try to improve it.

"Mrs. Mac, I used to be a very good forger."

McGraw and I started charting Jack's moods, his ups and downs. His pattern was erratic.

Every other day we would visit the inn to see how he was progressing. Progress had stopped. Nothing was happening, but Jack was full of excuses, so we decided to try giving him deadlines. We started with a small bedroom. The ceiling of this bedroom was to be covered in Celotex. This is an easy enough job for a good carpenter.

We suggested Jack hire another carpenter by the day, to help him. Jack resented the suggestion.

"I don't need to hire a helper. It's child's play, Mrs. Mac, I can do it myself," he bragged.

Jack had to prove he could do everything on his own. Why? Each evening, Jack would give us glowing reports of his progress: first, how he shopped to buy the wallboard; then, how he

managed to cut the price into half of what any other carpenter
would pay. He didn't want us to see the job until it was all done.

We waited until Saturday. I was having breakfast in the
kitchen, discussing the week's menus with Elsa. Jack was out
on the terrace with Danny. Suddenly we heard a scream outside. Elsa froze. "That's my baby!"

We dashed out the door just in time to see Jack dive into the
ice-cold sound. Elsa and I raced to the sea wall and looked over.
There was Danny, screaming and crying as he floundered
around in the water.

Jack was swimming to him. He reached out and grabbed the
child and swam back. He handed the crying Danny over to
Elsa as he climbed up the rocks.

"Damn kid," Jack muttered, "Damn him, I told him a million times not to climb on the sea wall, or he'd fall in."

Danny was sobbing as if his heart would break. We couldn't
understand what he was trying to say.

"If I hadn't been there, he'd be dead," Jack said.

Elsa and I hustled both of them into the house. We ran a hot
tub for Danny and gave him a bath. Then we forced a whisky
toddy down him. Jack had already found the bar and
had taken four stiff shots.

"Sorry, Mrs. Mac, but I'm chilled to the bone." Once again
that shy smile. "I hope you don't mind."

One shot was O.K., but four of them seemed to me to be more
than was needed to take the chill off.

Terry Olga, hearing Danny cry, immediately burst into
tears, and I dashed to the nursery. I rocked her for half an
hour, calming her fears. Then Elsa came down with a warmly
pajamed Danny behind her.

"I gave Danny what for all right," she muttered darkly.
"He'll never climb on that sea wall again and fall in. Will you,
Danny?"

Danny sniveled plaintively. "I didn't fall in. I never fall in.
Uncle Jack pushed me!"

Elsa and I looked at each other.

"He pushed me," Danny said again. "He pushed me, he
pushed me. I hate Uncle Jack."

McGraw went downstairs to face Jack, who was in the bar,

warming up on a fifth shot. Jack held to his story of saving the
boy's life. His voice was thick. He glowered at us. McGraw
ordered him to his room. Elsa carried up a cup of black coffee,
which we forced Jack to drink. He drank it and passed out cold.

McGraw and I weren't quite sure what to do. It's easy
enough to say, "Let the boy go." But we had started out to find
the "why"—"Why do these boys do what they do?" Jack was
acting out the pattern all right, but why? It seemed to us he
could no more help himself than a baby can help crying. Was
it inferiority forcing him to overcompensate? What was he trying to prove? We were frankly afraid to let Jack go; his own
fear of the world could conceivably manifest itself in violence
to others.

And then we had that funny little nagging feeling. Were
we accusing Jack of being a liar when perhaps he did save the
child's life?

In the excitement of the day, we had forgotten all about the
inn, and the ceiling of wallboard. But that night McGraw
and I walked over to the inn. The back bedroom had not been
touched. The ceiling had not been started. And there were no
wallboard, no nails, no preparation.

"He's afraid of it," McGraw said.

Now we speculated, "Too much responsibility?" Perhaps,
if we hired another carpenter to do the job and assigned Jack
as assistant, it would work out better. We examined the inn
and found that Jack had completed cutting out all of the
inlets and outlets that the heating company requested. Working
under direction he was successful. Perhaps our mistake with the
boy was allowing him too free a hand. We decided to talk it all
out in the morning. Jack was still sleeping when we got home.

The next morning, at breakfast, Jack was sullen and ashamed.
He stood, hangdog fashion, unable to look at us, and then burst
out, "I bet you think I'm sick in the head, I bet?" He turned his
back to us, and his voice was cold. "I'm moving to the inn.
I'm going to start my book and I'm really going to start that
ceiling in the bedroom. But I'll need help. I can't do it alone. I
don't know why I say things I do—they're outright lies. I won't
lie again if—if I choke on it." Without waiting for an answer, he
walked from the room.

McGraw shrugged his shoulders. "Another chance?"

I nodded in agreement. "Maybe we can still find out why?"

The next morning, I put in a call to a psychiatrist. We made a luncheon appointment to discuss Jack's problem. I felt better.

We had an agency meeting that afternoon on a new show. The meeting started at one. At four, while it was still going strong, we received a call from Elsa.

"Something's wrong, Mrs. McGraw," she said.

"With Baby?" That was always my first thought.

"Jack. He's not at the inn. He didn't show up for lunch. They say he hasn't been there all day, and his clothes are gone. He has the car. I would not worry, except we got a call from the florist. The florist wanted to know if it was all right to deliver two dozen orchids to me. It was charged to your account, but the card read, 'You won't forget me, Jack.'"

We told Elsa to get on the phone as fast as she could and notify every tradesman in the neighborhood to watch out for bad checks. Elsa had already called the Connecticut state police; then we started home.

Home was a nightmare. Elsa greeted us at the door, white as a sheet. "I called the tradespeople, but I was too late. He forged twelve checks, Mrs. McGraw."

"Where did he get the checkbook?"

Elsa didn't know. Then she started really to weep. "I had just taken my money out of the bank today and it's gone. Jack took my savings. Oh, Mrs. McGraw, how could he?"

McGraw and I started to check the house. What else was gone? One fur coat, one wrist watch, my Socony Gas charge card, a whole stack of credentials out of McGraw's wallet, two cases of beer, and a scattering of odds and ends of gin, rum and cordials, not to mention the car.

We went over to the inn to examine the apartment he had been working on. The sidewalk was littered with broken whisky bottles. His apartment was a shambles, chairs broken, drapes torn down, furniture upside down, violently smashed as if a madman had smashed it. We went through the drawers. We went through the closet. We found what we were looking for. A whole packet of .32 snub-nosed bullets. Except for Elsa, Jack had succeeded in hurting only himself.

The police came to see us. So did the FBI. In Jack's papers we found the names and addresses of several girls who lived in Long Island. We found a Marilyn, who swore she barely knew Jack and he was a pest. Another greeted us with, "You must be Jack's aunt and uncle. He told me he was living with his wealthy aunt and uncle and promised to introduce me sometime. I expect to see him today or tomorrow." And a third, pretty tough on the phone, "Sure I know Jack. But I think he's nuts." We got from all the girls, however, a fourth girl's name. She was supposed to be a very, very good friend of his and, more than likely, we could find her there.

We gave our information to the Connecticut state police. If Jack was on Long Island, the police informed us, then the problem of capturing him was New York State's. Frankly, I wasn't interested in protocol at that moment; I only wanted Jack safely in hand. I tried interesting the FBI in the project of a trip to Long Island, but the FBI had to ascertain whether or not Jack had violated a federal law, and that is a time-consuming project. They didn't want to move in on something that might be ruled strictly a state affair.

All the officials agreed, however, I had nothing to worry about. Jack would undoubtedly commit another crime before the month was over and he would be apprehended for that. He could get involved, they told me, in anything from auto theft to a homicide. Our concern turned to anger. Jack, under control, was no problem to anyone but himself; but drunk, running berserk with all controls off, this was another matter. I couldn't help but feel that protocol wasn't quite as important as Jack's next victim.

Then we heard news from the nearby town of Darien. Jack had been seen there in the local Howard Johnson's, drinking a soda. One of the men to whom he had passed a bad check, recognized him, collared him, got his money back in cash, and calmly let him go. "After all," he said later, "I believe in minding my own business."

A few days later the call we were waiting for came in. Jack had been found. He had already spent two days in a Long Island jail before they found out that he was wanted in Con-

necticut. He had been arrested for careless driving—of a second
stolen car—and violation of the Sullivan Act. They had found a
new gun in the glove compartment of the car, loaded and ready.

One phase of our life was drawing to a close.

Jack was sent to the New York Federal Detention Headquarters.

Peter was still coming into the office to give McGraw
his weekly haircut. He took the news of Jack calmly. "Thank
heaven that's all he did, Mr. Mac. I was tellin' the truth, you
know."

We knew.

"Would you think I'm nuts, Mr. Mac," Peter asked, "if I
wanted to go to school and be a radio engineer? I've been doin'
a lot of thinking since I left you."

"It's a long course. Do you think you can take the discipline?"
McGraw said.

"I can try."

McGraw and I grinned. We took Peter's hands; they were as
cold as lumps of ice.

"Will you help me enroll?"

We called the RCA Institute and made the arrangements.
Peter went down and took the entrance exam. It is tough. He
called us afterwards. "I did it, Mrs. Mac, I passed. Goddam,
maybe I'm as smart as I think I am. I start September seventh.
I got all summer to save my money."

We wanted to see Jack again. We called Warden Thompson,
a fine, intelligent man, at the Federal Detention Headquarters.
We introduced ourselves and asked about the boy. He invited
us down to lunch with him and some of the officers. After lunch
he called Jack into his office and left us alone with him.

Jack kept his head down. "You're mad at me," he started.

We weren't mad.

"You probably want to know why I did it."

We shook our heads again. Why wasn't important.

"I want to tell you," Jack started, "it was because you didn't
really want me—it was because you didn't really—" He broke
off and looked down. "I'm lying, you know that."

We smiled. "Why is not important now," I said.

Jack chewed nervously on his lip. He started to pace the office. "It *is* important, Mrs. Mac. It's damn important to me. Why? Why am I going to give up maybe five more years of my life. Why couldn't I make it outside?"

We waited for him to finish.

"I know why. I've been in institutions so long, I don't know how to get along in any other kind of place. I've spent most of my life in one institution or another. It's like home. The whole time I was out I guess I was just waiting for a chance to return." He hitched up his jail trousers and faced us at the door. "Write me, huh? I'll write you."

That perhaps is part of the "why." Warden Thompson sent Jack to have a thorough psychoanalytic test. After a long discussion with us, some of the officials felt perhaps Jack was psychotic.

He was held for testing for three weeks. Then he was returned to the Federal Detention Headquarters to await trial. He wrote us a letter on his return. It was an interesting letter. He said he learned a lot about himself during the test and now he was all grown-up. The test did him a lot of good because now he understood himself.

But what Jack said was much less interesting than how he said it. Jack's normal handwriting is right handed. When he forges checks, he uses a left-hand backstroke. The letter was completely written in a left-hand backstroke.

The result of that psychiatric exam was even more interesting. They found Jack to have an antisocial reaction. He was disassociated. He was confused. The report summarized that the prognosis for his future is very poor. But he was not psychotic (legally insane); therefore, nothing could be done for him medically. Since medical help is not available, Jack has been sentenced to three years at Lewisburg Penitentiary.

Is he a criminal who will respond to punishment? Figure the crime: a drunken wild kid goes on a spree, smashing his security. He cashes a flock of forged checks. He steals a practically useless old fur jacket, a beaten-up wrist watch, a typewriter, four hundred dollars, and whisky. With that money, he goes on a drunken spending spree and is picked up without a cent. He bought nothing with the money. It had no value for him. It represented neither security nor power, only the stealing of it brought satisfaction. He didn't take his packet and hide out cleverly from the police. He drove around with a gun in the glove compartment of a car, waiting to be caught.

He'll do well in an institution; he did well before. But what happens this time when he comes out? Punishment didn't work before, will it now? Last time he only bought, or stole, a gun and loaded it with bullets. The next time he may use it.

The experts themselves say, "Prognosis is poor."

McGraw remarked, "A young Earl Ward."

As for Peter, he came into the office just the other day with a big box all wrapped up in tissue paper.

"I got a present for you, Mrs. Mac, but you gotta pay me for it."

He started to undo the package. It was a handsome glossy picture of Peter and his Suzanne. Not an ordinary picture by any means: she was wearing a wedding veil.

"You took the big step, Peter!"

Peter grinned. "I figure with all this studying I'm doin', I ought to have someone by my side to appreciate me, and Suzanne sure thinks I'm great. I don't tell her how stupid I really am. I'm havin' a rough time with mathematics."

We knew how rough it was. Peter is holding down a job mornings and evenings, and going to school in the afternoons. He's paying his own way through. He wants it that way, and he has his report cards sent to us in the office. He's doing fine.

I held my hand out for the wedding picture. Peter shook his head, "You're just tryin' to wiggle out of the payment, Mrs. Mac, and I'm not gonna have it."

"What are you trying to con?"

Peter shook his head violently. "We don't use that language anymore, Mrs. Mac. We talk legitimate."

"All right, what are you trying to do me out of?" I legitimized.

Peter looked embarrassed. He shifted his weight and then grinned. "I'll give you this weddin' picture of me and Suzanne,

in return for a picture of Terry Olga. She's my mascot, Mrs.
Mac. Whenever I get that itchy feelin', I stop and think about
her."

When I get that itchy feeling, born of disgust and despair
thinking of Jack and all the other kids who are cut from that
same pattern, I stop and think of Peter.

are riots necessary?

. . . McGraw Reporting

WHILE WE WERE DISCOVERING THE WORLD'S WORST WAY OF running a home, we were also trying to put our radio series into final shape. Every show shaped up without too much trouble save the last one. How to end a series is always a tough problem, but, now that we had the answers, we knew that our prison story had no happy ending. We had been investigating riot spots and, although we had heard of good prison systems in various states, those were not the ones we had covered. "Federal" was the only system we had investigated that seemed good and even there so much remained to be done if the 97 per cent of the inmates who come out were to come out better than they went in. Pitifully few men seemed to be fighting for good prisons. So we decided to make a summary of the whole mess and call it "Are Riots Necessary?"

We had planned, after our first visit to New Jersey, to use that title for the first program in the series, but the answers we received there were not adequate to the question, so that we did not dare use it. We found that New Jersey inmates felt riots *were* necessary because by no other means could they get their complaints before the public. Smitty had admitted to us that the leaders of the main riot had been impressed by the publicity given the psycho riot, but they felt that this type of publicity should be directed to their complaints. Jersey was no exception. In Michigan, Ward talked of "the crusade to let the people know." In every other spot rioters said to us, "If the people only knew . . ."

Convict contacts with the outside world are necessarily limited. Some prisons do not allow newspapers, magazines, or radios; others circumscribe the use of them considerably. Consequently, it is not surprising that the world shrinks, in the inmate's mind, to a size not much larger than the diameter of the plant's outer wall. With little else to think of but his own problems the inmate cannot understand why his problems would not be as important to everyone outside, "if they only knew . . ."

The attitude of many prison officials, whose philosophy is summed up in the statement, "A good prison is any prison that's kept off the front pages," adds fuel to this smouldering inmate feeling. A warden with this attitude may have a "loose" prison. His staff is underpaid, so he lets the officials and guards augment their salaries with such petty grafts as selling whisky and dope to inmates, making bank and "kiting"* letters. Satisfied with their rackets, the prison staff wants no more publicity for the prison than does the warden.

From the point of view of the rich inmate and the professional crook, this also makes an "easier go." * These men are quite content with their lot, and, if they wield enough power, they will keep a prison quiet. However, if what Smitty called the "underprivileged element" breaks loose from its bosses, the prison may riot.

Wardens are trapped into this situation by that old bugaboo, politics. Usually politically appointed, they owe it to the state's political bosses to incur no public attention to any prison problems. This can trouble even a sincere, well-trained warden, because he is still beholden.

I remember a warden, for whom we have great respect, standing in the ill-equipped shambles of his outdated, inadequate bastille, pleading to us: "Make it clear that the governor has given me everything I've asked for." He said this after telling us all the necessities he lacked to run his institution on any but the most minimal basis.

But we could not blame him for this. With too critical an attitude he might no longer be a warden. Strangely, and tragically, the closest he had come to getting the things he had asked for was after his prison had gone up in riot. We did not ask this warden if he thought riots were necessary.

We did, however, ask that of other prison officials in other states, and the answer was not always "No." Many guards, whose salaries had been hurriedly increased by panic-stricken state legislatures, were quite frank in their statements that riots could do some good. There were even rumors in two states (we could never prove them true or false) that guards had committed the cardinal prison sin of encouraging demonstrations.

Among prison officials Vernon Fox of Michigan made the strongest statement which might be said to be in favor of riots. He pointed out that a wave of riots sometimes frightens wardens of nonrioting prisons into pushing through improvements to prevent their own houses from going up. But, he went on, riots usually do nothing but harm in the prisons where they take place, because the public looks at riots only in terms of tax dollars spent for repairs and turns against the rioters. Conditions then become even worse than before.

This was partially true in Michigan. However, an outside investigation, at least, was made there and in New Jersey; and perhaps something will be done. Ohio and Illinois also have taken first steps in changing conditions, but the acid test is that in most states the professional criminal would still rather get a state rap than a federal. Not only name racketeers, but former federal judges and ex-congressmen have been shocked to find that "Federal" never bothered to buy a red carpet and that they cannot buy an easy go there.

The story is told of a state superintendent of prisons who was taking a tour through a federal prison. In the yard he spotted a former congressman of his party and federal authorities saw the work of months shot to hell when the state "penologist" kowtowed to the inmate in front of others, calling him with deep respect, "Congressman." Perhaps this, as much as anything, typifies the difference between the federal system and many state systems.

But there are other differences. For instance, in every state system we investigated prisoners told us why the prison was bad, and usually administrators told us why it was good, no matter what the facts might indicate.

However, in "Federal," one example of a good system, everyone from the guard at the front-hall desk in the United States Penitentiary at Terre Haute, Indiana, to bureau director, James V. Bennett (recently called "America's best prison man" by Attorney General Brownell), told us how they would like to see the system improved. They detailed experiments they had tried, told us why some had failed and others had succeeded. They had an almost religious fervor when they detailed what they are now trying.

Interestingly enough, the best sales pitches we heard on the federal system came from inmates and ex-inmates. It was they, not the officials, who tried to alibi failures in "Federal." The inmates knew some of the problems and, though some of their own proposed solutions were pretty bizarre, they did not blame the officials for what was not being done. They even excused some of the officials they unanimously disliked by saying, "He reads too much—he ain't practical, but he tries."

The federal system differed from the other systems we investigated in yet another respect: it alone took immediate steps to rectify the cause of a riot. "Federal" had a riot in the reformatory at Chillicothe, Ohio. Assistant Director Myrl Alexander, who looks like a poetic Pat O'Brien and talks like a college professor turned convict, gave us the story:

> At Chilly, on September 8, 1952, at the time of the evening meal, the steward discovered that someone had put soap in the food being served on the meal. A substitute dish was hurriedly prepared.
>
> However, when the inmate body began coming down the walk toward the dining hall, they turned right to the recreation field,

rather than left to enter the dining room. This was permitted since inmates who didn't care to eat an evening meal were allowed to go on out to the recreation field.

The two associate wardens conferred and decided to allow the men to remain on the athletic field till the normal time to return to quarters, just before sundown. And so the recreation period went ahead with all normal appearances. When recall sounded, the entire group began to move off the yard.

Suddenly a group of problem inmates began yelling, "Let's don't go off the field." A few of them began to threaten others. Suddenly the movement off the yard turned, went back to the recreation field, and there began to be a milling about of inmates. Over in the center of the yard, a group of Latin American inmates, who had one of these rhythm bands with tom-tom type instruments, began, in a slow movement, to play. Gradually the crescendo of that tom-tom beating increased . . . slowly, gradually, and inexorably. Inmates began to mill around more and more, and then a cry went up, "Let's take the administration building!"

Mob psychology seemed to take over, and a large group began a mad rush toward the administration building.

The associate wardens signaled for tear gas, and the barrage stopped the movement. The men began to saunter back, talking, some laughing. But all the time the tom-toms were beating, louder . . . louder . . . and in a moment another group at the far end of the field said, "Let's take the warehouse!"

A tower officer laid down a barrage of tracer bullets through the twilight and that movement stopped. But there was one inmate who ran into that line of tracer bullets and was hit. A lieutenant came out and asked several inmates to help take him off the field. Immediately a group of the inmates said, "Let's get the officer. They're trying to kill some of our boys."

One inmate with a club attempted to hit the lieutenant, and finally the officer said, "Look, boys, one of your guys has been hit here. He ran into the line of fire. We're going to get him off now. I'll come back, but first we're going to get him off."

The inmates allowed them to take the boy off the field. The lieutenant then came back and, lo and behold, nobody troubled him. Apparently they respected the action he had taken.

After that it became apparent that the thing was getting entirely out of control. The tom-toms continued to beat, yelling took over, some of the boys started some wild dances to this music. A group went over to one of the dormitories, broke in a door, began breaking window glass. They dragged mattresses out of dormitories, started bonfires, and so it went from that time, which was perhaps eight o'clock, until shortly after midnight.

By that time, some of the boys who hadn't had anything to eat —the evening's fun wearing off—came out of the group and said, "We think we can get this settled if certain propositions were made, such as no reprisals."

The acting wardens sent back word that there would be no physical reprisals. The inmates well knew federal policy on that score. But they could be assured that there would be an investigation, that the leaders would be held responsible, that good time would be forfeited, and that the normal disciplinary procedures of the prison system would be exercised to the fullest.

Within a few minutes after that, the inmates said, "What the heck—we're tired, we're sleepy," and they went in and bedded down for the night, leaving the smouldering mattresses out in the yard, broken windows in the dormitory.

At about daybreak, I arrived at Chillicothe, having flown out during the night from Washington. Immediately we sat down to discuss what had caused it, what needed to be done. The first thing we did was get a representative group of inmates together, about thirty-five or forty of them.

I said, "Well, what's all this about?"

All seemed to agree that the complaint had been one of light evening meals—in their judgment, too light; as the inmates put it, "No chewing meat." In looking over the menus, we did find that the evening meals were light, much lighter than the noon meal. We made changes in the distribution of food between the various meals. It cost us no more, and generally that is pretty much the story.

We had damage out there in the neighborhood of $4,000, which was really exceptionally light. It took a few days to get the institution back to normal, but now one would never know that this group of seventeen, eighteen, nineteen year olds, a thousand of them, had pulled a riot.

The fact that we have made some adjustments in the menus indicates that there were reasons for complaint. But one very interesting finding of our investigation was that the demonstration did not start off to be a riot at all. Some of the more stable inmates had reached a decision that the only way to call attention to the food problem would be to stage a nonviolent demonstration. That's the way it started, and that was the only intent.

But then this group of more unstable youngsters saw an opportunity to really let loose. Perhaps only twenty or twenty-five of them began yelling and suddenly the leaders of the nonviolent demonstration completely lost control, the less stable took over and this riot was on our hands.

When Alexander told us this story, we felt it was too pat. We investigated. Without hearing Alexander's tape, ex-inmates told us their side of the story. It was exactly the same as Alexander's in every detail, except that they admitted that what he called "wild dances" were in reality a sex orgy. It was this orgy that tired the men out and led to the end of the riot.

"I guess we were just too ashamed to go on," said one kid. "None of us had ever seen anything like that—hundreds of . . . things going on at once. It was hard to look anyone in the face the next day."

This came from a known punk.

This was the only riot that stemmed solely from the question of food, though no riot leader omitted food from his list of riot demands. Where men have little else to occupy them, food assumes tremendous importance. And any institution will have "institutional food," be it school, hospital, army, or prison. However, it can be good institutional food. "Federal," under a man fortuitously named Shadrack "Chic" Sale, has the best food we tasted in any prison system, despite the fact that we ate "warden's food" elsewhere and "off the line" in "Federal." Sale told us:

Often we find that the so-called paper work in institutions may look very good, but it's back on the firing line, in the kitchen, where attention is needed.

The three important things in feeding incarcerated people is not so much what they get to eat, but how it's prepared; the cleanliness of the department; and the way it's served in the dining room. The food department must be always on the alert for new ideas and new dishes and lack of repetition on the menus, doing away with monotony so that the inmate can't tell the day of the week simply by looking at the menu.[2] It's well to plan menus on a ten-day plan, instead of a seven-day plan for that specific purpose.

---

[2] This was Smitty's complaint in Jersey.

Sale also deplored the fact that, while protein and calorie charts look good, the best food often goes out the back door of many prison kitchens instead of into the mess hall. He also pointed out that, when a prison claims that most of its inmates go out weighing more than when they went in it may be a sign that money is being saved by the serving of too many cheap starches.[3]

What happened at Chillicothe was pure carelessness. One of the officials, a man notorious for his personal disinterest in food, just could not understand anyone else being interested. Result: riot.

But unlike other riots, officials in the federal system admitted the reason for the riot and did something about it. In the other riot spots that we covered, usually top officials hedged. But Bennett said, "For every riot there are reasons."

His assistant, Frank Loveland, expanded on this when he said:

> For years we have been trying to tell the public what is wrong. We have been trying to point out that the very conditions that make prisons inefficient and ineffectual as correctional institutions are the same that generate prison riots.
>
> While the public has reason to be concerned over riots and their results, they should have even more concern over the prison product, the sixty thousand persons released each year from prisons throughout the country. The penal institutions of this country are not doing the best job society has the right to expect. This is emphasized by the fact that 60 to 70 per cent [4] of the offenders committed to prison have already had previous prison or reformatory records. This failure rate, though it does not make the headlines and lacks the dramatic effect of riots, is many times as costly in both life and property.

This was backed up by the American Prison Association, an organization dedicated to the study of crime and prisons, which put out a report on the riots. In its preface this report states:

---

[3] In a well-run prison with good food, regular living will also put pounds on the boys.

[4] In 1952 the figure was 60.6 per cent.

It is believed, by some, that prison riots are at least partially related to mass rebellion. . . . This thesis . . . should not be seized upon as a convenient excuse or a pat explanation for prison riots.

We believe that . . . prison riots are . . . the direct result of shortsighted neglect . . . amounting to almost criminal negligence . . . by governors, legislators, governing boards, directors, wardens. . . .

Prison riots should be looked upon as costly and dramatic symptoms of faulty prison administration.[5]

Strangely, one of the signatories to the above is that staunch advocate of the "mass rebellion" theory, Sanford Bates.

Admitting that any breakdown in listing riot causes would have to be artificial because "there is obvious overlapping between categories," the report "for emphasis and convenience" divides riot causes into seven categories:

(1) Inadequate financial support and official and public indifference.
(2) Excessive size and overcrowding of institutions.
(3) Substandard personnel.
(4) Enforced idleness.
(5) Unwise sentencing and parole practices.
(6) Lack of professional leadership and professional programs.
(7) Political domination of management.

The overlapping quality of that categorization is obvious, even at first glance. And no state-prison riots we investigated stemmed from any one thing. Each was always the product of all seven of these administrative, legislative, and public failures working in concert. We found also that these failings could be found in prisons where riots had not happened, but these prisons were considered, by penologists, to be poor. Here are the seven deadly sins of our American prisons. They are worth studying.

---

[5] "Prison Riots and Disturbances," prepared by the committee on riots under the auspices of the American Prison Association. Pp. 5, 6.

(1) *Inadequate financial support,
and official and public indifference.*

Probably the single statement most often made to us was:
"Prisons are the last thing on a budget to receive money and
the first thing to be cut. People don't want to spend money on
prisons."

And it was pointed out that anyone who advocates more
money for prisons is immediately accused of wanting to
"mollycoddle" convicts. Seldom heeded are the arguments that
it is false economy to let men out who are prepared for no
life save one of crime. However, it has been proved that money
properly spent on men in prison saves more money later. It
costs less to treat a man than to pay insurance on his later
crimes, to pay police to catch him again, courts to try him
again, and prisons to board him again.

Michigan, despite its present rejection of this argument, has
figures to back it up:

> In 1942, when there wasn't a treatment program at Jackson,
> of all the men that came into that prison, 58 per cent had been
> there before. In 1951, after a treatment program had been in ef-
> fect, of all the men that came in, only 42 per cent had been
> there before, showing a drop of 16 per cent. If you take the cost of
> that 16 per cent in terms of damage done to society, you'll find
> that a treatment program is economical.

Going about it in the opposite way, Ohio also proved that
being penny-wise on treatment is being pound-foolish in subsequent costs. At the state maximum-security prison in the heart
of Columbus, Warden R. W. Alvis had tried to initiate a treatment program, but he had a riot caused almost entirely by the
shortness of his budget.

"Big Red" Alvis taught us one important lesson. Peg and I,
like almost every layman we met, felt that, given a prison of our
very own, we could do a much better job than those now
bumbling through the job. Alvis showed us what crazy, mixed-
up kids we were.

Big Red has every attribute considered necessary for an
ideal warden. He is, first of all, a *man* in the convict sense of

the word. Most inmates, being emotionally immature, admire physical strength. But more, they respect self-confidence and a definite personality. A man who says "no" to an inmate request is better liked than one who says "maybe" or "yes" without meaning it. When Red says something, he means it.

Physically big, he has a florid, honest face. An ex-football player (pro and college), ex-construction worker, and ex-state cop, he has had many years of penal experience. When he took over at Columbus, he did more than talk prison reform; despite handicaps he got results. As he put it:

> It has been my philosophy that each inmate is subject to return to society. The treatment he receives in prison will have a direct bearing on how he will act when he does return to society. If you treat a person like a dog, he will react like a dog.
>
> With that in mind, we have established many changes for the betterment of the inmates. We doubled the number of inmates that were in the educational program. In our hospital we have increased the outside clinics so that we have practically all the specialists in Columbus holding clinics for the men. At the beginning of our administration we eliminated the lock step and allowed talking in the mess hall. We have inaugurated an entirely new prerelease program.

Further, Alvis became one of the few Ohio wardens who could go anywhere in the prison without a bodyguard. On the debit side of the ledger, however, is the prison itself. Said Alvis:

> Our plant was originally built in 1831, and since 1930 there has been very little building or remodeling. We are set up to handle twenty-five hundred inmates. We have forty-seven hundred.
>
> Our cells are seven feet wide, seven feet high and nine feet deep. In these cells, if two men want to go to bed, all four have to go to bed. These cells have a maximum cubic air space of some six hundred cubic feet. The state law of Ohio requires that at least three hundred cubic feet of air space be supplied for each prisoner. The warden of the Ohio penitentiary is probably the largest law violator of the state because he has twenty-four hundred men incarcerated in violation of the state law.

This is not a new situation. For years Ohio prison men have asked for money to either build a new prison, or better, several new prisons, to house the inmates not only more comfortably, but in a manner that will allow for segregation and treatment. Supporting these demands have been the citizens of Columbus. However, their motivation was not prompted by worrying over inmate welfare.

Columbus is a city gripped by fear. An inmate escape will start a panic, and in 1930 a fire sent the citizenry into a state of shock from which it still has not recovered. But in 1930 it was prisoners, not Columbians who were hurt. Sugar Bill Baliff, a bank robber doing fifty years told us:

In 1930 we had 5,126 men in the place. They lived under the hospital, they lived in the corridors, they were scattered all over, because we didn't have enough of blocks of cells. That was the reason they started to build a new block. In one hundred years they built just one new block, and that was the block that went on fire Easter of 1930—a beautiful day.

The fire started between half-past four and five o'clock in the afternoon. Every man was in his cell block. I was in the old block that's been standing there for over one hundred years. Smoke was seen coming out of the new block. A cry went out. Men were yelling to be taken out. They didn't have automatic locks in that prison, where you would pull the bar and it would spring all the cells at one time. The main key was in the guard room. A guard asked the warden for the main skeleton key and he refused. He was worried about some men going over the wall.

First they called for the Columbus police department to surround the prison. Then they got some young sailors that were training around Mansfield, Ohio. And, only after they surrounded the prison, a few guards had the courage and the guts to open the cells.

By then, in the sixth range, the fifth range, and the fourth range, the men were dead already—gassed to death. The framework of this new block was that Georgia pine, the cheapest kind of wood, full of knots and rosin; and they had paper, a heavy black paper, to hold the wood. Naturally, when that started to burn, it was nothing but a deadly poison. And that's what killed—it wasn't the fire. A few were burned, but the rest were gassed to death. We all admit that the sixth range was already gone, but they could have saved the men on the fourth range; they could have saved some men on the fifth range, but there was no move made.

In my cell block, we was getting the smoke from the other block and we started to shout to be taken out. Finally two men came along with sledge hammers, and we started to break the locks. Then a few guards came around and started to open up our block, which was not on fire, and we all started to run into the block where it was burning. We started to move the men. We didn't have enough of stretchers, so we used blankets. Some of the boys died locked together. After we got them all out in the yard, we counted them—322.

Well, the recap was that they said two men set the fire; but, according to the grapevine of the institution, that wasn't so. It was poor wiring that caused it.

Evidently discouraged by the loss of its new block, Ohio passed a law forbidding any new building inside the penitentiary—only "repair and maintenance" work, which kept the place in condition to allow more men to be crammed within the walls.

True, there was much talk about the need for a new prison, but the legislature did not want to be rushed. For twenty years it showed such admirable control that it only once came close to appropriating funds for the purpose. But then it was only kidding, for while money was designated for a new prison, no money was allocated to buy land for it nor was any land available. When time ran out on the appropriation without anyone's solving the architectural problem of hanging a prison from sky-hooks, the legislature felt that there had been enough activity to warrant its relaxing a while longer.

It was during this period that Alvis became warden. Despite petitions against it, he found a way to relieve overcrowding in a small way. He instituted minimum-security camps* around the state. Their continued existence was touch and go for a while, until Alvis was able to appeal to Ohio's great big soft heart by showing that camps saved money for the state.

But he still had too many prisoners in Columbus for the equipment and money he was given to handle them. Conclusive proof of this came on Halloween, 1952, when the Ohio

State Prison formally joined the list of "disturbed" institutions with one wingding of a riot.

Here again, it was the usual story of destruction, fires and vendettas. The inmates started to throw cabbages at the guards. As one guard said:

"What could we do? When I got hit by a salt cellar I sat down over in a corner, put salt on a cabbage, and ate it."

While guards ate cabbage, Big Red strode out into the mess hall (where, as usual, the whole thing had started) stood upon a table and outyelled the rioters. He succeeded, by pure force of personality, in quieting a few; but the hysteria had spread to the yard, and it took the combined forces of the state and city police to finally herd the inmates to their cells. Since most of the locks were broken by this time, state police kept the place quiet with leveled guns. Due to the steel shortage, many of the locks still had to be replaced when we got there.

But by that time, Alvis had become a legend with the inmates. Despite the fact that several inmates themselves had told him (not threatened him) to get out of the yard because he might accidentally get hurt, he stayed there. They swore that at one time he tried to settle the thing by offering to "take on" any six rioters at once. This Alvis denies, although guards told us the same story. At any rate, no six inmates took him up on it, but some forty-five hundred of them worship him for the offer.

Most of the inmates we talked to realized what Alvis was trying to do inside the walls, especially by his abolishment of the guided tours that had, for the sake of additional prison income, let teen-age babes in shorts tour the prison to see the funny animals in their cages.

But few of the inmates could understand why Alvis still had a bad prison. One kid, brought out of the hole in handcuffs to talk to us, asked why a swell guy like Alvis hired the guards he did.

"Is Warden Alvis so stupid he doesn't know what these bastards do when he's not around?" Maybe the kid was dangerous, maybe he did have to be handcuffed as he sat in that heavily barred room with us, but tears ran down his face when he choked out those words.

Alvis is not that stupid. Despite the fact that he never asked us to, we later played back that tape to him. He blushed as only a redhead can, and halfway through he banged his big fist on the table.

God damn it, what can I do? If a guy can dig a ditch, he doesn't become a prison guard, because he doesn't make as much money. I've had guys leave here after one day because they could make more money downtown. And right now, if they take the state troopers away, I won't have even what I've got for guards. Do I know what's going on? God damn it, what am I supposed to do?

Alvis is a redhead who has learned to control himself, but when he does let loose, it hurts. He banged out of the room without another word. Later, on tape, he gave us a very controlled statement about how guards needed higher wages. He would not criticize his personnel. Nor would he condemn those who, with a sixty-million-dollar surplus in the Ohio treasury, gave him pennies when he needed dollars.

"After all," he smiled wryly, "I got to work with what I've got."

(2) *Excessive Size and Overcrowding of Institutions*

This riot cause is, of course, tied closely to "inadequate financial support." Despite an ever increasing crime rate, little new money is being spent to house the growing convict population. Instead, inmates are continually being crammed into big houses that are, at the same time, not big enough to house them adequately and too big to do a job of rehabilitation.

Since its riot, Ohio has again appropriated money for a new prison and this time the legislature has even provided for some land. But Peg and I found it hard to get information about this action. Often quoted to us was: "Ohio is the cradle of the presidency." The main trouble we found in the Buckeye state was that almost every public official felt that the cradle rocked only for him.

Already in 1952, state legislators hesitated to make statements because, as they explained in hushed tones, 1956 was coming and they did not want to commit themselves on anything as unpleasant as prisons.

Governor Lausche's secretary made this quite clear when she said: "Governor Lausche will be a strong contender for the Presidency in 1956, so he could not comment on prisons. However, he has issued some bulletins on the subject, which he has sent to the press."

Thus we never received the answer to the question we most wanted answered. Building a new prison is important, but even more important is the type of prison to be built. A maximum-security prison can be one of the world's most expensive edifices. The tons of concrete, brick, and tool-proof steel that go into a wall surrounding acres of land and into more walls surrounding inside escape-proof cells cost enough to give pause to the richest of states.

The rub lies in the fact that, despite the propaganda of steel and concrete salesmen, using these 100 per cent maximum-security fortresses is as efficient as swatting flies with a steamroller.

The leadership toward more efficient, less costly prisons, is, at the present time, in the hands of the federal system. James Bennett is a stubborn man, and, despite contrary pressures, he has held on to the idea of less and less costly security and more and more treatment efficiency.

The penitentiary at Terre Haute, Indiana, is an example. Instead of an expensive concrete wall, it has an inexpensive double barbed-wire fence with accordion rolls in the center. Besides being less expensive than concrete, this provides perfect visibility for guards and no hiding places for escapees. However, since it has no wall, old-time prison men do not consider Terre Haute a maximum-security house, despite the fact that there has never been an escape over this fence. This is a claim few of our "escape-proof" bastilles can make. Much of the planning of Terre Haute came from "federal's" senior architect, Robert Barnes. He told us:

> Too many state prisons are old and have not been kept up to date. They're too large and have been a football for political people rather than being planned and handled by trained prison administrators and builders.
>
> Thirteen per cent of the prison buildings in use in the United States are over one hundred years old. Most of them have large

cell blocks, no recreational areas, and too many prisoners. They have a preponderance of steel cells, steel bars, cut-off grills, and not enough light or air. From an architectural point of view, the worst thing on the American scene is these old patched-up prisons. Take the New Jersey State Prison, which was started in 1836. It has had seventeen additions over the years, and it is most inadequate for any good treatment program. Prison planners must stop the extending of old institutions and must start planning small diversified institutions having only a minimum of maximum-custody facilities, where treatment can be carried out.

After all, the architecture of a penal institution reflects the philosophy of the group running it. Having just returned from a two months' visit to the prisons in Germany, this was brought home to me. In Germany it is felt that prisoners must be in solitary confinement, that it is harmful for them to talk to each other. This reflects itself in buildings consisting of single rooms where prisoners are held in solitary confinement, working and eating only in his cell. Walking in the courtyards constitutes their only outdoor exercise.

This is opposite to the federal system's way of thinking. Our idea is that we have people in prison to make them better. To accomplish this we have a variety of housing, using not only cells, but dormitories, cubicles, honor rooms. We have day rooms where people can congregate and talk over their problems, indulge in games. We have athletic fields instead of exercise courts. We have large industrial buildings where people can work together. We use mass feeding—we use large mess halls and central kitchens.

It is our belief that prisoners should be taught to work with the most modern equipment and in the most efficient manner, and they should work as close to eight hours every day as possible. Our whole institutional program and our design of the buildings is based on that premise. Many of these men have never worked, never held jobs, have not been taught to work; and we must not only teach them new trades, but we must teach them the most efficient trades on the most modern equipment.

Also, we do not believe that all inmates have to be housed in inside cells or even outside cells. This has made it possible to open up our plans and change the character and the appearance of the physical buildings, especially since we use much cheaper materials than tool-proof steel. During the period 1938-40 the Bureau of Prisons constructed about fifteen million dollars' worth of prison buildings and probably used only about $500 worth of tool-proof steel. During that time we also constructed not over two hundred cells with steel walls. We usually used concrete blocks, which in many cases were made on the institution grounds."

Bennett agreed with all that Barnes had to say, with one reservation. A plant, he pointed out, was less important than personnel. If he had to make a choice, because of a limited amount of money, between plant and personnel, he would use existing facilities, relieve the crowding by opening up camps (it has been found that only about 20 per cent of all prisoners need maximum security anyway), and splurge on personnel.

"If you have the right people and can keep from being too crowded, you can run a good prison in a barn," he concluded. "It's harder if you have a bad plant, but it can be done."

Bennett has proved this, literally. The Federal House of Detention in New York is housed in an old garage, yet Warden Thompson has one of this country's few good jails, one that proves that the city and county monstrosities that we have come to know need not exist.

The Federal Bureau is trying to do something about jails. Part of Myrl Alexander's job is to inspect them and run an educational program for their personnel, but he points out:

The jail is usually administered by a sheriff, who serves only a two-year term of office. If he is defeated, another man comes into office. Jail personnel changes constantly. They're untrained; they simply are people who come into work in the jail for a few years. By and large, we can say that the average jail is little more than a moral cesspool in the community.

Yet there are hopeful signs. Some of our jails are putting in intensive training programs for personnel, and we are very hopeful about the program that we have been carrying on of making available a correspondence course to any jail official in the country. So, while progress is slow, while the jail remains at the lowest level of modern correctional practice, there is hope and progress is being made.

What can any individual citizen do about the total prison problem? First of all, in his community there is a jail. He can visit the jail, he can help his sheriff learn about the training facilities that are available and the advice he can get. Perhaps, if you do this, it may not be too long until jails, through which pass all people who go to prison, through which go somewhat more than a million people a year, can become much more constructive instruments in the community than they have been in their long and pretty sordid history.

(3) *Substandard Personnel*

As we saw in Ohio, this is a direct outgrowth of too little money, as are the inadequate plants. But, as Bennett said, personnel is the more important consideration.

We found around the country that guards, in many ways, have a worse life than inmates. Dr. Teeters of Temple University told us:

> I saw a man in an observatory tower in Eastern.[6] He's been there thirty years, every day, doesn't see a soul. Goes up there in the morning, away up there in that tower. He eats his lunch up there, he has no radio, all he does is stand up there or sit on a stool and he's been in that prison since 1920.

Big Smitty said, "At least us guys get out. Screws end up with nothing."

Some states pay guards as little as $100 per month. Then, more often than not, what men they can have at the price receive no training even in the prison. Said an Illinois guard, "I was given a block by myself my first day. I had to ask the cons where the keys were."

This man, more intelligent than the usual guard we met, had quit prison work to go into a factory, as had his boss, the captain of the guard. The pay was better. The amount of self-respect most guards have can be judged by the fact that they call themselves "screws." Yet it is these screws whose job it is to rehabilitate as they guard. Only in the federal system did we find guards that showed promise of being more than "screws."

The federal civil-service exam is hard enough so that only the qualified make it. These men are then made into "officers and gentlemen" as "Federal" weeds out all but the "career" man

---

[6] Eastern State Penitentiary in Pennsylvania.

by intensive on-the-job training that gives each recruit a taste of every aspect of prison work. Bennett says proudly, "Our future wardens are at this minute walking the walls."

Warden Paul Madigan, now at the federal penitentiary at Terre Haute, started as a "screw" at Alcatraz. When he was introduced to us, he was associate warden in charge of custody, and we could imagine this tough Irishman practicing rehabilitation with a "club alongside the head." But practically the first thing he said to us was, "The tremendous need we feel here is for more intensive psychiatric treatment for the inmates."

This, coming from a custody man, was a new experience. We were used to such reactions as we got from Commissioner Mike Seyfrit of Illinois, who said, "We don't bother to IQ 'em much in Illinois."

We grew to have tremendous respect for Madigan. He had been known as the toughest guard at Alcatraz when he first came into the federal system because of the depression. Expecting to be a guard only until he could find a "decent" job, he was not too happy when Bennett began his campaign of rehabilitation by working with the inmates rather than by working them over. Then, much to his surprise, Madigan found out that he liked working with men. Mark Richmond, Terre Haute's associate warden in charge of individual treatment, said that by the time Madigan got to Terre Haute, he spent more time treating individuals than almost any other man on the staff.

Inmate reaction to Madigan was consistent on two points. He is still tough—the toughest official at Terre Haute—but every inmate went out of his way to extol his fairness and the fact that he was a "man." The screw had developed into an officer. Bennett's theory that officers too need rehabilitation paid off.

Though his story is dramatic, Madigan is not exceptional in the federal system. Richmond is a serious hard-working student. Former warden Overlade, who became interested in prisons when he was a bookkeeper for the federal system, knew enough practical psychology to keep his budget up by coddling congressional investigators and his recidivist rate down by

knowing when not to coddle inmates. He defined his job as
being part salesman, part administrator, part foxy grandpa.

A Mormon by religion, he is religious in his work. The
only time he stood us up on an appointment was when he was
stuck for four hours in the hole with an inmate he felt was
psychologically ready to go back into general population and
start some training classes. We asked if he thought the boy
was rehabilitated. He shook his head sadly:

"No. He'll be back in the hole again. But he goes back less
often now than he did. He'll come along. But sometimes it's
so slow."

Captain of the Guard W. F. Anderson is the best pistol shot
in the system, having defeated FBI men and T men in inter-
bureau competitions. He is now an associate warden, and, like
Madigan, he is as much a treatment man as he is a custodian.

We looked for men like these in the riot spots we investigated,
but there the constant cry was "too little money to get good
people." However, we also found that some of the rioting
prisons had higher budgets per inmate than federal prisons.
The difference lay in the handling of the money.

Bennett says:

> Of course a prison man must have a good salary. That's im-
> portant. But, also important, there must be tenure of office, and
> personnel must not be subjected to the political whims and vicis-
> situdes of changing administrations.
>
> The federal system is able to attract able men because the
> average salary is now about $300 a month. An officer receives
> leave at the rate of twenty-six working days a year and, most
> important, can retire at the age of fifty after twenty years of serv-
> ice. That brings into the federal prison system able men who
> learn to appreciate the importance of their jobs.
>
> Around our institutions, however, I find men who stay in the
> service because of the satisfactions and rewards that come be-
> cause they are able to shape and mold and condition other men's
> lives. It's surprising how many of our officers will receive a letter
> from a discharged inmate, treasure it, and carry it about with
> them to show to their friends. It's their compensation for what
> sometimes is a disagreeable and, not infrequently, dangerous
> job. But in no other field of work can those inner satisfactions
> come in the degree to which they occur in a well-organized prison.

Bennett broke down his costs for us: "Operating federal institutions costs $3.55 per man per day. Two dollars, or over half of that money, goes toward paying personnel."

Bennett puts first things first.

(4) *Enforced Idleness*

The federal system has another feather in its cap. Against odds, it has been able to keep prison industries going to the extent that, at Atlanta, the over-all cost of operating the institution is completely offset by money made out of its industries. Atlanta does not cost the taxpayers a dime, but unfortunately it is the only self-supporting prison in America.

Most state houses are having a difficult time even keeping their industries going, much less make much money out of them. This is harder on the inmate than the taxpayer.

The American Prison Association says:

> When agitators strike the spark that starts a riot, idle prisoners flare into revolt as dry and crumbling tinder bursts into flame. . . . In spite of the solemn sentencing of prisoners to "hard labor," the most striking characteristic of the great majority of our prisons . . . has been an atmosphere of dry rot.

As we saw in New Jersey, this is a dilemma that the public itself has forced on the prisons. While it does not want to pay taxes to "coddle the bastards," it resents a prison's competing to make money for self-support. Federal and state laws reflect the farmers' opposition to prison agriculture, the manufacturers' dislike of prison industries, and the unions' refusal to allow in-service training of inmates. Many states allow prisons to sell only to state agencies, but even this last outlet for prison goods is being outlawed. Metal workers and manufacturers want license-plate stamping given to private industry; printers resent even the printing of prison forms inside the walls; and national lobbies battle every can of food that comes off institutional land into a prison commissary. Even during the war, with labor and material at a premium, the prisons were often prevented from supplying for national defense those items with which they were overstocked.

Faced with a diminishing market, prison-industry men have fewer and fewer jobs with which to occupy their ever growing populations. This mounting idleness not only increases tensions but defeats any training that might prepare the inmate for release. He comes out with no training at all; or, worse, he comes out with years of training for a trade only to find that this training did him more harm than good because he was working on inefficient, outdated machines. If the prisons spent money for efficient machines (an expense legislators view dimly) then even fewer men would be kept busy.

A survey might be valuable if it compared the rate of returnees to the disappointment suffered by inmates who are victimized by this basically dishonest practice.

I asked one inmate about his earlier term in a reform school. Did he have any vocational training—did he learn anything he could use when he got out? "Yeah," he said, "I learned how to start a car without the key and how to jimmy a window."

He is now in a federal prison for interstate transportation of a stolen vehicle. Ironically, his earlier incarceration had been in California. Recently, due to yeoman work by Earl Warren, this has become the only state where the unions and the manufacturers' associations have decided that crime costs them more in the long run than prison competition does in the short view. There only has anything like a solution been worked out. But then too, California is more advanced on other phases of penology, as, for example, in its sentencing procedures.

(5) *Unwise Sentencing and Parole Practices*

There is enough to be said about this particular riot cause to fill many volumes—and it has. But no real solution has been worked out yet, although there are some hopeful signs. James V. Bennett points out:

> Courts and judges approach from many viewpoints the matter of disposing of the offender. There's the factor of deterring others from crime, and there is punitive or retributive justice. This is the Mosaic concept of justice, the doctrine of an eye for an eye and a tooth for a tooth. Another important consideration

is social protection against the offender. This factor looms large in the cases of narcotic and sex offenders. We try to protect the public by quarantining the offender. Incidentally, this is the factor which underlies much of the European theory of protective custody.

Another factor is the extent and the nature of the injury caused by the offender. This, of course, partially overlaps the idea of punitive justice, but the fellow who steals only ten dollars is not considered in the same category as the man who steals half a million dollars.

Now the factor that judges should take into account is the salvageability of the offender. Is the man worth spending some money on and worth saving? A young person may commit a relatively minor offense. His whole background may show that he is in need of training, and therefore the judge should determine how long it would take to teach him to be an automobile mechanic or a good welder.

And I think the judge should take into account the attitude of the offender, the extent, for instance, to which he cooperated with the government in the solution of the crime, his degree of remorsefulness and sincerity.

Sentencing has been debated and tested and considered ever since society began trying to find a formula for enforcing its laws. Time was when reliance was placed almost entirely on striking fear into the heart of the offender. Later we had the theory that the prisoner had to expiate his crime, that he owed a debt to society that he had to pay off. Of course, that's a false philosophy. No man can possibly pay a debt for bringing human suffering and harm upon some other individual, and he doesn't owe a debt to society as a whole. That theory has been pretty well relegated into limbo.

In our whole field of law enforcement, there's no problem more baffling. Unfortunately, views vary widely, which means that sentences are widely inconsistent. Inconsistent sentences spell trouble in prisons. Men compare their sentences; and, if one of them feels that he has been unjustly treated, then bitterness arises in him, and that gives place to frustrations that break out into disturbances and maladjustments. Prisoners rationalize their crimes. Each thinks he's an eight-ball Willie who just happened to get caught, and he thinks he just had a poor attorney or he didn't have the right connections because he sees other men in prison who did worse than he did and yet received shorter sentences.

There is not very much that the prison warden can do about this problem. A great many people feel that the solution to the problem of sentencing lies in the indeterminate sentence and in the so-called sentencing tribunal. The late Governor Alfred E. Smith of New York believed that the courts should be relieved of meting out specific sentences, that the legislature should merely specify the maximum sentence for a particular offense. The judge would determine the issue of guilt or innocence and a group of experts would gather information concerning the offense, would analyze the character and the behavior of the offender, would determine the extent to which that person might be dangerous to society, and then determine just how long he should remain in prison.

Substantially that system is in effect in the state of California, where the judge merely determines the maximum period to be served by the offender and turns the prisoner over to an adult authority. This authority gives the prisoner an interview at the time he is admitted to the institution; its members examine the reports of the doctors and the psychiatrists and the case workers, and then they decide when the prisoner will come up for parole and just how long he will have to remain in the institution. The system has been in operation in California for some years now and is generally accepted as a progressive and forward-looking system.

But in most states, as was often pointed out to us by prisoner and prison official alike, the sentences are entirely up to the judges, who are influenced by the volatile and changing tempers of their electorate. This can result in situations such as the one concerning two chicken thieves who went to trial in the same state before judges in different counties. One was given a term of ten years (in a chicken-raising county); the other, a term of ninety days (in a nonchicken-raising county). Legal technicalities can also work great unfairness. There was the man given a federal rap of up to twenty years for stealing one can of beans. The country store this hungry bum chose to burgle was also a rural post office. Though he touched no mail and robbed no money, a judge used a legal technicality to "make an example" of him.

In an attempt to tailor sentences to the needs of the individual offender, many states have "indeterminate sentences,"

which gives maximum and a minimum number of years to be
served. But this plan has not worked out too well.

Judges have often let their sentencing lose the elasticity the
indeterminate sentence is supposed to have. While it is legally
"indeterminate," a sentence of thirty to thirty-one years bypasses
the purpose of the law. A single sentence of one year to life
for all felonies has been suggested as the most useful of indeterminate sentences. This would then leave a man's release up
to the prison and the parole board working together.

But here again, this could work only if more intensive work
were done with inmates. As it is, inmates show little understanding and much resentment of the indeterminate sentence.
Often they presented long quasi-legal arguments showing us
why they should automatically be released at the end of their
minimum sentences no matter what their record in or out of
prison. They feel that, when they are imprisoned past that
minimum, it is because they lack connections to get through
to the "crooked parole board." The fact that, by law in some
states, they cannot be paroled simply because they have become "institutionalized" and have never been sent to the hole,
is lost on them.

Then too, several men gave us an almost irrefutable argument when they said: "The parole board ain't supposed to
let us out until we're rehabilitated—we know this. But the
prison does nothing to rehabilitate us, so they gotta parole all
of us or none of us."

Since in many prisons there is no recognizable rehabilitation
program, it is understandable that these men are puzzled when
some men are paroled and others are not. But then too, we also
found many puzzled parole officials. Too often, for instance,
parole boards are forced to consider not prisoners but the latest headlines about one of their parolees who has committed
a murder. Then they begin to feel that they are paroling many
too many men rather than that they may have paroled the
wrong man because of inadequate study or understanding.

Parole boards suffer most of the same inadequacies as do
prisons, and they have the additional stigma of public disfa-
vor. Said Frank Loveland, assistant director in charge of parole for the federal system:

Parole is usually thought of as clemency, as just a way for a prisoner to leave the prison before his term expires. This is not true. The real purpose of parole is to better protect the public by releasing the man when he is best prepared to accept the responsibilities of citizenship, when he can best support himself in the community.

Another important element of parole is that the inmate should receive supervision while he is in the community. Statistics show that at least 50 per cent of all ex-convicts who break laws and come back to prison do so within the first few months after their release. That indicates very clearly that the early period after release is a very critical period in the offender's life. It is the time when a released man most needs supervision.

I would say that, for an efficient parole system, there are four important requisites:

First, there must be a competent board of parole, composed of members who have an understanding of human nature and of the factors making for criminality.

Second, the board must have adequate information about the offender: his background, his accomplishments, his weaknesses, and his strengths. This information must be largely submitted by the prison.

Third, the institution program must prepare the man for his release. In too many prisons over the country the man is released with five dollars, an obviously prison-made suit of clothes, and he is expected to make his adjustment in the community without committing any further crime.

The fourth requisite is that there be competent, trained parole officers who can supervise him, assist him in making an adjustment in the community and who can report him back to the board of parole if he becomes a danger to the community.

But, as in prisons, that competent personnel is lacking. Although it costs as much to keep one man in prison as it does to keep many on parole, the economy of so doing is seldom considered in the form of adequate salaries for parole officers. We end up with substandard personnel enforcing unrealistic parole regulations. As Loveland said: "Some parole boards have rules that are excessively restrictive, which were written . . . years ago, when it was felt that every man who was released from an institution should be in by curfew time."

It was all of these factors working—or not working—together

then, that prompted riot leaders to include in their list of demands one that asked for the elimination of the indeterminate sentence and the abolition of the "crooked parole board."

Despite the fact that "crooked" was associated with "parole board" in prison much as "damn" is tied to "Yankee" in the South, we found no evidence of dishonesty—in fact quite the contrary. But the boards, overworked, underfinanced, have become trapped into unfairness, as MacCormick pointed out in Michigan, or the hurried job he decried in New Jersey.

Smitty came up for parole in Jersey and his description of the interview is revealing. He was asked: "Do you know this is the parole board?"

Said Smitty to us, "I been waiting years to talk to these guys. Do I know this is the parole board?"

Next question was, did he want a parole?

"I'm going to say I'm hungry to stay in?"

Did he have anything to say?

Smitty admitted he had escaped once, had held an honest job for two years before being caught again, and had served three years flat for that escape. He now had only two years more to go on his original sentence, and he had never served time in the hole. It took Smitty some thirty seconds to say this, but he said he noticed the board members looking impatiently at their watches. He shut up.

"We'll let you know," he was told.

They did. He served the two more years flat. Perhaps they were justified in their decision but the reason was never explained to Smitty. He says now:

> They just want that place crowded so they can get money for a new prison. Look, Bates started the theory of short sentences and long paroles but his parole board sees that you get a long sentence and a short parole. The main reason for the riot in Jersey was the parole board.

True or not, Smitty was one of many who said much the same. It is unfortunate, because parole, the indeterminate sentence, and probation are considered the most progressive steps that can be taken by penology. But, until part of each inmate's program is education and training for parole, these devices will

neither serve the public nor help the inmate who fights them
to the extent of rioting in protest.

In Ohio, incidentally, we found that Alvis, in his new pre-
release program, starts teaching his "short" men about parole
months before he hits the bricks. Each inmate is put in civ-
vies, is given money to carry, and participates in round-table
discussions with Columbus businessmen who tell about life
and jobs outside.

Ohio was the only state where we heard no complaints
about parole. Inmates there seemed to understand it.

(6) *Lack of Professional Leadership*
and Professional Programs

Under this riot-cause heading, the American Prison Association points out that due to the lack of any program for the
training of penologists, prison jobs, "especially . . . the important posts of warden and department head," are filled "all
too often from the ranks of plain politicians." It goes on to
say that these men go into a prison and serve "their apprentice-
ships at the top and not at the bottom . . . often bringing
disaster." [7]

We found Illinois to be the best example of this. There
Mike Seyfrit was the director of public safety, and he ran
the prisons along with such things as the state police. Before
taking this job, he had been a small-town lawyer and he had
helped Adlai Stevenson campaign for the governor's chair.
Once governor, Stevenson put Seyfrit in charge of Illinois'
prisons. At the Menard Division of Illinois State Penitentiary,
Seyfrit in turn appointed Browning Robinson as warden.
Then Robinson, according to the guards, instituted "Democratic Civil Service," in contrast to the years of "Republican
Civil Service" they were used to under previous administrations.

This lasted until an investigation by Senator Peter J. Miller.
He told us:

We found generally unlimited laxity all through Menard . . .
specific instances of brutality, favoritism; the brewing and drink-

---

[7] "Prison Riots and Disturbances," pp. 12, 13.

ing of intoxicating beverages by the inmates; lack of discipline
among the employees; no supervision over trustees; agitation;
fraternizing of guards with inmates; violation of civil-service
laws; and many complaints as to the quality and quantity of
food, even though the food budget was overspent by $140,000.

And it was found that the warden used the prison bull to
service his own cows.

Robinson was put to pasture at the Illinois State Farm and
Jerome J. Munie took over at Menard. When we met Munie,
he had survived two riots and a scandal involving "voluntary
contributions" to the Stevenson gubernatorial campaign fund.
These contributions were so voluntary that, when they did
not come in fast enough in the assigned amounts,[8] Captain
Wood told us he was given the job of "talking to" those who
had not yet volunteered their contributions.

Part of Menard's program of rehabilitation consisted of giving the inmates who worked in the quarry all summer one bath
a week, keeping the place in a condition filthier than any slum
I have ever seen, and manufacturing products in the prison
industries that were turned down for use in other state institutions because of bad quality.

Mike Seyfrit could not understand why these products were
so bad despite the fact that, unlike other Illinois prisons including Joliet, the men were given no pay for working in industry at Menard. This puzzled him almost as much as the
fact that he could not hire good guards for Menard despite the
fact that they were paid not only less than they could earn in
industry, but even less than guards in other Illinois prisons.

However, it was during the riots that Menard officials
showed their professional leadership. Dick Dudman of the St.
Louis *Post-Dispatch* covered both Menard riots and he told us:

> One difficulty that the guards faced in attempting to quell the
> first riot was in connection with the water supply. The convicts,
> in taking over the cell house, got hold of a fire hose and squirted
> it out through the broken windows at the state police and the
> guards holding them at bay. Warden Munie right away sent for
> the head maintenance man of the prison. The maintenance man

---

[8] Guards, $20; sergeants, $25; lieutenants, $35; captains, $50.

at first couldn't be found. When they finally found him, he reported that he couldn't find the right wrench to turn off the water and stop the fire hose. When they finally found the wrench, then he couldn't find what valve to put the wrench on. They never did get that water turned off.

The riot finally ended after about thirty hours, when the state police fired riot guns at the men who were squirting the fire hose. Finally one of the shots hit a man, and with a blood curdling yell he dropped the hose, continued to scream and moan in agony for about twenty seconds, and the fire immediately went out of the convicts. Then state police and guards were able to enter the cell house and restore order.

After this riot, Seyfrit investigated his own department to see if it was in any way to blame for the riot. Seyfrit cleared Seyfrit but the ungrateful inmates went up again. The second riot became a national crisis.

(7) *Political Domination of Management*

Illinois exemplified this riot cause in more ways than one. Not only did politics touch prison personnel, but inmates at Menard admitted to us that the timing for their second riot was determined by the national presidential campaign. By that time Stevenson was off the state ticket and was campaigning for the Presidency. They felt they could embarrass him into conceding quickly to their demands just to shut them up.

With no results forthcoming from their earlier riot and their demands for better food, adequate clothing, and more baths, inmates felt they could not depend on Seyfrit to better conditions. One evening they took some guard hostages to the top tier of their block and threatened to throw them down on the concrete floor below unless Adlai Stevenson himself flew back from his campaigning and heard their demands. Seyfrit tried to avoid this by handling things himself; but, when the inmates of the mental institution (also located on the Menard prison grounds) started a simultaneous riot in their own building, Seyfrit gave in by bringing the inmates a lieutenant governor, Acting Governor Sherwood Dixon.

This was sufficient for the rioters in the mental hospital. Despite the fact that they had taken possession of a kitchen, where they spent their time eating and brandishing butcher knives at their hostages, they gave up easily when Dixon agreed to hear their demands for less brutality and better food.

But even in this surrender, Illinois' comedy of errors went on. Reporter Dudman told us:

> One of the complaints in the psycho riot was that the grievance box was not available to the inmates, that they could not send a complaint to the warden. Warden Munie said this was nonsense.
> One of the inmates said, "Look, our suggestion box is taped over." He pointed across the room, and, sure enough, there was tape across the slot in the box. Somebody went over and tore the tape off and it was obvious the tape had been there for months and months.

Once the riot in the mental hospital was settled, Dixon and Seyfrit met with a committee from the main prison riot. Dixon started out by telling the rioters he represented the millions of citizens of Illinois. One rioter stepped up and said, "I represent the poor bastards they got stuck in here." These two statements marked the end of constructive discussion.

Warden Munie said the conference with Dixon got nowhere because the rioting whites and Negroes could not come to any agreement. Munie attributed the whole riot to "the blacks and the whites not getting along."

Inmates denied this in exactly the same words used in Michigan when the race issue was brought up, but in Illinois, unlike Michigan, newsmen did not contradict the inmates.

Inmates contend the conference came to nothing because they did not trust either Seyfrit or Dixon. They felt Stevenson was a man of his word, and, if he promised to do something about conditions, he would. Cheers went through the rioting block when their radios told the inmates Stevenson was flying back.

But by this time Seyfrit had decided that, hostages or no hostages, force was the only way to stop the riot. When the governor arrived, it was to watch Seyfrit, complete with a portable P.A. system, let loose a string of invective, curses and threats that would have given an inferiority complex to a sailor's parrot.

While Seyfrit amazed the rioters with his fluent profanity, state police blew off the blockaded cell-block door and rushed the place, bullets flying. One by one the hostages came down the stairs and the rioters went into cells. Results: One inmate shot, no hostage hurt, nothing done about the complaints despite another Seyfrit investigation of Seyfrit and Munie.

"The inmates didn't have any real complaints," said Seyfrit. "Those damn billy goats will do or say anything for attention."

The inmates said many things to us. They said inmates had been beaten by Assistant Warden McCarthy. McCarthy said they were lying, but ex-Captain of the Guards Wood, said he knew that McCarthy beat prisoners on two different occasions, once as two guards held the inmate.

The fact that individual guards were afraid of the inmates, however, no one denied. None of the hostage guards wanted to talk about their experiences on the radio because, "the inmates hear these damn things, you know."

While we were talking to one prisoner, he asked us to turn off the tape machine. Then he turned to the guard Munie had posted to monitor the proceedings and said, "Look you. I'm going to say some things Munie won't like, but he'll be out of the joint by the time this goes on the air. Meanwhile, don't you open your mouth about a thing I say, see."

The guard mumbled a shamefaced, "No, sir." He later asked Peg to assure any other inmates we talked to that he would not quote them to Munie.

Munie, however, asked us about what went on tape. His only question was: "Did they say anything about me?" Actually, most of the inmates talked only of the system and the department of welfare, which they designated with the name of the state capital, Springfield. They made "Springfield" sound like a four-letter word.

When we met him, Munie's position was weak with both guards and inmates. Dixon, who had taken Stevenson's place on the Illinois ballot, was defeated and Republican William G. Stratton was going to take over as governor in about a month. Munie expected to be fired "because of politics," Mc-

Carthy told us he was tired of prison work anyway, and the lower echelons were wondering how they would fare under what they called "Republican civil service."

To find out about this we made appointments, through their press representatives, with both Stevenson and Stratton. But it turned out that Stevenson was too busy with vital state business to see us. However, we did get to interview Dixon, who made an excellent impression on us by suggesting that the inmates should be moved and Menard burned to the ground.

That afternoon we went to Stratton's office. We had to wait an hour to see him, although his secretary told us he was never late to appointments. It seems that at the last minute he had been called to the governor's mansion for an important meeting.

Stratton finally showed up, full of apologies and mad as man can get. His secretary later told us why. On a day when it was public knowledge that Stratton had a budget meeting in addition to all his other preparations for taking office, Stevenson had insisted he drop everything to go to the governor's mansion. Stevenson's vital business concerned the ultimate fate of the mansion's dining-room draperies.

But Stratton, who had been the youngest man ever to be elected to the legislature and one of the youngest governors ever elected in Illinois, wanted to talk to us about prisons. He threw away the carefully prepared statement his press secretary handed him to read, with the comment, "They want my opinions—not this."

He then proceeded to put himself out on a limb. After telling us he would try to get the mental hospital moved away from the prison to a spot where better psychological facilities and personnel would be available, he said:

> I'm of the opinion that we must make a definite effort to keep politics, political pressure, and political methods away from the guards and from the management of Menard. As far as I'm concerned, the guards will be kept free of politics. There will be no assessments levied on their salaries for political purposes. We won't tolerate the usual political pressures being put upon them. I think by increasing the morale of the guards (and of course getting some professional management for the institution itself) we

will help to solve the problem of the morale and the conditions among the inmates themselves.

I suppose that sometimes prison riots may occur for no apparent reason. However, at Menard there were reasons for the riots. You can be sure that as the new governor of this state, wherever we do have good prison conditions (such as Stateville),[9] I hope to continue to support those people who have made such fine records, irrespective of political affiliation. In the case of Menard, however, I believe that one of the first necessities is a complete overhauling of the personnel and the management of that institution.

This promise was fulfilled. Stratton appointed a new director of public safety, Joseph Bibb, a Negro.

Warden Munie told us that, if Stratton appointed a Negro to that job, Menard would go up in immediate riot. "After all, how would you like taking orders from a black? The whites won't stand for it. Stratton ought to pay off his black vote some other way."

However, Dr. Bibb has not had a riot at Menard.

As warden there, either Bibb or Stratton appointed Ross Randolph, a man with long penological experience. Stories out of Menard are changing. Instead of taped suggestion boxes, we hear of the warden's office being open to any prisoner with a beef. I talked to Warden Randolph after our program on Menard. The first thing he said was, "Come on down and go through here again. Be as rough as you want, but I think we'll surprise you."

Evidently, Stratton is living up to his post-election promise in every possible detail. It is significant to note that the man appointed to replace Warden Munie is a registered Democrat.

Will there be more prison riots? No man, penologist or prisoner, said "no" to this question. In fact, they usually anticipated it by predicting more and bloodier disturbances, not only in many of those spots already hit by riot, but in other prisons that have not yet gone up but where the riot causes listed in the A.P.A. report also exist.

---

[9] Joliet-Stateville Divisions of Illinois State Penitentiary, under Warden Joseph E. Ragan, a Democrat.

Is there any way to prevent more riots? Within the prisons themselves, there are two possible ways. One is to keep prisoners under such tight custody that they cannot riot. This would mean reverting to solitary confinement with individual cell feeding, the elimination of industries, industrial-training programs, and education programs. But this failed completely when it was tried before, and, if it is tried again, penologists say, "We'd better never let these men out again."

But as long as we do allow 97 per cent of our prisoners to return to the streets, a solution that is economically and humanly less wasteful should be found. We had better look for some way to cure the comparatively few criminals we catch. It has been proved that only a good treatment program in our prisons will do anything to bring down the constantly rising rate of recidivism.* And it is by this rate that any prison system must finally be judged.

Meanwhile, progressive penologists, no matter how sincere, are handcuffed. As James Bennett has said:

Prisons are a series of paradoxes. On the one hand, we, as prison men, are expected to punish; on the other, to reform. We are expected to discipline rigorously, and at the same time to teach self-reliance. Prisons are built to be operated like vast impersonal machines, yet we are expected to fit the men in them to live normal community lives. We must operate in accordance with a fixed, autocratic routine, and yet we are supposed to develop individual initiative. And, all too frequently, laws force our inmates into idleness, and yet we're supposed to teach them a trade and how to hold their place in a production line.

To some people prisons are nothing but "country clubs." To others prisons are charged with rancor and bitterness and an all-pervading sense of defeat. And this whole paradox continues on and on, because the ideas of the public and the views of the law-enforcement agencies regarding the function and the purpose of the prison in our society are confused, fuzzy, and nebulous.

Americans must realize we get the prisons we deserve. A prison administrator is only a product of his times. He must do his job in the way he believes the public will approve. Therefore, the public must be educated to the fundamental purposes of prisons and what they should be seeking to achieve.

All this is not to say that prisons should become country clubs, coddling the prisoner and catering to his every whim. As a matter of fact, prisons, no matter how well run, are places of punishment.

To prove this point, Bennett read a letter sent him from Alcatraz by a man once in the headlines as Public Enemy Number One:

> Maybe you have asked yourself how a man of even ordinary intelligence can put up with prison life, day in, day out, week after week, month after month, year after year. To put it more mildly still, what is this prison life of mine like? You might wonder whence do I draw sufficient courage to endure it.
>
> To begin with, these words seem written in fire on the walls of my cell: "Nothing can be worth this kind of life I am leading." No one knows what it is like to suffer from the intellectual atrophy, the pernicious mental scurvy, that comes of long privations of all the things that make life real. Even the analogy of thirst cannot possibly give you an inkling of what it is to be tortured by the absence of everything that makes life worth living. A prisoner cannot keep himself from being haunted by a vision of life as it used to be when it was real and lovely. At such times I pay with a sense of delicious, overwhelming melancholy my tribute to life as it once was!

Yes, even in federal prisons (which are the ones most often labeled with that favorite tabloid phrase, "country club,") men are still being punished, but Negley Teeters says:

> I am satisfied that the concept of punishment is a failure. You can't rehabilitate men and punish them at the same time.
>
> And the two hundred years' history of imprisonment has shown that prison too is a failure. Instead of rehabilitating people, it debauches them.
>
> We've simply got to develop something else. What that is I don't know, but I suspect that some kind of community treatment like probation is the answer. Today probation is financially starved, and yet it is the hope of the future.[9]

---

[9] Chief Justice Irving Ben Cooper of the City of New York Court of Special Sessions recently stated in a special report that his court, "due to an understaffed Probation Department," is "often driven to sentence acts rather than persons" because of an inability to determine who among his youthful offenders

As we saw all over the country, Teeters' solution will work for many of our safer prisoners, but is prison the answer for those who are too dangerous to be loose in society? MacCormick admits that a certain number of offenders will always have to be locked up, but he points out that you can lock them up in hospitals as well as prisons. This is a vital difference, he goes on, because:

> The function of a hospital is curative, it's therapeutic. The word *prison* connotes punishment: *hospital* does not. By thinking of hospitals, we can get away from the prisons we've known in the past.
> We should work to have in the future a series of small institutions with specialized functions and with varying degrees of security: maximum, medium, minimum. Some of them will be agricultural; some, industrial; some, fundamentally training; some, medical. But we'll stop using the term *prisons*. We'll use titles which will indicate the purpose for which these institutions exist, and that purpose will be a lofty one and not simply a punitive locking up of men in cages.

But how far into the future do we have to look for that "prison of tomorrow"? Answer that, prison men say, and you have the answer to how long it will be until recidivism and riots are lessened.

Are prison riots necessary? No they are not; but then neither are many wasteful things in our world. Little is being done to eliminate any of them. For instance, I found one riot cause not mentioned by the A.P.A.

I saw this when I spent a week end in a small Southern town. When I went into my hotel room, I found on the telephone a note which said "For liquor, call—" and there followed a telephone number. As I went around town I found this same notice stuck on public pay phones.

This is good advertising, but consider that I was in a county that, by local option, was dry. When I asked why it voted dry

---

"can be safely returned to the community" and who are the "hair-trigger, perverted, or psychopathic . . . who need institutionalized care." He decried the fact that "the courts can do little to minimize recidivism."

every election, I was told, "Hell, in wet counties, you have to go out and buy your whisky at state stores. Here we can get it delivered right to the door any time, day or night. And besides, we keep everything under control. We only got one bootlegger operating."

The payoff to this story came when I parked behind the local police station just at quitting time for the force's day shift. I watched beaten and battered old Fords, each with a large white "Police Department" lettered on its sides, chug into the parking lot. I saw the officers, notoriously underpaid, check out for the day and drive away in their own cars. They went home in brand new Lincolns, Buicks, and Packards.

Here too is a cause for our prison troubles. Prisons are but one phase of our total crime problem. As long as we close our eyes to the whole problem, this small, dark, crowded closet where we lock up the few lawbreakers we catch is not going to be cleaned up, no matter how noisily those inmates pound on the door.

But the attitude we have toward our prisons is symptomatic of our attitude toward crime as a whole. We are interested in hearing about it, but it is too much effort to do much about it. Consequently, the James Bennetts, the Austin MacCormicks, and the other crusading prison men cry in the wilderness as the men with the well-paying jobs and the political plums work at the easy task of persuading the public it can forget prisons along with society's other failures. You can mark these men because they are the ones who act only when the public is in danger of getting the facts.

8

assignment complete

. . . **Peg Reporting**

"FIND OUT WHY THERE ARE PRISON RIOTS. GO OUT INTO THE field, talk to the officials and the inmates. Bring back the truth, not a whitewash." That was the assignment given us by Bud Barry, vice-president of NBC.

We had waded through darkest penology with microphone and tape recorder, and we had the facts. We incorporated all we had learned in the field and at home into the narratives as we scripted our programs.

On February 7, 1952, we had just completed the first draft of the New Jersey story, a most unsatisfactory show since it came to an inconclusive end. "We need another statement, Peg," McGraw decided. "Perhaps something from Governor Driscoll telling us of their future plans."

Since I had tried to see Governor Driscoll some months before with no luck, I hadn't tried again. But McGraw was persuasive. So I called Governor Driscoll for the fourth time. Governor Driscoll, unlike Governor Williams of Michigan, is a formal man whose inner sanctum is as easy to get into as Fort Knox.

We had discussed our proposition with the governor's executive assistant, Mr. Donald S. Benson, who promised to look into the matter. He looked, because within a few days Commissioner Bates called us on the phone.

The entire matter had been turned over to him. It seems the governor could not make an appointment to record his opinions, but he had written a letter. This letter had been sent to the commissioner for approval, and it was to be sent on to us. "You'll receive it in the next day or two," Commissioner Bates promised.

Five days before broadcast date the letter arrived. We read it carefully. Governor Driscoll had written:

February 9, 1953

Dear Mrs. McGraw:

When the disturbances occurred in New Jersey correctional institutions, we were fortunate in having two internationally known penologists, Commissioner Sanford Bates and Dr. F. Lovell Bixby, in charge to handle the situation.

On Commissioner Bates' recommendation, I appointed three outstanding men, including Supreme Court Justice Harry Heher, to conduct an independent inquiry in the belief that this would show our sincere interest in ascertaining the facts and providing remedies.

The findings of this distinguished committee confirm our conclusions:

1. We need a new prison.

2. We need to attract and hold professionally qualified employees.

3. We need to eliminate unintentional inequities in the parole procedures.

We are taking affirmative action to remedy all these deficiencies. In many instances, such action had been taken before the committee began its study.

In 1952, New Jersey voters approved a second bond issued of $25,000,000 for capital improvements. In my Annual Message to the Legislature this year, I recommended that some part of that amount be used to start construction on a new prison. An allocation bill has been introduced and a site for the new prison will soon be selected.

Thus, steps are being taken to build a modern prison. Additions to our other correctional institutions will also help to eliminate evils with which we have long been familiar and which the committee of inquiry commented upon: the lack of constructive employment for inmates; and the lack of facilities to permit more effective classification* of inmates.

With the exception of the State Prison, our penal institutions have for several years had career superintendents. Before the new Constitution was adopted in 1947, the central office of the department had little control over the State Prison. Since 1951, when the constitutional status of the Principal Keeper terminated, the appointing authority, on my insistence, has resided in the Board of Managers of the Prison. The one condition I imposed upon the appointing authority was that appointments be based upon merit. A Principal Keeper and an Associate Warden, experienced and qualified, were appointed and the prison was thus well on the way to improvement even before the committee of inquiry made its report.

(This paragraph, of all paragraphs in the letter, interested us. The body known as the board of managers was handed the hot potato known as Trenton, and the letter literally took the commissioner off the hook. The board of managers is composed of a group of civic-minded citizens who control the money. Those who control the purse strings also control the way the money is spent.)

In addition to the foregoing measures, we have substantially increased the remuneration for prison personnel. A training program for new correction officers has been carried on and will be continued.

Inequities in parole procedures have been eliminated by administrative direction and remedial legislation.

It is helpful to us to have the sound recommendations of this competent investigating committee which will materially assist us as we seek public support for our correctional program.

Sincerely,

Alfred E. Driscoll
GOVERNOR.

McGraw pointed out that with the exception of the reference to the board of managers we were back to the mimeographed form. "What's it say that the commissioner hasn't said already?"

"This time the governor says it, McGraw," I pointed out. "Out of fairness to the commissioner we ought to put it in. Let someone else defend the situation."

McGraw gave a nod, and the letter was inserted in the show.

It was on that same fateful Monday that Jack Cleary, who supervised the project for NBC, called us and asked us to report to the publicity department for some preshow publicity.

We went in and submitted to the kind administrations of a publicity department's inquiry. Where had we been, what had we done, who had we talked to? They shot a couple of pictures of the McGraws, asked us about our findings, and started to send out advance promotion.

After the publicity meeting Jack Cleary suggested that we set up a meeting for NBC's legal staff to hear not only the tapes, but the written script as well. They rule on every word that goes over the airwaves. After a long session with the legal staff, exploring the dark and cavernous byways of New Jersey's penology, the ruling came through—we were approved for air.

Thursday dawned bright and cold and very bitter. A pre-broadcast rehearsal was scheduled for that night. The call was in for a full orchestra, complete with director-composer Morris Mamorsky, four narrators, two tape machines, and the usual complement of engineering personnel. McGraw and I were sipping coffee, contemplating the world with a kind of rosy disregard for things to come, when our telephone rang. Joan came in quite unperturbed to announce that we had a long-distance call from Commissioner Bates of New Jersey. "He seems somewhat disturbed," she reported.

Bates *was* disturbed. "I told you, Mrs. McGraw, I specifically told you that I would not allow you to talk to inmates inside Trenton penitentiary."

McGraw and I answered, quite honestly, that we had not talked to any inmates inside Trenton.

"The newspapers here in Jersey have an article which I will read to you. It specifically states that you talked not only to our department, but to guards and inmates."

McGraw apologized profusely for the error, but it was an error. We couldn't control what the newspapers said about us.

The commissioner didn't believe us.

We pointed out that under any circumstances it had been impossible for us to talk to Trenton's inmates since we couldn't get in to talk to them without permission. McGraw added, "Commissioner, you don't think much of your own security precautions if you think a reporter complete with tape recording equipment and an engineer can wander at will inside the walls."

The commissioner paused for a moment and then calmly, "I think I have the right to ask to hear the entire program before it is broadcast. I assure you that I will not permit inmates to dispute my word." He hung up.

Then Jack Cleary called. He was puzzled. "What's going on?"

We gave him a rundown on what we knew. Bates wanted to hear the show. We felt this was a bad idea. Since not only the ex-convicts, but many of the quotes from the official report disagreed with his findings, we couldn't expect the commissioner to approve our New Jersey story.

"What do we do?" McGraw asked.

"I don't know. Bud Barry is in Hollywood. The problem has been turned over to the treasurer of NBC, Mr. Joseph A. McDonald, who is also a lawyer. Mr. McDonald feels that we ought to be fair to the commissioner and allow him to hear the show."

We both asked, "Why?"

McGraw said, "Jack, as reporters we're given a job and we do it. Bud Barry knew, as well as everyone else at NBC, that this investigation was sure to step on somebody's toes. We didn't know when we started whether we would be antagonizing the inmate population, the guards, or the officials. We don't want to hurt anyone, we have no axe to grind. But if someone is hurt by the facts, Peg and I have to live with it."

Jack listened, and there was another long pause while he considered the situation. "Don't worry about it," he said. "I'll get back just as soon as I find out what to do."

He called back in less than half an hour. "Commissioner Bates and his attorney will be at NBC this evening at seven-thirty," Jack said. "They want to hear the show."

McGraw and I took the news resignedly. The order had come from above. We pointed out that at seven-thirty we would be in the middle of rehearsal and unavailable.

Jack suggested we join them after our rehearsal in case there was anything to discuss.

Rehearsal for most shows is a complicated procedure, but rehearsal for "Challenge of Our Prisons" was halfway between a magic trick and a Shakespearean drama. Full orchestra, narrators, and tape-recorded voices are rehearsed and delivered with split-second timing. Only McGraw's steel constitution could take it. I huddled in a corner and shook. The show ran a full hour; preliminary rehearsal, three hours, and those three hours left some forty people limp while last-minute changes were made. At the conclusion of rehearsal time the stamp was added: READY FOR AIR.

It was 9:30 P.M. when rehearsal finished. I felt the need of a few minutes of rest before joining the boys. McGraw insisted we pause only long enough to rearrange his mustache into a bristle. Then we went in.

The editing room had become a hearing room for the evening. Crowded around an oblong table was a roomful of people. Jack Cleary was reading the script. Commissioner Bates, red-faced, hot-eyed, and burning, listened across the table.

Our entrance was not greeted with enthusiasm. Cleary glanced up and introduced us to Mr. McDonald. Joe McDonald, a slight, wiry man in his forties, has dignity and authority. He's a stickler for details. He wanted to hear the entire story before he made any decisions. He was sitting calmly at the head of the table, concentrating on his fingers, which

were playing an imaginary piano. He glanced up and acknowledged us. "Join us, Mr. and Mrs. McGraw, we are in the middle of hearing your New Jersey report, and there seems to be
some discussion as to its factual content."

The commissioner could control himself no longer. He
raised a shaking finger at me, and said, "You—you double-
crosser, you."

"Commissioner—" I started.

Mr. McDonald took over. "We have just finished hearing a
man named Smitty who allegedly reported on conditions as
he found them. Shall we continue?"

Mr. McDonald signaled to the engineer, who started the
tapes again. Smitty was suggesting at that moment the riot
was well planned, not a spontaneous combustion as had been
suggested by the department.

The commissioner's face mottled as he slammed his fist
forcefully on the table. "I know that man." He fixed me with
a sharp eye. "I know that voice. He was one of the worst of
the group who rioted. Don't think I don't know why he says
what he said. He would say anything, anything to embarrass
the administration. And yet you try to tell me that you didn't
use inmates."

"Commissioner—" I began again.

Joe McDonald rode over me quietly but competently as he
addressed McGraw. "Mr. McGraw, as I understand it, you had
promised Mr. Bates not to use the voices of inmates. Is that
correct?"

McGraw, who matched Mr. McDonald in control and formality, nodded his head gently. "Quite correct, sir. And we
have not violated our promise. The man we call Smitty is a
former inmate of Trenton, who is now out on the streets, having completed his term at Trenton. He was at Trenton during the riots. He came out shortly after the riots. He did not
participate in the actual riot at any time. He was in another
cell block."

"You're lying," Commissioner Bates accused. "I recognize
him because he had some of those same arguments during the
riot."

"Sorry, sir," McGraw answered. "We are not lying."

There was silence at the table. McGraw looked toward Mr. McDonald for a signal.

Mr. McDonald said, "Suppose, commissioner, you suggest to us some way that we can reach a solution to this problem. This report is scheduled to go on the air in less than twenty-four hours."

Bates now faced McDonald squarely. "There is no solution. I tell you I will not have my word questioned by convicts. I'm a respected man with a history of accomplishment. Where do convicted felons come in to criticize me? These men by definition are convicted liars! That's what the law says. Do you point that out in the script—does that script say anywhere that they are liars?"

Mr. McDonald nodded to McGraw to answer. McGraw took over. "We screened the statements made by these former inmates carefully. We used only samples of inmate opinion that could be termed examples of what the report was citing as fact."

"Those inmates lied," Commissioner Bates doggedly went on.

"If they are lying, then the governor's report, which was written by State Supreme Court Justice Heher, Mr. Asche, and Mr. MacCormick is also a lie. Is that true?"

Mr. McDonald interrupted and suggested evenly, "Suppose we go on with the show. Let's listen to the entire show and then discuss it." He signaled Jack Cleary who continued reading from the script, knitting together the various tapes as they appeared.

Jack was reading the section on sanitation, direct from the governor's report, where the members of the committee had seen rats by direct observation. Once again the commissioner stood up, fists clenched, and burst out, "They saw one rat!"

We were all concerned for him. McGraw cautiously began, "Commissioner, it is not our aim to be unfair. If you feel we are telling half the story—if you have more to add—"

"Mr. McGraw, you ignore the fact that most of New Jersey's institutions are far above the average. Do you mention our

fine women's prison, our delinquency-control group, our reformatory at Annandale, or even Menlo Park? No, no, all you
do is look for something rotten to say about me."

There was a long pause in the room. All of us understood
the commissioner's point of view and sympathized with it. But
McGraw pointed out, "Commissioner, our assignment was to
find out 'Why Riots?' We came to you and asked you, why a riot
at Trenton. You told us 'spring fever.' Perhaps that is the answer. We gave you the opportunity of offering this suggestion
to the public. Others disagree with you."

"Of course, convicted felons disagree."

"But the governor's report disagrees. Surely they are allowed to express their opinion. Our job as investigators of
prison riots is not to go out and compliment New Jersey's nonrioting prisons. It is not our job to examine Menlo's great
diagnostic center, nor is it our job to present only one side of
the question. We were told to get all sides of the riot story
and that's what we did."

The commissioner shook his head resignedly. "Let's continue hearing the show."

Once again the engineer pressed the *go* button on the
tape machine. Now we had come to the life story of The Professor. The commissioner listened in silence for three minutes, and then, unable to control himself longer, burst out.
"That entire tape is a lie, a lie. That swan song of the dying
fawn. We do not shave heads in prison. Either that tape is
out or I'll get an injunction against NBC."

Now the hearing broke up into piecemeal comments. Ted
Kupferman, of NBC's legal staff, pointed out that he didn't believe there was basis for an injunction. The attorney accompanying the commissioner, New Jersey Deputy Attorney General Eugene T. Urbaniak, argued the point. The commissioner
was going to take the case to the highest court in the land.
Joe McDonald, soft-voiced and steady, placated, "Wait a minute, commissioner. There's no point to this argument. I'm
sure we can work this out to everyone's satisfaction."

The commissioner's lawyer suggested a break in the meeting while he and the commissioner talked the matter over.
The commissioner walked heavily from the room. His attor-

ney followed him. The meeting was adjourned for fifteen minutes.

Now our group sat down in discussion. "Perhaps," Mr. McDonald suggested to us, "we could make certain changes in the script and tapes to give Commissioner Bates more time to express his feelings, to have a complete say."

McGraw began to point out how we could retape the commissioner along different lines, when the commissioner and his attorney re-entered. The commissioner was calmer now as he took his seat.

McGraw opened the meeting by trying to re-outline the show along the lines we had suggested, but the commissioner broke in. He wasn't interested. The only way Commissioner Bates would allow the show to go on the air was "to divide it into two distinct sections."

His attorney took over. In the first section the commissioner would make a satisfactory speech explaining the entire situation in New Jersey. In the second section we could use our inmate voices if we informed the public that these men were "convicted liars."

McGraw listened and then countered that it was impossible; it couldn't be done before air time.

"Perhaps you could just cancel the show," the commissioner suggested pleasantly. "After all, the situation in New Jersey had already had enough publicity. More publicity," he pointed out grimly, "could start another riot, and it very well might."

The idea of an NBC broadcast kicking off a million-dollar prison riot was not pleasant to contemplate.

"Commissioner," I answered, "There's one thing you've overlooked. You are not the only man who read the advance publicity on the New Jersey story. The inmates at Trenton read it too. They get newspapers too. What happens tomorrow night when the clock strikes nine and an announcer goes on the air saying, 'For reasons beyond our control the broadcast originally scheduled for this time has been canceled'?"

"It seems to me," McGraw said quietly, "the fact that there is no broadcast might incite a riot a lot faster than a frank and open airing of the story." [1]

---

[1] The inmates of Trenton listened, and there was no riot or display of any kind.

The commissioner's lawyer glanced quickly at his client and suggested, "I don't think it's necessary to cancel the show at all. Frankly, neither does the commissioner. We feel the important point here is not to put the commissioner in a spot where his authority is challenged by convicted felons."

Now it was only some twenty hours before air time. Jack Cleary took over. "I think that can be worked out practically. Suppose we start going over the script line by line and figure out the changes."

The scripts were passed out. Now the commissioner took over and line by line began fighting for changes. He insisted on branding the ex-convict voices as convicted liars. "Untrue," he claimed when he read the section on heterogeneous population. "A lie," he said when Dancer's picture of the first offender was spoken. "Dope, sex, homebrew—all overemphasized."

He insisted on deletions not only from the inmate voices, but from the actual report which had been made by the governor's committee. Most important of all was the deletion of that one lonely rat that had been spotted inside Trenton by the investigating committee. The commissioner's last request was for us to delete the entire testimony of that "swan song of the dying fawn," and make room for him to give to the radio audience a fifteen to twenty-minute speech.

McGraw and I argued every point. We had to give in on some to win others. The "dying fawn" stayed in, and we compromised with an eight-minute speech for the commissioner. Mr. McDonald made an appointment with the commissioner in his office for the following morning to write and record the commissioner's final speech.

The meeting broke up. Jack Cleary, McGraw, and I wandered out into the foggy night, aimless and depressed. None of us had had lunch or dinner. We weren't hungry, either; but McGraw and Jack agreed we'd need nourishment to go through the night. We ate, then Jack, McGraw and I went to a hotel for what remained of the night. McGraw and I went to work on the script, rewriting and revising.

At 4:00 A.M., as I was finishing the last two sentences, I said, "I can't help comparing the job we do, McGraw, and the job a newspaper reporter does."

McGraw lit his eightieth cigarette.

"Maybe," I started, "a network has no right to participate in this kind of report. Maybe that's the problem. Maybe that's why they have to compromise."

McGraw smoked in silence, thinking it over. Then he said, "I think you're wrong, Peg. The question really is, has a network any right NOT to participate?"

He crushed out the cigarette. "You're not going to solve anything at this hour, honey. Let's get some sleep."

The next morning, back on the job, I headed for Mr. Mc-Donald's office while McGraw retired to the editing room to try to figure out some way of deleting more minutes from the tapes to make room for Bates' speech. "I'll cut all I can, Peg," he warned, "but try to keep the commissioner as short as possible without being unfair."

When I arrived, Commissioner Bates was already locked in with Mr. McDonald, reviewing the entire subject again. Finally I was called in to join them. The commissioner was ready to start his speech. He didn't want my help, but I was welcome to stay and listen as he dictated it to Mr. McDonald's secretary. He had been promised an opportunity to say anything he wished to say, and he was going to say it. I didn't argue.

He sat back and started dictation. I only timed him. Bates started:

> I understood that this was to be a discussion of facts and circumstances connected with last year's disturbances at Trenton prison and I must say I'm at a loss to understand why it was considered proper to permit certain anonymous critics to make statements about matters that have already been repeatedly investigated.[2] A prized American tradition is that neither a person nor a group, or an institution private or public can be condemned in any such manner.

The commissioner glanced toward me meaningfully. If that was what he wanted to say, I had no argument. He continued:

---

[2] This was the same statement Bates had made when the guards made their statements to Reporter Gregory.

Now I don't know whether these persons are inmates or on parole or discharged—

I interrupted to add, "Former convicts—out flat, commissioner." He continued without pause:

But certainly it cannot be claimed that the inmates at Trenton need a forum. They've had it. They've had it before various tribunals including the impartial committee that's been referred to, who filed its document with Governor Driscoll. Now this document is certainly no whitewash; it clearly points out the deficiencies of the prison as it was formerly administered.

I interrupted again to point out that we had no argument on that point. But the committee had also taken under consideration conditions at Trenton at the time the riot occurred and that, if Bates was rebutting fairly, that point should be included.

The commissioner flared up to remind me that he was supposedly to be allowed to say what he pleased, and he was going to say it. I nodded half-heartedly.

The commissioner continued:

The board of managers of the prison, an unpaid group of distinguished citizens whose right to appoint the warden of their own institution was only recently confirmed, has likewise listened to the complaints and grievances. Our department has spent several days with the committee of inmates, encouraged them to list the grievances, and we've given a prompt answer, yes or no, to such as could be answered. I think that most of our inmates are well intentioned. They acted well during the riots, which were participated in by a small proportion. I still think that the majority of the prisoners now think that changes for the better have been made. And I think they propose to cooperate.

We of the administration in the institutions of New Jersey are, I may say, determined not to permit these incidents to dissuade us from the belief that most prisoners do have some good in them that can be reached with patience and understanding. We should certainly regret it if these recent widespread disturbances should have the effect of alienating public support.

The commissioner placed especial emphasis on alienating public support.

I interrupted only to ask a question. "Do you really think, commissioner, that publicity alienates support?"

"I do," he responded promptly.

"It's an old newspaper truism," I pointed out, "that there is nothing like the white-hot glare of publicity to clean up sore spots. I think you might find that publicity rightly used by your department might gain public support for many of these things you have crusaded for in the past."

Commissioner Bates stopped for a minute, only to ignore me and start again.

We hope these broadcasts, by presenting facts, not rumors, will assist in a proper understanding of the almost insuperable difficulties in administering a prison.

I wanted to point out that we were trying to present all sides of the facts, but I was fighting a losing battle. I just sat back and listened and wondered.

And so I don't propose to answer these anonymous criticisms. They contain no new disclosure. And I think the public will remember that a prison is a place where, and a few of the persons in it those to whom, criticisms come naturally. Instead, New Jersey proposes to let its actions speak for themselves. Here are some of the actions:

On Tuesday Governor Driscoll signed a bill appropriating $4,800,000 as the first installment toward a replacement of the "old bastille." Extra guards have been authorized, and on July first their salary will become the second highest in the United States. Parole administration has been improved. New bills removing inequities which developed when a new legal system of parole was superimposed upon what was, in effect, a pardon system, are now before the legislature with Governor Driscoll's assent. A new acting warden is in charge. Many necessary improvements as well as restrictions have been established and are recounted at length in the committee report. I think I may also say that the sensational charges referred to here tonight with reference to the inevitable problems of dope, sex, and con-

vict rule have been referred to by the commission as grossly exaggerated. And the actions which New Jersey has taken, which I
think speak louder than words, are not confined to actions taken
since these disturbances.

The handbook of correctional institutions, published by the
Federal Bureau of Prisons, which was quoted in the Heher report,
says this: "The State" (meaning New Jersey) "has plodded along
with an antiquated and overcrowded plant for nearly eighty
years and still has this penal mosaic as a millstone about the neck
of one of the most enlightened systems of correction institutions
and administration in the country."

That "enlightened prison system" referred to by the federal
bureau includes such outstanding installations as the Diagnostic
Center at Menlo Park; the State Home for Boys at Jamesberg;
the Home for Girls at Trenton; the Open Reformatory at Annandale, which is known pretty well throughout the world as an
unusual experiment in this type of institution; the Intermediate
Reformatory with its excellent educational and therapy projects
at Bordentown; the High Fields' experiment, which won the
Reader's Digest prize for its director, Lloyd McCorkle, now
warden at the prison; a full-time parole board and a state-wide
supervision of parole, are parts of this organization for which we
have no apologies to make.

Of course, one can speculate at length on the basic unrest in
prisons. One can point to an epidemic of violent reactions in our
schools, in our colleges, and in our industrial relations; to the
unprecedented number of escapes from correctional schools all
over the country. And one could make a fairly good case for the
statement that prison troubles are, to some extent, a reflection
of this tendency. But the outstanding and unique reason which
had bearing on the disturbances at Trenton was, as referred to
above, the lack of control over the institution by the department.
We now have a career warden. The prison, under its new management and in a new location, with a trained and efficient staff,
with cooperation from the inmates, will soon take its place in a
constellation of correctional institutions in New Jersey, which,
under the control of the state board, has won acclaim throughout
the civilized world.

The commissioner stopped. He gave the nod to the secretary
to type the speech up. It was now two hours prior to dress
rehearsal and five hours before the show.

The speech was typed in record time. The commissioner wanted an hour to study it and make any necessary changes. I left him alone and joined McGraw in the editing room and gave him a copy.

McGraw read it. "Y'know, Peg, if this is what he wants to say, by all means let him say it."

I agreed with McGraw. The commissioner's speech was good. "Now he admits Trenton state prison needs a change. And, McGraw, changes are proposed, some of them have been made."

McGraw nodded. "But why does Commissioner Bates fight the presentation of what was wrong at Trenton? He objected to the Newark *Star Ledger* stories. From what we hear, the Senate investigating committee had a problem with him. He objects to point after point in the governor's report. Now us." McGraw shook his head. "Why does he resist allowing the public a chance to know why a new prison is urgently needed? Why doesn't he want to give the public the reasons for the money they are going to pay out?"

We both sat and thought. Finally McGraw said, "Maybe we'll never get the answer to that."

I got up wearily to leave the room. "Maybe he's just a real good fighter. What's the difference, McGraw? Despite everything, the story is in and it's going on the air."

One hour before rehearsal we escorted the commissioner into a studio and recorded him. He wanted to hear his broadcast played back. We played it back and took notes on the pauses and mistakes that were to be edited out. McGraw, complete with notes, rushed to the editing room.

The commissioner and I sat alone in the studio. Both of us tired, emotionally spent. And I still wondered, why was he defending Trenton?

Almost to himself, Commissioner Bates said, "Why does this have to happen to me? Why, at my time of life?"

I had no answer.

The studio doors opened, and the musicians began coming in, setting up their music racks; the engineers began to prepare the studio for broadcast; the narrators began trooping in, still with their old scripts in their hands. Joan was in the mimeograph department collating the new scripts.

McGraw came in with the final reels of re-edited tapes. Rehearsal was about to begin. He faced the commissioner. The commissioner, sagging with weariness, stood up. "I think I've taken as much time as I should." He smiled, "This has been hard on all of us." McGraw shook hands. I felt rotten, depressed. We weren't attacking the commissioner—there was so much that was fine about the man—we were attacking a system, but he had made it a personal war.

"The Challenge of Our Prisons" went on the air at nine o'clock that night. At ten the phone calls started coming in. The friends we had made on our trip around the country called to congratulate us. But it was the ninth phone call that was impressive. McGraw answered it. It was from an official in New Jersey who called to say he thought the show "stunk." McGraw thanked him and relayed the information to us. Joan agreed quietly, but added, "He should have heard the one that got away."

Once "Challenge" was on the air, the rat race began. One hour of exposé material had to roll out every week, and we had had our fiery initiation with New Jersey. What would the federal prison system do when publicity broke; what about Michigan, the Ohio report, or the bitter commentaries we had recorded of the politically hog-tied Illinois story? Publicity kept pushing material out to the local papers, and the papers gave it space.

Between editing, rehearsals, and production we waited for phone calls, but those phone calls never came. Instead, letters by the thousands poured in to the network: prison systems requested transcripts of our shows for instruction material; the United States Army requested a copy of each hour as it rolled off the line to use in their instruction lectures to training personnel for their prison camps; investigating committees wanted our material for study and research; and the great listening audience wrote in to ask what they personally could do. Then a steady stream of men and women started pouring into our office, prefacing their entrance with a telephone call, saying, "You don't know me but I gotta talk to you." They came not for help or personal gain, but only to say, "Thank you. You said what we want to say and you said it good."

On April 21, 1953, Assignment Prison Riots was completed. The rest of the story you've read here. The people we met and worked with touched our lives briefly but unforgettably: the governors, the officials, the guards, and the boys like Jack, Smitty, Mac, The Professor; and the men like the Indiana bank robbers living in their houseboats as they travel easily down the Indiana river; and, most of all, Peter, who found himself and helped us find an answer.

Authors' Note: Despite the words of Sanford Bates and Governor Driscoll's letter to us, now that the "hot glare of publicity" has died down, the one-hundred-eighteen-year-old New Jersey State Prison at Trenton has had another stay of execution. The newly elected democratic governor, Robert B. Meyner, has indicated that he will take the $4,800,000 appropriated to start a new prison at Arneytown and use it to fix up the old prison at Trenton. The land purchased for the new prison site will be sold.

Somehow it seems that this is where we came in.

glossary

Prison jargon is part the words used and part the intonation. For instance, there is the word *good*. Nonprisoners will say, "I had a *good time*," stressing the last two words equally; but inside the walls time off for good behavior is *"good* time," with the accent on *good*. This carries over to *"good* pay," money received for working in prison industries.

Go is another mixed-up word. *"Easy* go" is time in prison with no problems and a soft job; *"tough* go" is the opposite.

Besides general expressions that are fairly universal in all prisons, each house has its own expressions, and a man with a good ear will tell by an inmate's language where he has spent time.

Below is a list of most often used prison expressions. In the text an asterisk after a word indicates that that word is included in the glossary. Throughout the book misspellings in the taped stories are deliberate in order to show their pronunciation.

Arctic:	*See* Hole.
B&W:	Bread and water, still given as a punishment in some prisons.
Block:	A group of cells, either in a separate building or separated from other groups or cells in the same building for security or segregation purposes. Convictese will express it as "Fifteen Block," or simply "Fifteen."
Boy:	Usually applied to an inmate, no matter what his age.
Boy-girl:	Homosexual.
Bum rap:	As a noun, an unjust accusation or sentence; as a verb, to accuse unjustly: "Don't *bum* rap me."
Check:	A disciplinary report written by a guard against an inmate.
Classification:	A grouping of prisoners on the basis of their records, crimes, and ages for the sake of segregating old timers, sex offenders, and the more easily rehabilitated. Separate classes are theoretically placed in different prisons or segregated sections of the same prison.
Count:	An inventory of inmates, which may be taken several times a day.
Double-team:	Noun: a team of two men, either guards or policemen, who beat up an inmate or a suspect; verb: to beat up, two against one —"I was *double*-teamed."
Drawer:	Inmate's record.
Easy go:	Imprisonment without problems and with a soft job.
Felony:	Usually a crime for which a sentence of more than one year, or a year and a day, may be given.
Flat:	Used in connection with serving a sentence completely in prison rather than partially on parole: "I went ten years flat."

Flop *or* flop-over:	A term of years designated by a parole board before which an inmate cannot have another parole hearing.
Fragile:	Unstable.
General *or* general population:	The majority of prisoners, who are not either in segregation or quarantine.
Get out of my face!	"Go away!"
Going home:	Getting out of prison (either by release or escape) even if the inmate has no home to go to.
Good pay:	Wages for working in prison industries.
Good time:	Time deducted from a sentence in acknowledgment of good behavior.
Hit the streets *or* Hit the bricks:	Be released.
Hold:	A detainer against an inmate by another law system on other charges.
Hole:	Solitary confinement cell or a block of them, used for punishment or segregation.
Hot box:	A box or cell heated to high temperature and used to torture inmates for punishment. Has often been fatal.
Installment plan:	A number of years served in the same prison on different sentences for separate offenses.
Isolation:	Solitary confinement, either for punishment (as in the hole) or for protection of other inmates. In some prisons psychopaths or sex deviants are kept in isolation.
Jail:	Not a prison, but a place of detention for suspects awaiting trial, sentence, or transfer to prison. Also used to imprison misdemeanants for sentences that are usually shorter than a year or a year-and-a-day. Usually run by county or city governments rather than state or federal, although there is one federal jail.

Kite:	An uncensored letter either smuggled outside the walls or an uncensored note to an official from an inmate.
Kiting:	Smuggling a letter out of prison.
Klondike:	*See* Hole.
Lag:	A jailbird, usually of long standing.
Max *or* maximum:	The longest time a man can serve under the terms of his sentence.
Maximum-security prison:	A prison designed to keep the most dangerous and unmanageable men from escaping.
Medium-security prison:	A prison with less formidable safeguards against escape than a maximum-security house. Usually has a fence rather than a wall.
Min *or* minimum:	The shortest time a man can serve under the terms of his sentence.
Minimum-security prison:	A prison, or more usually a camp, with little safeguard against escape.
Misdemeanor:	Usually an offense calling for a term of less than a year.
Nothing shaking:	"Nothing is happening," *or* "It's not true."
On the carpet:	Disciplinary action. This expression originated in prison because of the custom of making an inmate stand on one square foot of carpet while he was sentenced to the hole. This was a safety precaution, since the carpet was kept far enough away so that the inmate could not hit the warden.
Over the wall:	Escape.
Package:	Inmate's records.
Plant:	The prison.
Punk:	Homosexual.

Quarantine:	Segregation, usually of new inmates who are being classified before being let into the general population.
Rack it up:	Equivalent to "blow your top."
Recidivism:	Falling back into prior criminal habits, especially after punishment.
Recidivist:	Prison returnee.
Rumble:	News or rumor.
Screw:	Guard.
Shakedown:	Search.
She-boys:	Homosexuals.
Shiv:	Knife.
Short:	Coming close to the end of a sentence.
Shortitis:	Nervousness of a prisoner who is short.
Shot:	Discipline report.
Ticket:	Inmate's record or a discipline report. (Varies in different houses.)
White Banner:	Edict from the warden.
Wing:	*See* Block.
Wolf:	Aggressive homosexual.
Yard:	Recreation area.
Yard Out:	Recreation time.